PORK BARREL POLITICS

JOHN A. FEREJOHN

PORK BARREL POLITICS

Rivers and Harbors Legislation, 1947-1968

Stanford University Press, Stanford, California   *1974*

Stanford University Press
Stanford, California
© 1974 by the Board of Trustees of the
Leland Stanford Junior University
Printed in the United States of America
ISBN 0-8047-0854-1
LC 73-89859

TO SALLY

PREFACE

In the preparation of this study I incurred more debts than I can repay. The largest one is to my wife, Sally, for her assistance at each stage of the research and writing, as well as for her encouragement and support. Of course, since this book would not have been written without her help, she must share some of the blame for its existence.

I should also thank my good friend, perpetual critic, and sometimes collaborator, Barry S. Rundquist. Many of the basic ideas in this study emerged from thousands of hours of discussion and argument between us over uncounted bottles of beer.

My friend and adviser, Raymond E. Wolfinger, is also due special thanks for stimulating my interest in congressional policy-making, responding to my confused letters with insightful comment, and providing a catalogue of useful ways of improving this study. No matter what you might think of the present version of this book, at one time it was much worse!

J.A.F.

CONTENTS

Introduction   1

PART ONE. *How Projects Are Chosen*

1. The Evaluation of Water Projects   15
2. Benefit-Cost Analysis   25
3. Political Benefits and Political Costs   47

PART TWO. *The Appropriations Process for the Corps of Engineers*

4. The Making of the Corps of Engineers' Budget   71
5. The House Response to the Budget Request   87
6. The Senate's Response to the Corps' Budget   106
7. The Conference Committee   116

PART THREE. *The Distribution of the Corps of Engineers' Construction Projects*

8. Committee Effects on Project Choice:
   The House Public Works Committee   129
9. Committee Effects on Project Choice:
   The House Appropriations Committee   157
10. The Senate Committees and the Corps of Engineers'
    Expenditures   195

Conclusion: Comments on a Theory
of Congressional Behavior on Divisible Policies   233

Appendixes 255   *Notes* 267   *Bibliography* 277   *Index* 281

FIGURES

1.1 Procedures for Evaluating Projects for Federal Funding   16–17

2.1 The Relation Between the Benefit-Cost Ratio and the
Discount Rate   31

4.1 The Fair-Share Hypothesis, 1948–68   78

4.2 The Effect of Unemployment on Budget Size, 1948–66   82

4.3 Inflation in the Construction Industry and Budget Size,
1948–69   83

4.4 Relation Between Budgeted and Congressional New Starts,
1959–70   84

4.5 Total New Starts as a Function of Budgeted New Starts   85

5.1 Appropriations as a Percent of Estimates: H.A.C. Decisions,
1948–62   94

5.2 Budget Requests and H.A.C. Recommendations for the
Corps of Engineers, 1948–69   98

5.3 H.A.C. Cuts in the Budget and Number of Floor
Amendments   100

5.4 House Floor Changes in H.A.C. Recommendations on the
Corps' Requests, 1948–69   102

5.5 Number of Amendments on Appropriations Measures in the
House, 1947–62   104

7.1 Conference Disagreements and Senate Victories, 1951–67   120

7.2 Percent of Splitting the Difference out of Total Disagreements
Between House and Senate, 1951–67   124

9.1 Percent Cuts in Construction Budget Requests: States
Represented on the H.A.C. Public Works Subcommittee
Compared with States Not So Represented, 1949–64   176

9.2 Average Budget Requests per District for the Chairman of the H.A.C. Public Works Subcommittee Compared with All Other Members, 1949–68   186

9.3 Average House Changes per District in Budget Requests for Members of the H.A.C. Public Works Subcommittee, 1949–68   187

9.4 Average Budget Request per District for Members of the H.A.C. Public Works Subcommittee, 1949–68   188

10.1 Percent of Senate Increase over the House Budget Estimates: States Represented on the S.A.C. Public Works Subcommittee Compared with States Not So Represented, 1949–68   204

TABLES

2.1 Opportunity Cost as a Percentage of Dollar Cost for Five
Project-types   41

3.1 Classification of Projects   53

5.1 H.A.C. Budget Decisions: Fenno's 36 Bureaus and the Corps
of Engineers Compared   88

5.2 Floor Reception of H.A.C. Recommendations   97

5.3 Amendments to Appropriations Bills   99

6.1 S.A.C. Budget Decisions: Fenno's 36 Bureaus and the Corps
of Engineers Compared   108

6.2 Percentage of Line Items in the Corps' Construction Budget
Changed in the House and Revised in the Senate   110

6.3 Planning and Construction New Starts Initiated by the
House and Senate from 1951 to 1969   112

6.4 Senate Action on Fenno's 36 Bureaus Compared with Senate
Action on the Corps' Budget   113

7.1 Proportion of New Starts Initiated by the House and Senate
and Funded in the Conference Budget   123

8.1 Estimated Number of House New Starts for Fiscal Year 1967
for States Represented on the H.P.W.C. in 1956 and 1966   135

8.2 Estimated Number of House New Starts for Fiscal Year 1967
for States Represented on the H.P.W.C. in 1956 and 1966,
Controlling for Need   136

8.3 Budgeted and Congressional New Starts by Project-type in 1969   144

9.1 Relation Between House Success and Senate Success for
24 Bureaus   159

9.2 Some Effects of the 1955 Floor Revolt   165

9.3   Membership on the H.P.W.C. and Cuts by the H.A.C. Public
      Works Subcommittee   166

9.4   Constituency Benefits of Membership on the H.A.C. Public
      Works Subcommittee   167

9.5   Pork Barrel Orientation of H.A.C. Public Works Subcommittee
      Members   168

10.1 House Cuts and Senate Additions for States Represented on
      the S.A.C. Public Works Subcommittee   205

10.2 House Cuts and Senate Additions for States Represented on
      the S.P.W.C.R.H.F.C. Subcommittee   209

10.3 The Effects of Subcommittee Membership   210

10.4 Deviant Cases from the Appeals Court Hypothesis   211

10.5 House Cuts and Senate Additions for States Represented on
      the S.A.C. Public Works Subcommittee, by Party   213

10.6 Net Change in Budget Figures for States Represented on
      the S.A.C. Public Works Subcommittee, by Party   215

10.7 House Cuts and Senate Additions for States Represented on
      the S.P.W.C.R.H.F.C. Subcommittee, by Party   217

10.8 Net Change in Budget Figures for States Represented on
      the S.P.W.C.R.H.F.C. Subcommittee, by Party   218

10.9 Use of Seniority as a Criterion for Making Organizational
      Decisions Within Committees   221

10.10 House Cuts in Budget Requests for Chairmen Versus Other
      Members on the S.A.C. Public Works and the
      S.P.W.C.R.H.F.C. Subcommittees   223

10.11 House Cuts in Budget Requests for Ranking Minority
      Members Versus Other Members, Excluding Chairmen,
      on the S.A.C. Public Works and the S.P.W.C.R.H.F.C.
      Subcommittees   224

10.12 House Cuts in Budget Requests for Chairmen Versus Ranking
      Minority Members on the S.A.C. Public Works and the
      S.P.W.C.R.H.F.C. Subcommittees   225

10.13 Additions by the Senate over House Recommendations for
      Chairmen Versus Other Members on the S.A.C. Public
      Works and the S.P.W.C.R.H.F.C. Subcommittees   225

10.14 Relation Between Senate Additions and House Cuts for
      Chairman Versus Other Members on the S.A.C. Public
      Works Subcommittee   226

10.15 Relation Between Senate Additions and House Cuts for
      Chairman Versus Other Members on the S.P.W.C.R.H.F.C.
      Subcommittee   226

10.16 Senate Additions to House Recommendations for States
Represented by the R.M.M. Versus Other Members,
Excluding the Chairmen, on the S.A.C. Public Works
and the S.P.W.C.R.H.F.C. Subcommittees 227

10.17 Senate Additions and House Cuts for the R.M.M. Versus
Other S.A.C. Public Works Subcommittee Members,
Excluding the Chairman 227

10.18 Senate Additions and House Cuts for the R.M.M. Versus
Other S.P.W.C.R.H.F.C. Subcommittee Members,
Excluding the Chairman 228

10.19 Results of Regression Analysis for the Members of the
S.A.C. Public Works Subcommittee 229

10.20 Size of House Cuts Necessary to Ensure That the Senate
Addition Remains Below the Original Budget Request:
The S.A.C. Public Works Subcommittee 229

10.21 Results of Regression Analysis for the Members of the
S.P.W.C.R.H.F.C. Subcommittee 230

10.22 Size of House Cuts Necessary to Ensure That the Senate
Addition Remains Below the Original Budget Request:
The S.P.W.C.R.H.F.C. Subcommittee 230

PORK BARREL POLITICS

Introduction

Every action taken in the House of Representatives is shaped by
that body's structure of influence.   *—Richard Fenno*

In the late summer or early fall, the Conference Report on the
Appropriations Bill for Public Works is considered on the floors of
the House and Senate. This bill contains the annual appropriations
for the Bureau of Reclamation, the Atomic Energy Commission, the
various power administrations and river basin authorities, as well as
the Army Corps of Engineers' civil construction program. In every
recent year the Corps of Engineers' portion of the bill has contained
funds for between 300 and 400 projects spread over perhaps 45 of
the 50 states. Every year, too, the House and Senate between them
have usually managed to add new Corps of Engineers projects to the
public works section of the President's budget (which has lately totaled around one billion dollars), increasing it by about half a billion dollars.

The Public Works Appropriations Bills are criticized as "pork
barrel legislation" by some and praised as "development bills" by
others, but both groups appreciate the fact that these bills are made
to a great extent in the Congress, principally in the various committees that share jurisdiction over the nation's rivers, beaches, lakes,
and harbors, and that over the years they can fairly be said to constitute the policy of the federal government in the area of water resources development exclusive of water pollution legislation. Each
year in the hearings before the appropriations committees and in
the floor debates, the senior members of what might be called the
water committees—men like Senators Ellender, Cooper, Randolph,
Stennis, and Magnuson, and Representatives Kirwan and Evins—

congratulate one another on the fine development bill they have produced and praise the worthy flood-control and navigation projects that will soon be built in Louisiana, Kentucky, West Virginia, Mississippi, Washington, Ohio, and Tennessee. The casual observer sees that, yes, the Red River (in Louisiana) has been programmed by the Senate committee with the concurrence of Congress to receive 100 million dollars over the next few years, and that there are ten to 15 projects receiving federal funds in Kentucky as well as large projects in Ohio and Washington.

Members of the presidency, congressional opponents, and even some congressional supporters have referred to this bill privately as a pork barrel, a product of logrolling, a "Christmas tree" bill, and a boondoggle for certain powerful members of both houses. Yet each year a bill that looks very much like the one that passed the year before appears in the Congress and is passed without much general debate or comment on its propriety, though with considerable discussion of individual projects. The result is that more cement is poured, more rivers are dammed, and more streams are straightened. And everyone knows that it will all be about the same next year.

Is this what really happens? Are a few powerful senators and congressmen actually able to treat the public purse as a development fund for their states or districts? After all, unless these people constitute a majority in the House and Senate, they can be prevented from regularly enacting such legislation by a majority of either chamber. Yet the process continues unchecked in the public works area. This study is an investigation of why such a system exists and how it functions in the federal government.

The Theory

The Congress is not an anonymous group of men and women who occasionally meet to pass legislation by majority vote. On the contrary, it has an elaborate formal and informal structure, traditions, norms, and agreed-upon practices. The institutions of the Congress establish among other things a division of labor—routine methods of assigning jobs and of working out procedural matters—and complicated systems of status and influence within each chamber.

The distributions of influence in the House and Senate arise from several sources: from institutional prescriptions about who shall have authority in particular fields, from the skills of different individuals, from traditional practices and habits, and from common agreement. The congressional institutions that interest us in this study are the committee system, the seniority system, and the separation of the authorization and appropriations processes. Together these institutions produce forms of cooperation by dividing the work load by issue areas in Congress and by encouraging specialization, reciprocity, and deference to expertise. At the same time, they produce certain kinds of conflict between the two chambers, between authorizing and appropriating committees, and between the committee leadership and the party leadership on particular issues.

Committee chairmen usually exert a good deal of influence over legislation within the jurisdiction of their committees, but some exert more than others. Their influence results from several factors:

1. Control over committee staffs.

2. Control over the organization of their committees (formation of subcommittees, allocation of jurisdictions).

3. Committee members' respect for values and norms such as expertise and apprenticeship.

4. Ability to work with the House and Senate leadership and the committees on committees in recruiting members to their own committees.

5. Individual expertise in the issue area.

6. Reputation in the chamber as a whole and ability to get committee bills passed on the floor.

This short list indicates how much room there is for individual variations of influence over a particular issue within the committee's jurisdiction. Customs and routine procedures give each committee chairman potential influence, but they do not ensure that he develops that influence.

Many of the committee studies produced in the past few years contain examples of the wide range of variation in the chairman's power. For example, several chairmen have effectively lost control of the organization of subcommittees and the allocation of jurisdictions.[1] Others have not been able to control who goes on their committees.[2] A more ambiguous concept, one frequently talked about in newspapers and periodicals, might be called generalized influence. This term as used here does not connote influence over any particular issue. Some chairmen are more influential than others simply because the issues they deal with are more important (perhaps to the other members of Congress) than those other chairmen deal with. Indeed, in this generalized sense, some subcommittee chairmen might wield more influence than many committee chairmen. For example, Fenno claims that certain chairmen of House appropriations subcommittees are more influential than many full committee chairmen. He would receive little argument on this point from other experts on congressional politics.

The major institutions of Congress and the primary methods of recruitment into them (seniority for the committee system, caucus votes for the party leadership systems) form an "initial" distribution of resources that should constitute a relatively strong constraint on the actual distribution of influence in the Congress. Although most scholars would agree that this institutional distribution is likely to be relatively more binding on the real distribution of influence in the House than in the Senate, it should be important nonetheless in both chambers. Casual observation indicates that chairmen are considered powerful and influential in both House and Senate, and that only rarely does a nonchairman gain the same kind of influence in comparable legislative areas as a chairman. At the same time, a necessary condition for influence in a particular issue area is membership on an appropriate committee.

A hypothesis can therefore be formulated stating that the "initial" or institutional distribution of influence will have a *measurable effect* on the kinds of policies produced. On the face of it, there would appear to be substantial difficulties in testing such an assertion. After all, how can one hope to say that because some small set of individuals in the Congress had more say over federal policy toward higher education than other members, such policy took on a particular form? Yet the hypothesis formulated above is the central concern of this book, and in the course of the succeeding chapters we shall seek to demonstrate that in the presence of geographic representation and the committee system (and its associated norms and practices), congressionally made policies tend to take on a peculiar and identifiable form. This form does not bear any necessary relation to who occupies the positions of influence. Whether a strong-willed, conservative Southerner with political inclinations or a distracted big-city liberal more interested in city politics than the pork barrel chairs the House Public Works Committee, the same outcome is to be expected. The chairman's state might reap more benefits in one instance than in another, but certain general patterns will still appear.

To examine the effect of the structure of Congress on its output, an issue area was chosen deliberately that offered the widest possible amount of latitude for conformity of the pattern of expenditures to any particular distribution of influence. The most important policy characteristic for our purposes might be called "divisibility." A pol-

icy area is considered to be divisible if the amount of funds or benefits, however measured, going into one district (or state) can be varied
without affecting the amount going to others. If a policy area is characterized by divisibility, then it is possible that the distribution of
funds will correspond to the distribution of influence over the policy. The area of public works, and in particular the civil works program of the Corps of Engineers, seems to be characterized by almost
perfect divisibility, for the benefits of each project are localized,
whereas the costs are so spread out as to be nearly invisible to non-
beneficiaries. In addition to exhibiting this geographic divisibility,
public works projects can be made large or small* and can be constructed quickly or slowly.† These characteristics give congressional
decision-makers a broad range of choices on a project in any particular year. Thus the malleable nature of the Corps of Engineers'
construction program makes it a natural choice for the research purposes of this study.

It has been necessary throughout to make an assumption about
what members of Congress want. When Lasswell remarked, "The
influential are those who get the most of what there is to get,"[3] he
was referring to many different values. For our purposes, congressmen and senators are assumed to want to maximize the flow of expenditures into their districts and states; a later chapter will be devoted to a full-scale analysis of this assumption. For now, let us
simply assume that since each district and state is taxed by the federal government in order to pay for the public works program, members of Congress attempt to get as much as possible back for their
constituents.

This assumption is restrictive in several ways. First, the public
works budget is not the only distributive expenditure available to
a member. Early in his career, for example, he may face a choice between concentrating on getting more public works spending and
working to get more post offices or defense contracts for his constituents. By focusing on one issue, this study will miss the implications of such choices. Second, some districts, owing to the absence
of waterways, simply cannot receive very much in the way of public

---

* Chapters 2 and 3 will spell out in some detail how project size can be varied
by adding project features. For example, a flood-control dam might be altered to
include recreational features by building an upstream dam to help regulate stream
flow and thus obtain a relatively constant water level for the reservoir.

† The speed at which a project is built is heavily influenced by technical factors, but Congress can exercise a large amount of discretion within technical
constraints.

works expenditures.* Third, a member may have higher policy preferences—he may be willing to forgo an increase in public works expenditures in his district or state to increase the chance of passing a civil rights bill or of enacting a right-to-work law. Fourth, he may believe in certain criteria or standards for public works spending that the projects in his area fail to meet. He may then choose to stick to his standards rather than to press for the projects. Although these four factors are undoubtedly important, there is no way to take them into account in our initial assumption without also taking into account *all* distributive issues and how they affect every congressman and senator. Consequently, we have to accept our initial assumption about what members of Congress want, reassured by the statements of members themselves and by the observations of others.

In examining the way in which public expenditures reflect the institutional distribution of influence in the Congress, we also examine some political (as opposed to economic or technical) bases for policy decisions. We shall see that certain public expenditure decisions are regularly made on the basis of political considerations rather than of any desire to further the public good. Of course, political considerations and the public good are not always in conflict; but the extent to which they are is of some interest in itself. When decisions are made that openly violate economic principles, we find an opportunity to measure political influence.

The influences exerted by the distribution of power in Congress are complex and vary according to both issues and external circumstances. However, two broad and interrelated effects of these influences should occur and should be amenable to systematic study. First, if a program has geographically divisible components (as does the construction program of the Corps of Engineers), the members of Congress who are most strategically situated should receive a disproportionate share of its benefits. Second, among all programs, those sufficiently divisible for the members of Congress with the most leverage to get a disproportionate share of benefits should receive favored treatment by the Congress. Budgets for these programs should be found to be seldom cut deeply; they should also have powerful congressional support in struggles with the Budget Bureau and with other agencies. This study will attempt a systematic analysis of these twin hypotheses.

---

* Core city districts that do not border on navigable waterways are not eligible for funds under the program of the Corps of Engineers.

The book is divided into three parts: Part One (Chapters 1 through 3) is preliminary to the main investigation and deals with the decision-making structure for individual projects. Several questions are treated in this section. First, what are the formal criteria for project choice? Second, at what stages are "real" decisions actually being made? Third, which decision-making bodies have discretionary authority over projects, and which ones exercise it? Fourth, what is the relationship between a Corps of Engineers project and the local congressman? Part Two, which focuses on the second of our two key hypotheses, illustrates the handling of the Corps' budget over time. Part Three examines the distributive hypothesis (hypothesis number one) and demonstrates that a change in the distributive pattern in 1955 accounts for the change in the handling of the Corps' expenditures over time.

The first hypothesis is essentially static in nature. Among its implications are that members of the public works committees, and members of the public works subcommittees of the appropriations committees, should receive disproportionate benefits from their shared jurisdiction over the Corps of Engineers' construction program. In addition, senior committee members should benefit more than junior members, and the chairman and ranking minority members should receive large benefit shares relative to other senior committee members. Of course there are many additional hypotheses that can be advanced with some study of the unique formal and informal institutional configurations surrounding each of the committees. Chapters 8, 9, and 10 are devoted to setting forth each institutional hypothesis and testing it with appropriations data from the Corps' construction program.

An examination of the second hypothesis can be made through a comparison of the periods before and after the 1955 floor revolt in the House, which caused a permanent change in the House Appropriations Committee's attitude toward the Corps of Engineers' budget. Fenno's seminal work on the appropriations process offers a wealth of valuable data on congressional treatment of agency budgets that can be used as a basis for comparisons.

The Choice of a Policy Area

The nature of the questions we are posing makes the choice of a policy area for investigation particularly important. As mentioned above, it was considered desirable to choose as divisible a policy as possible so that there would exist an opportunity for variations in influence to be reflected in variations in public-policy outputs. The civil construction program of the Army Corps of Engineers seemed to be particularly suitable as such a policy for several reasons. First, the congressional policy-makers actually specify project by project exactly what will be built and the pace of construction on each project. Also, the traditional practice, codified in law, is for all projects to have their origin in the Congress. House and Senate committees in some cases determine when construction activity is to begin on particular projects. In summary, Corps policy is eminently divisible and is made to a great extent in Congress.

The Corps of Engineers, established more than 150 years ago, initially had as its mission the undertaking of internal improvements such as building canals and improving navigable waterways. Late in the nineteenth century the Corps began to enlarge its mission to include flood control, and over approximately the next half century the occurrence of several disastrous floods in the Mississippi Valley gave the Corps the opportunity to take over all projects having to do with flood control.

During the same period, the growth of another water resources agency, the Bureau of Reclamation (whose initial mission was literally to reclaim lands by providing irrigation water), began to threaten the Corps' primacy in the water resources field. Tales of battles between the two agencies are recounted elsewhere—for example, in Maass's *Muddy Waters*—and any discussion of them here would entail a description of the curious comparative statutory prerogatives of the agencies. It is sufficient for our purposes to say that during this period the Corps was permitted by Congress to claim irrigation and electric-power benefits in justifying its construction projects. Thus by 1936, the Corps' mission had expanded from the improvement of navigation to include flood control, electric-power production, and irrigation.

The Corps' function has expanded even more dramatically in the last thirty years. Projects for the protection of wildlife, the construction of recreation facilities, the improvement of water supply and quality, and the stimulation of regional economic development have all been authorized by Congress for the Corps of Engineers during this period. Although this expansion has enabled the Corps to avoid cutting back its budget and staff as earlier functions have declined in importance, it has also brought it into conflict with other federal agencies.

It would be misleading, however, to give the impression that the

Corps has been successful in enlarging its mission solely because of its close association with the congressional committees that share jurisdiction over its programs. A good part of its success has been the result of the high regard on the part of the official presidency and outside interest groups for the Corps' engineering competence in comparison with that of its rivals. The Corps' engineering or cost calculations are frequently regarded as more believable than those of the Bureau of Reclamation or the Environmental Protection Agency by members of the Office of Management and Budget or the White House staff.

It is well known that Congress's official attitude toward the Corps as expressed through the supervising committees can only be compared to its attitude toward the F.B.I. There has been a constant tendency on the part of the relevant committees to see a community of interest between the Corps and the Congress in opposition to the cold and frugal Budget Bureau, which seems unaware of the improvements in human life wrought by water projects.

The Data

In order to examine the hypotheses of interest, we must locate a set of discretionary decisions by Congress about which projects are to be built. This set of decisions must be in a divisible policy area and must prescribe the geographical distribution of benefits within that area. The principal criterion our set of decisions must meet is that they must actually be discretionary decisions, with a significant amount of the discretion resting with Congress. By choosing the program of the Corps of Engineers as a focus, the policy choices are already guaranteed to possess divisibility, as we have seen.

As will be demonstrated in Chapters 1 through 3, Congress is intimately involved in many decisions about which proposed projects will be built by the Corps of Engineers. Congress, through its committees, must initiate consideration of a project by requesting a study, must pass legislation authorizing each project (by name) to receive funds, and must provide appropriations for the individual projects. Some of the decisions are properly speaking not really decisions at all, since they involve no discretion. If a project meets a certain objective test, then it receives an automatic favorable decision from the appropriate congressional committee (see Chapter 1); if it fails this test, it is automatically rejected. Thus for our purposes we must isolate a set of decisions involving significant discretion on the part of congressional actors.

Appropriations decisions appear to meet this requirement. No single set of characteristics of a project dictates that the project must receive appropriations or, conversely, that it must not receive them. To be sure, there are exceptions to this statement (in particular when disastrous floods occur), but they are rare enough relative to the total number of appropriations decisions that they may be safely neglected.

Technically, the appropriations for the construction program of the Corps of Engineers are made in separate lump sums for planning and for construction. The Corps receives a certain amount for each of the two functions and then must divide that up among several hundred separate projects. However, the "Reports" accompanying the Appropriations Bill contain specifications detailing how much each project is to receive. Though these "Reports" do not have the full force of law, agency personnel regard them as binding. If the Corps desires an exception to a specified allocation of funds for a project as written into the "Report," the Chief of Engineers contacts the chairman of the relevant committee to obtain explicit permission to disregard the specification. This is a rare occurrence, and by and large the amounts written in the "Report" accompanying the Con- ference Bill are accurate indicators of what is actually spent during the fiscal year.

The principal data base for this study is the project-by-project appropriations recommendations contained in the "Reports" that accompany the House, Senate, and Conference Appropriations Bills. Data are available for the years 1947 to 1969, but changes in account- ing procedures occasionally make it necessary to omit certain years when longitudinal data are employed. In each of the chapters in which these data are used, aggregation procedures were employed to make them more manageable for our purposes. These procedures are described whenever they are used.

In addition to the appropriations recommendations, several other kinds of primary source data were collected and employed in a less systematic fashion. Several years of House and Senate hearings on the Appropriations Bills were read in their entirety, and many more years of hearings were consulted occasionally. Quotations from these hearings have been used where appropriate. Interviews were con- ducted with various participants and observers of the appropriation and authorization processes.[4] Hearings before the legislative com- mittees have been consulted and are quoted occasionally. The "Re- ports" accompanying the 1968 Rivers and Harbors and Flood

Control Bill were analyzed in some detail and material from this analysis is used where it seems helpful. The *Congressional Record* was employed to obtain the floor debates on the various authorizations and appropriations bills.

The rather extensive congressional literature of the last twenty years has yielded a rich source of interview material available in published and unpublished works. Various scholarly books, autobiographies, biographies, dissertations, articles, and papers have been consulted and quoted when it helps sustain an argument or ground a hypothesis. In addition, Donald Matthews of the Brookings Institution has generously allowed the author access to a set of interviews that he (and Professor James Stimson of the State University of New York at Buffalo) conducted with a sample of 108 congressmen. Of course when using interviews or quotations from interviews conducted by other researchers interested in other questions, care has been taken to avoid using material out of context. Whenever possible, several sources have been used to buttress the same point (if it is an important one), and hopefully these secondary materials are not made to bear too great a weight.

The interviews, the hearings, and the secondary source materials were used in making decisions about how to aggregate, analyze, and interpret the data. Those respondents who consented to several interview sessions were especially helpful in choosing how to interpret (or how not to interpret) some of the results of the statistical analyses. This study attempts to knit the material from all these diverse sources into a single fabric—to the extent that that is possible. The frayed or loose ends that remain are both mysterious and maddening.

PART ONE

How Projects Are Chosen

1

The Evaluation of Water Projects

The planning process appears to be specifically organized in response
to the need for an adjustment of group interests at the general
levels at which these interests may become articulate.
                                                —*Arthur Maass*

The Congress has long recognized a responsibility of the federal
government to undertake or to assist in undertaking the development
of water resources. This recognition began in the early 1820's and
has for many members of Congress as much urgency today as ever.
The requirement of undertaking only those projects in the public
interest has resulted over a period of time in the development of
procedures for routinely evaluating projects proposed for federal
funding. These procedures have remained remarkably stable since
World War II. This chapter will outline them and attempt to show
how they operate (see Fig. 1.1 for a flow chart of these procedures).*

Maass observed that each project must go through 32 separate
stages of consideration. At some of these stages no decision is made
and all projects pass through unaffected. At others, discretionary
decisions are not really made, since projects that meet some "objective" criteria are automatically passed and the rest are rejected. But

* There is no consideration here of the requirement that the Corps file an
environmental impact statement prior to initiating construction on a project.
This requirement became law in the National Environmental Policy Act of 1969
and has had severe consequences for many Corps projects otherwise eligible for
construction funds. Since nearly all of the data that form the basis for this study
relate to the period before this act went into effect, and since little is known as
yet of its consequences for the Corps of Engineers' construction program, the requirement has been omitted from this study. There is a growing congressional
sentiment either to repeal the specific section of the act requiring impact statements of a particular form or to pass laws granting exemptions for various types
of projects. In the 92d Congress, at least twelve bills were submitted to exempt
certain types of policies from the requirement of filing an impact statement.

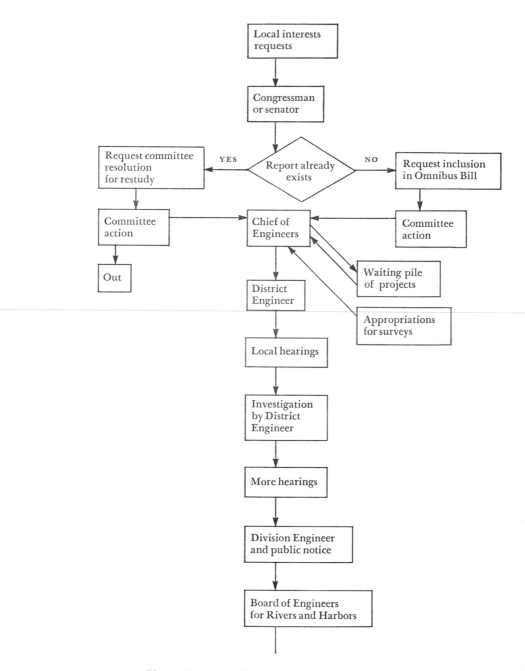

Fig. 1.1 Procedures for evaluating projects for federal funding

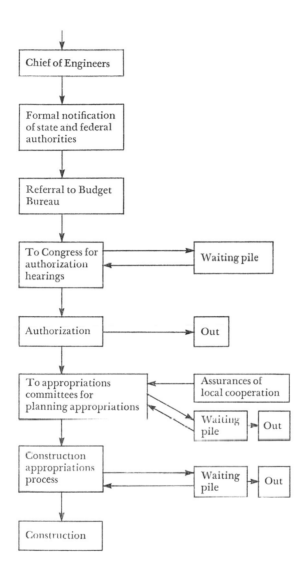

Figure 1.1 (*continued*)

at certain stages decision-makers exercise formal discretion over the fate of projects. We will not attempt at this point to systematically evaluate the characteristics of the decisions made stage by stage.

President Kennedy is quoted in *Senate Document 97* (issued on May 29, 1962) as saying: "The basic objective in the formulation of plans is to provide the best use, or combination of uses, of water and related land resources to meet all foreseeable long-term and short-term needs. . . . Well-being of all the people shall be the overriding determinant in considering the best use of water and related land resources."[1] Certain formal procedures constitute the Corps' and the Congress's tests of whether or not a project is in accord with this end.

The first stage is a request by a local group to a congressman or senator for an investigation of a proposed project. If no feasibility study has previously been done, the congressman or senator asks that the study request be included in the next Omnibus Rivers and Harbors Bill.* If the project has already been examined and an authorization for a study exists, a committee resolution is required for another study. Maass has studied committee resolutions and cites a 1935 manuscript.

During the 74th Congress, first session, the committee on Rivers and Harbors passed 117 resolutions calling for reviews of reports on rivers and harbors projects. Just about one-third of the 204 projects authorized in the current rivers and harbors act [1935] originated as favorable reports transmitted to Congress by the Corps of Engineers. Nearly two-thirds of the improvements authorized in the current act represent projects which were originally turned down by the Corps of Engineers or projects which have been modified by them upon review under committee resolutions.[2]

Maass also found that three-quarters of the Corps' investigations completed in 1946 were made under committee resolution and were not included in the Omnibus Bill. In the Rivers and Harbors and Flood Control Act of 1968, approximately 85 percent of the projects were investigated under committee resolution.

Once authority for an investigation is given (either by legislation or committee resolution), the project will eventually undergo a feasibility study. Appropriations for these studies are given in a lump sum and allocated among projects by the Corps of Engineers. The Corps exercises discretionary choice at this stage in deciding which projects will receive funds for investigations.

The preliminary examinations are carried out in the field by the

* Until the mid-1960's, the Omnibus Bill was reported out of the public works committees of the Congress and passed biennially. Since then an Omnibus Bill has passed each year.

Office of the District Engineer. Hearings are often held at this stage and local interests are invited to express their views on the proposed project. The report of the results is forwarded to the Chief of Engineers. The Chief of Engineers has a great deal of freedom of choice at this stage. Since no detailed plan exists, estimation of "expected" benefits and costs is approximate at best. Projects are eliminated if the Chief of Engineers judges that they are not economically justified. Maass states that for the period 1941–48, 478 of the 914 project reports from the Corps recommended against federal activity.[3]

If the report is favorable, project supporters must obtain appropriations for general investigations, which will make possible a more detailed study. Hearings are held and a fairly specific "plan of improvement" is drawn up. A meaningful benefit-cost ratio is computed at this point; if it is favorable the District Engineer recommends construction. There are reviews by the Division Engineer, the Chief of Engineers, and the Board of Engineers for Rivers and Harbors.

At this point other agencies are notified of the recommended plan, as are the Budget Bureau and those state governments affected by the project. Each will usually submit statements to accompany the project recommendation and will send representatives to the authorizations hearings before the congressional committees concerned with public works. All reports are submitted to Congress whether the associated project is recommended for construction or not; a recommendation at this stage is based solely on the benefit-cost ratio.

Hearings are held on the projects by the House and Senate committees on public works. In the House, the subcommittees for Rivers and Harbors and for Flood Control meet jointly to consider the reports. Each report, published as either a House or a Senate document, is referred to as the "project document." At the conclusion of project-by-project hearings, one or the other of the public works committees draws up an Omnibus Rivers and Harbors and Flood Control Bill. There are minor additions and deletions on the floor, and the bill then moves to the other chamber.

The authorization stage is not generally a point of critical decision on a project. Almost any project with a favorable benefit-cost ratio will eventually be authorized, even in the face of intense local opposition within the Congress. For example, in the hearings on the 1968 Omnibus Bill one of the projects under consideration was at Port Jefferson Harbor, New York, in the district of Representative Otis Pike (Republican–New York).* Pike testified before the House

---

* The bill had passed the Senate, and the Senate version recommended authorization of the project in Representative Pike's district.

Committee on Public Works that "in my opinion, this particular project which is located right smack in the middle of my own district, and is not near to anyone else, is not particularly justified at this particular time. I think if the committee in its wisdom saw fit to remove it from the bill the Nation would survive and so would I."[4] Nonetheless, the Corps recommended the project because it had an extremely high benefit-cost ratio of 6.0. Although the House version of the bill did omit the Port Jefferson project, it was restored in conference.

An examination of the 1970 Omnibus Rivers and Harbors and Flood Control Bill supports the thesis that decision-making at the authorization stage is largely automatic. Thirty projects were recommended in the House bill and 34 in the Senate bill; the final conference bill included all but one of the House's recommended projects and all but one of the Senate's as well. Thus in every case but two, apparent disagreements between the chambers were resolved by authorizing the projects in question.

In authorizing projects the Congress seldom seriously questions the benefit-cost analysis provided by the Corps of Engineers. Yet the methods the Corps uses to compute benefits and costs are open to objection on several grounds (see Chapter 2). There is a tendency to overestimate benefits and underestimate costs in the Corps as in other agencies, but even in the face of objection to the economic evaluation of a project congressional authorization tends to be automatic. There is one exception to this rule, however. In recent years the Congress has required that proposed projects undergo a preauthorization review by the President. Controversial projects are sometimes challenged at this stage by the Budget Bureau or by someone on the White House staff. The President might then object to the authorization of the project, which is almost the only way for the authorization decision to become a crucial one. In the 1970 Omnibus Bill, one of the projects not finally authorized although included in the Senate bill failed because of objections to the benefit-cost analysis by the Office of Management and Budget (O.M.B.).

Congress does not rigidly refuse to consider projects that have not received presidential clearance. On the contrary, committees frequently consider such projects and even authorize them—subject to the requirement that the President eventually clear them. Members of the institutional presidency are critical of this practice. A high-ranking O.M.B. official said in a personal interview, "We take a dim view of the inclusion of any project in the Omnibus Bill on which the President's review is not complete. . . . It really puts us on the spot. It puts the President out there in front of God and everyone." There is little doubt at the O.M.B. that this method of authorization subject to presidential clearance makes it politically difficult to object to a project at the preauthorization stage.

It is even more unusual for a project to be struck from the authorization bill as a result of an objection by a member of Congress. In the Senate debate over the Flood Control Act of 1962, Caleb Boggs (Republican–Delaware) attempted to remove a project at Knowles, Montana, partly on the grounds that the Corps of Engineers had incorrectly computed the benefits and costs of the project. Senator Robert Kerr (Democrat–Oklahoma), the floor manager of the bill, replied.

I wonder if the Senator from Delaware knows that most of the assignments to the Corps of Engineers are made from the top ten per cent of the graduating class each year at West Point. If there is a highly trained, competent group of engineers in the United States . . . they are to be found in the Corps of Army Engineers.

The project which the Senator from Delaware seeks to strike from this bill was evaluated by the Corps of Engineers, the Board of Rivers and Harbors, the Chief of Engineers, and then by the Director of the Bureau of the Budget of the U.S. Government.

All of them said that it was economically feasible. Under that circumstance it would be a little presumptuous of me to say it was not economically feasible.[5]

Boggs's attempt to strike the Knowles project failed.

These remarks indicate the strong presumption in favor of authorizing projects with favorable benefit-cost ratios. This is not to say that all projects with favorable benefit-cost ratios are immediately authorized. In every Omnibus Bill there are a few controversial projects, and some of these are refused authorization. However, the vast majority of projects recommended by the Corps do get by the very low hurdle that is the authorization stage.

In the next stage after authorization a project must receive a "definite project report." Since 1958, Congress has appropriated planning funds, which go toward drawing up these reports, separately for each project. Before that the Corps had wider discretion in deciding the pace of project planning. The decision about appropriating planning funds takes place within the budgeting process, and for the first time in the formal procedure the project is considered in a context of scarcity, both of funds and of capacity for resource use. For this reason, the planning appropriations stage is a significant bottleneck. At any given time there are usually hundreds of projects with authorizations but without completed definite project reports. Some projects are held up at this stage for years, and many never get beyond it.

In fiscal year 1969, for example, there was a backlog of 381 authorized active projects (those eligible for construction without reauthorization or restudy).* In addition, planning on 150 projects had not been initiated. In fiscal year 1970, of 452 projects planning was completed on 102 and had not been initiated on 198.

Scarcity of funds alone is not sufficient to explain why some projects are delayed and others die at this stage. The formulation of the definite project report entails determining what land must be taken out of private hands, how much local governments will contribute, which roads and bridges must be moved, and so forth. Local people are able to obtain a pretty good idea of who will benefit from the project and who will not. Consequently, local opposition materializes to a much greater degree at this stage than at previous ones. The repeated local hearings and extended consultation between the Corps and local interests allow opponents plenty of opportunity for organizing opposition groups, for hiring lawyers and engineers to evaluate the project and delay it, and even for testifying against the project at hearings before the appropriations committees in Washington.

The number of planning new starts undertaken each year is fairly small. In the last ten years the President's budget has generally contained between 20 and 45 planning starts. Congress will frequently add on another 20 to 40, and sometimes more. In fiscal year 1970, with a total of 198 projects awaiting planning starts, there were 58 starts. The number has ranged from 78 in fiscal year 1964 to 10 in fiscal year 1971. The planning stage, then, is one of the real points of decision for a project. Few projects are actually "killed," but most must wait in limbo (sometimes for years) for opposition to die and for their turn to receive appropriations.

With the completion of the final plan, the project is ready for construction appropriations. Only rarely is construction money appropriated without the definite project report's being completed.

* The classification of authorized projects into "active" and "inactive" projects is done within the Corps of Engineers and is occasionally published in the appropriations hearings. Projects are considered inactive if they require reauthorization or restudy. A project will require reauthorization if construction costs have increased or if it requires some major modification prior to construction. Projects may require restudy under similar circumstances.

The decision process at this stage has many of the characteristics of the previous stage. Scarcity of funds and of construction resources is, if anything, more of a consideration here than when the project was awaiting planning money.

Each year the Budget Bureau gives the Corps a budget ceiling and the Corps presents the Bureau with an allocation package consisting of construction appropriations for ongoing projects and a list of new construction starts. The Budget Bureau evaluates the new starts project by project and comes up with a list of those to be submitted to the Congress. The Budget Bureau customarily holds informal hearings on a state-by-state basis. During each hearing a delegation from the state concerned and its congressional representatives customarily appear to plead for particular projects. The Budget Bureau has criteria for determining project priorities independent of the benefit-cost ratio, and consequently the project list it sends to Congress will not include solely those projects with high benefit-cost ratios.

The Corps budget is presented to the House Appropriations Subcommittee on Public Works as part of the Public Works Appropriations Bill. This House subcommittee holds hearings and reports out a bill, itemized project by project, which contains many additional new starts for both planning and construction so that the total obligation on the Treasury is generally increased. The Senate Appropriations Subcommittee on Public Works holds hearings at the same time as the House. Generally, a witness will appear in the House on one day and then go over to the Senate on the next day to testify there. In both the Senate and the House the hearings follow the procedure of first receiving testimony from the Corps on a project-by-project basis and of then obtaining testimony from "outside witnesses" who generally support the budget request or ask for more money on some projects. In the Senate, there is generally a second period of hearings right after the House committee reports out their bill for the Corps to ask for "reclamas,"* or to support new starts added by the House or asked for in the Senate. These second hearings are usually brief and only agency witnesses appear. The Senate subcommittee reports out a bill that is generally larger than the House's. The bills then go to a conference where compromises are worked out project by project.

Once a project receives its first construction appropriation the

* A "reclama" is a request by an agency to the Senate Appropriations Committee to restore funds cut by the House from the agency budget.

expenditure stream becomes fairly determined.* However, when a project has many small separable components there is some discretion over the timing of the construction program, i.e. there is an opportunity to affect the speed of the process. Very few projects that receive initial construction funds are not completed though.

The appropriations process for construction contains several points at which real decisions are made. In general, if the Budget Bureau, the House Appropriations Subcommittee, or the Senate Appropriations Subcommittee decides to start a project, it will be constructed. This is so because projects are rarely struck from the budget once they are put in. The Budget Bureau is the tightest of the three bottlenecks. One result of this is the fact that of the total of 674 new starts between fiscal years 1959 and 1971, 376 were unbudgeted, i.e. originated in Congress. The completion of these projects will require a total outlay of about $10.5 billion by the federal government. Of this amount, $5.5 billion was committed by unbudgeted new starts.

The Budget Bureau can delay a project but it cannot stop one if the Congress wants to put it in the budget. In 1970 and 1971 the Budget Bureau impounded funds for congressional new starts. A responsible official in the O.M.B. commented, "We sure got a lot of heat on that. We had to let that money loose on June 30 (1971), but we made sure none of those projects was in the fiscal year 1972 budget. We stalled them for another year anyway." The same official alleged that extending the impoundment of funds would have been politically impossible and that the O.M.B. had done very well to hold up the projects for a total of three years.

This description of the project approval process indicates that most of the really important decisions taken on projects occur in the budgetary process. For this reason, most of the analysis in this book concentrates on decisions made within the various institutions involved in budget-making.

* Appropriations for Corps projects are made strictly on a year-by-year basis. The Corps is the only agency in the federal government which receives construction appropriations on this basis. Some implications of this method of funding are explored in Chapters 4 and 5.

2

Benefit-Cost Analysis

Unlike most policy decisions made in the federal government, the public investments undertaken by the Corps of Engineers undergo elaborate technical and economic analyses in order to determine whether the project will contribute to the "public good" (as defined by Corps practice and by statute) and whether the projected scale and services are the optimum ones given the alternatives available. The techniques used in such an investigation are generally known as benefit-cost analysis. The theory of benefit-cost analysis is relatively well-developed, although substantial disagreement remains among economists on several issues, as we shall see. The exposition of the theory of benefit-cost analysis in this chapter will introduce a useful (and relatively noncontroversial) necessary condition for a project to be considered in the public interest, i.e. the concept of efficiency. In practice, the results of a benefit-cost analysis are sensitive to several methodological decisions made by the Corps. We shall take a hard look at some of these decisions. In the course of investigating the basic benefit-cost theory we shall be able to examine the important hidden political decisions that underlie the actual application of that theory. At the end of the chapter the concept of efficiency will be used to analyze some institutional practices associated with benefit-cost analysis and will provide an answer to the question of whether there really is a "pork barrel."

Since the passage of the Flood Control Act of 1936, which required that for a project to be authorized its benefits must exceed its costs, the Corps of Engineers has engaged in what is now called benefit-cost analysis. In practice, economists have different opinions on exactly how such analysis should proceed, what variables should be taken into account, and what values should be assigned to some of the crucial parameters. There is more agreement on the theory, however; so we shall begin there and then proceed to an examination of issues that arise in practice.

The theoretical justification for the benefit-cost analysis of projects is found in welfare economics. There are two areas that concern the welfare economist: first, efficiency (the size of the pie); second, distribution (how it is cut up). Now in the interests of separating ethical questions from questions of fact, the economist traditionally has restricted his domain to the first of these areas—questions of efficiency. The theoretical definition of efficiency follows: a project is *efficient* if it will make everyone either better off or at least no worse off than he would have been without the project. However, this criterion is impossible to apply in practice. An example will illustrate some reasons for this.

Let us suppose that a public project has been proposed that will entail building a small dam on a river in order to prevent flood damage to people living downstream. Further, this dam will be built entirely on the property of one farm, which the downstream people who will benefit from the project must buy. They must also pay construction costs of building the dam. Let us suppose also that construction materials and labor are supplied competitively at known prices. Now if each of the N downstream people stands to lose $100 in the absence of the dam, and if construction of the dam costs m dollars, then the farmer who owns the land can get anything up to $(N \times 100 - m)$ dollars for his farm. If the farm is worth more than that to him, he will refuse to sell; if it is worth less, he will sell. Theoretically speaking, the project is efficient if he sells.

However, if we drop the assumption that each downstream dweller will lose $100 without the dam and instead allow each person to contribute as much as he wants, we get the following situation. The individual who lives downstream stands to lose a certain amount (a_1) known only to himself. If he claims to the other downstream dwellers that he stands to lose less than this and will thus put up a smaller amount of money (a_2) to get the dam built, then he has gotten $a_1 - a_2$ as a surplus from lying about his true preferences. The same incentive to lie confronts each downstream individual, so that in the aggregate less money will be collected than would have been the case if nobody had lied. In this situation the upstream farm-owner will want to exaggerate the amount he would accept for his farm, especially since he knows that the money raised downstream is going to be "too little." Consequently, we have a complicated bargaining problem among all of the actors. We can see that the dam might "really" be an efficient project, although it may never be built because in the presence of bargaining the real preferences of the actors are concealed, with the result that the costs apparently exceed the benefits. This problem is endemic in public projects involving required local contributions.

Leaving aside the problem of strategic behavior, the use of the concept of efficiency entails considerable computation on behalf of individual participants. In the previous example, a proposed project plus a transfer of funds from downstream dwellers to an upstream farmer might produce many effects other than simple flood control. For instance, among the benefits from building the dam in our example may well be the additional recreational facilities for swimming, boating, and fishing afforded by the presence of a lake. Such a lake would also provide a habitat for fish and wildlife (a habitat that might or might not be superior to the free-running stream), a stable water supply for a nearby village, and a reserve of water to augment stream flow during low-water periods and thus dilute effluents from farms and factories. Small variations in the physical characteristics of the project might have a substantial effect on one or more of the project's outcomes. In order to decide if it is efficient to build a certain project, we would have to examine various proposed ones (taking into account both physical descriptions and fund transfers) to see if any one exists that if carried out will leave each actor at least as well off as he was without it. Evidently, each individual must work out the consequences for himself of a proposed project to see whether it will improve his lot if it is built. This process may have to be carried out many times in the search for an efficient project. Thus, even if each individual were committed to revealing his true preferences, he would face a costly and time-consuming task.

In order to circumvent these difficulties, two compromises have been made. First, a less restrictive efficiency criterion has been adopted, the Kaldor-Hicks criterion. Second, in utilizing this criterion an effort is made to use market price information whenever possible. According to the Kaldor-Hicks test, a project is efficient if when it is completed it will be possible to compensate everyone in such a way that all will be either better off or at least not worse off than they would have been without the project. The compensation need not actually be carried out. Marglin puts it well: "Why not design public sector projects to maximize the size of the economic pie and rely upon pricing and fiscal policies to achieve the desired slicing?"[1]

The Kaldor-Hicks criterion requires only that the total benefits of a project exceed its total costs (according to some standard of value—say dollars), regardless of who receives those benefits. If we can utilize market data to estimate benefits and costs, then we need not consult each individual for his project evaluation. Of course, where market prices are unavailable we must use some method of ascertaining what each individual is willing to pay to have a particular project built. Such measures may be liable to strategic behavior and require expensive computations. Since the actual procedures followed in measuring benefits and costs are not of concern here, examples of estimation methods will not be given. It should be noted, however, that there are frequently benefits and costs that are not readily measurable by using market-like prices. These include aesthetics, national security, a general preference for hydroelectric power over fuel-generated power, preferred distributions of wealth, and the saving of human life. These "intangibles" qualify the use of benefit-cost analysis as the sole criterion for project choice.

The benefit-cost analyst's criterion is that if a project contributes more to the gross national product than it costs, it is a desirable project. Formally, if benefits − costs > 0, or if benefits ÷ costs > 1, the project should be adopted.

Investment projects, whether public or private, frequently produce benefits that spread far into the future. The Corps of Engineers often utilizes project lifetimes of one hundred years in its benefit-cost analyses. Consequently, even if the problem of measuring the value (in dollars) of the total benefits and costs of the project on a year-by-year basis is solved, there still remains the problem of estimating the total benefits and costs of the project in a single number aggregating over time. One solution would be simply to add up the benefits and costs of each year, obtaining

$$B = \sum_{t=1}^{N} B_t, \qquad C = \sum_{t=1}^{N} C_t.$$

This would imply that one dollar 20 years from now is to be counted the same as one dollar received right now; however, that is not the way human beings behave. For this discussion, risk and the possibility of dying during the 20 years shall be assumed away.

If a person is confronted with a situation in which he can receive a dollar now or a dollar in one year, he will choose the dollar now, other things being equal. There are many bases for this fact of *time preference*, and classical capital theorists have discussed them extensively. Among these are the diminishing marginal rate of utility of money—the consumer expects to be richer in the future than he is now so that a dollar will be worth less to him in the future—and the productivity of capital—if there is any place in the society where capital earns a positive rate of return (if for investing a dollar he can obtain $1.05 in a year), to refuse the dollar now for one in the future would be to forgo five cents. One can now define for an individual his riskless discount rate. If the individual is indifferent between a dollar now and $(1+r)$ dollars in a year, then we say he has a discount rate equal to r; this concept is defined for situations in which he knows with certainty that he will receive the $(1+r)$ dollars after a year. It is possible to define such a rate of discount for each individual in the society.

These individual rates of discount are actually revealed through the operation of capital markets in the following manner. An individual is faced with the choice of using his dollars to invest in various alternative productive enterprises. He will continue to invest additional dollars until the return he earns on his last dollar invested just equals the benefit he gets from spending that dollar on current consumption. The rate of return for this dollar is the individual's rate of discount on the margin. The individual discount rates will all be equal in the presence of perfect markets except when one of the following two conditions is true. In the first condition the individual has a small amount of current wealth and spends it all on consumption in the present. If he can borrow from the future he will do so until his marginal rate of time preference falls to the market rate of return. If his future income stream is small or if he cannot borrow freely, his marginal time preference rate will stay above the market rate of return. In the second condition, the individual may attach a small marginal valuation to increments in current consumption spending even though he is on the boundary of starvation; consequently he will have a marginal time preference lower than the market rate.

In a perfect capital market, competition among firms for investment dollars operates to produce *market rate of interest*. In equilibrium this is equal to the marginal productivity of capital in every firm. The precise conditions under which this occurs are not of concern here, but we can observe empirically that there are market rates of interest that confront firms and investors. The actual rate confronting different firms at a given time depends on the risk involved in investing in them. However, it is worth remembering that the individual's discount rates are in general different from each other (sometimes very widely so) even in equilibrium in perfect capital markets.

In choosing whether or not to invest in a particular project, the government must choose a rate for discounting both the cost stream and the benefit stream in order to decide whether the project is efficient. The government's choice lies in either using the market rate of interest or somehow arriving at a *social rate of discount*. There also remains the question of how to treat risky projects. These are controversial matters for the economics profession because the questions are as much ethical or political as economic. Before outlining the major arguments for each position, it is worth indicating why this disagreement, seemingly concerned with differences of only two or three or perhaps five percentage points, is of major importance.

Perhaps the best place to begin is with some empirical results. Irving Fox and Orris Herfindahl of Resources for the Future examined the Army Corps of Engineers' projects authorized in 1962. The discount rate in use at the time was $2\frac{5}{8}$ percent; 178 projects were authorized with benefit-cost ratios greater than one. The market rates of interest confronting firms borrowing money were between 8 and 10 percent pretax return. If the Corps' projects had been evaluated at discount rates of 4, 6, or 8 percent, then "the following percentages of initial gross investment would have had a *B-C* ratio of less than unity: 9 percent, 64 percent, and 80 percent, respectively."[2] It becomes apparent that project authorization (which depends on the *B-C* ratio) is extremely sensitive to the choice of a discount rate. Why?

Most water projects involve a substantial capital outlay before any of the benefits are felt. The costs are incurred very early in the life of the project and the benefits are spread out over a long period. A simple numerical example will illustrate this phenomenon. Suppose there is a project with initial capital costs of $100, net yearly benefits of $10, and an infinite project life. We can then graph the benefit-cost ratio against the discount rate (see Fig. 2.1). In this example the project is favorable as long as the discount rate is less than 11.1 percent. If the discount factor used were 20 percent the benefit-cost ratio would equal about .6. The choice of the discount rate therefore has a great effect on the pool of projects that can effectively be considered. Using a similar example it could be shown that

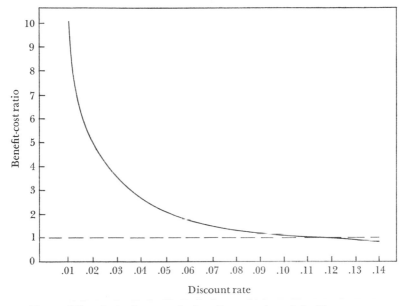

Fig. 2.1 The relation between the benefit-cost ratio and the discount rate

lower discount rates encourage the choice of greater scale within each project. If the discount rate is too low, though, too many projects are chosen and they are too big. What then is the "appropriate" rate of discount?

There is a basic conflict between those economists who believe that the market rate of interest is an appropriate rate of discount and those who believe it is too high. Economists in the first camp (Baumol, Tullock, and Hirschleifer)[3] as well as their opponents (Marglin and Sen)[4] defend their positions on primarily ethical grounds. We shall first examine the argument that the market rate of interest should be used for discounting public investments.

Political scientists sometimes think of expenditure and taxation decisions as entirely separate. And indeed the institutional configuration surrounding public budgeting as it has developed in the United States lends at least an aura of reality to this bifurcation. Clearly, the political processes at work in these areas are almost completely separated. The economist, however, his vision chiefly focused on the household as the primary economic unit, sees a basic unity between expenditure and taxation decisions that has to exist in the long run unless economic instability is to reign. A dollar invested in a public project is a dollar not invested somewhere else, he would argue. If the dollar were invested in a private enterprise, it would earn the prevailing interest rate; since the government obtained that dollar by taxation or other means (printing money, for example, which is also a kind of tax), a dollar more in a public project is a dollar less in a private project.

This simplistic argument is clearly wrong. What ought to be considered explicitly is what is called the *opportunity cost* of a public investment. Opportunity cost is defined as the amount that society forgoes by investing in a public project. Baumol summarizes this concept aptly.

The decision to devote resources to investment in a public project means, given the overall level of employment in the economy, that these resources will become unavailable for use by the private sector. And this transfer should be undertaken whenever a potential project available to the government offers social benefits greater than the loss sustained by removing these resources from the private sector.[5]

In a situation where all the factors of production are fully employed, Baumol's remarks are true: the opportunity cost of a dollar of public investment is a dollar that will not be available for private investment. In equilibrium, the market rate of interest that would be earned by a dollar invested in the private sector must be enough in excess of the government bond rate to make up for the taxes that the private investor must pay. Therefore, according to Baumol and his supporters, the discount rate that should be used is neither the rate at which the government can borrow money nor the "social rate of discount" (however this might be derived from the individual rates), but rather the market rate of interest. By using the market rate of interest, efficiency in resource allocation between the private and public sectors can be achieved. We shall see, though, that the efficiency question cannot be settled so easily. We must still ask what rate of discount should be used in order to achieve efficient resource allocation between the present and the future.

This brings us to a consideration of the position of Marglin and Sen, who argue that the market rate of interest is too high a discount factor. Marglin asks, "Why do governments require citizens to sacrifice current consumption in order to undertake investments that will not yield their benefits until those called upon to make the sacrifice are all dead?"[6] He argues that there are three possible bases for such behavior. The first is authoritarian rejection by the government of individual discount rates. The government simply decides that there ought to be a certain level of public investment irrespective of the wishes of individual citizens. Second, citizens are "schizophrenic" with respect to the choice of discount rates. The individual operates on the basis of self-interest when acting as a consumer, but when acting as a citizen he has a wholly different set of public preferences. This is similar to the Rousseauian distinction between the "will of all" and the "general will." Third, public investment is viewed as a collective good rather than as a private good.

Burke was perhaps the most persuasive advocate of the authoritarian position on this issue. He argued that the body politic is an organic unity and that those who have lived in the past, who are living in the present, and who will live in the future all have interests in how it is governed. The governors thus have responsibilities to future generations as well as to generations past. In representing the future, the government has an obligation to conserve resources and to provide for public investment that might favor future generations over the present one.

The schizophrenic view is well illustrated by Arthur Maass in a recent article.

Each individual plays a number of roles in his life . . . and each role can lead him to a unique response to a given choice situation. Thus an individual has the capacity to respond in a given case . . . in several ways, including these two: (1) what he believes is good for himself—largely his economic self-interest—and (2) what he believes to be good for the political community.

Now, the response that an individual gives in any choice situation will depend in significant part on how the question is asked of him. . . . The great challenge for welfare economics is to frame questions in such a way as to elicit from individuals community-oriented answers.[7]

Maass repeatedly drives home his point that the individual has two distinct sets of goals—public and private ones—and that he is really in consequence two different people—citizen and consumer.

The third position neither ignores the individual nor divides him in two. The individual is assumed, rather, to value others' consumption (in present and future) as well as his own. He is not completely altruistic, since he values his own consumption more than that of others in nearly all cases. Marglin presents this thesis as follows. "But here . . . the key is not that a change in the frame of reference occasions a change in individuals' preferences. Rather it is the difference between the machinery offered by the political process and the machinery offered by the market process for implementing one's preferences."[8] A little elementary algebra will illustrate his argument.

There are two generations, present and future, and no one in the present generation is alive in the next. All present individuals are alike and face the same sets of opportunities. For individual i, we denote his utility by u_i and his consumption by c_i. The total consumption of present and future generations is written c_p, c_f. We then write the ith individual's marginal utility as

$$(1) \qquad du_i = dc_i + \alpha dc_f + \beta(dc_p - dc_i),$$

where it is assumed that the marginal utility of an extra dollar of consumption to the individual is equal to 1. Both α and β are constant and generally less than 1.* The return a dollar's worth of investment now will bring in the future is $k > 1$. The individual will invest in the future only if $\alpha k > 1$. This means that he will invest in a long-term project only if he values the return the dollar will bring to the future generation more than he values the loss of the dollar in current consumption. If $\alpha = .1$, in which case the individual would seem to be extremely altruistic, and if $k = 2$ (a dollar's investment now pays off two dollars in the future), this calculation would mean that no one would invest in the long-term project.

Now suppose that some other individual, call him j, could invest a dollar in the project. Individual i values j's consumption at β according to equation (1), and so he would be pleased with j's decision if $\alpha k > \beta$. Of course, by the above reasoning individual j might not want to invest in the project anyway.

However, the political system, being in part a system of coercion, can provide a method for undertaking investment in the future. The ith individual might find it desirable to invest if he is convinced that others will also; this investment can be ensured by coercion (taxes). If everyone invests one dollar, then the ith individual's gain can be written.

$$(2) \qquad du_i = -1 + \alpha kn - \beta(n - 1).$$

Everyone is better off if $du_i > 0$, i.e. only when $\alpha kn > 1 + \beta(n - 1)$. If $\beta = .15$ (the individual is more altruistic toward his contemporaries than toward the future), one can see that du_i will be nonnegative as long as n is greater than 17. Therefore if the community is large enough, the political action of imposing taxes to benefit future generations can make everyone better off than would be the case if the market operated freely.

* The symbol α is the increment in utility that person i receives if the future generation receives an extra unit; β is the utility increment he gets if his contemporaries receive an extra unit of consumption.

We can translate this result directly to the discount rate by noting that the individual's private discount rate between generations is $100 \times (1/\alpha - 1) = 900$ percent in the example, whereas the social rate of discount for a large society is equal to $100 \times (\beta/\alpha - 1) = 50$ percent. It is evident that the social discount rate is much lower than the private discount rate.

This social rate has nothing to do with the rate of interest facing individuals. From this fact Marglin draws the following conclusion. "We reject the twin notions (1) that the rate of interest determined in an atomistic competitive market need have any normative significance in the planning of collective investment, and (2) that the market-determined rate of investment, and hence the market-determined rate of economic growth, need be optimal in any welfare sense."[9] Marglin's whole argument follows from his insight that public investment in the future is considered by individual consumers as a public or collective good. He therefore finds that individual consumers find it in their interest to act as citizens in the course of maximizing their own self-interest. This concept bears some resemblance to Hobbes's description of the origin of the state, and it is one that recurs in political theories developed from voluntarist or individualist ethics (as, for example, Dahl's and Lindblom's). From this position Marglin argues that the social rate of discount should be considered to be lower than the market rate of interest.

Thus two sets of eminent economists are in fundamental disagreement over the appropriate discount rate. We have seen already that the choice of a discount rate has a very important effect on the size of the pool of available projects. Baumol, partly conceding Marglin's point, states that ". . . no optimal rate exists."[10] The rate which leads to efficient allocation between public and private sectors is a different rate from that which achieves efficient intergenerational distribution where investment is considered to be a public good. The difference between the two results centers around the fact that Baumol's individuals are selfish whereas Marglin's are altruistic.

Tullock presents a persuasive argument against Marglin's model. Even if we admit that the individual has the capacity to be altruistic, Tullock argues that the individual generally displays this capacity when the gifts are to be given to the poor rather than to the rich. It is hard to imagine, he claims, a society of assistant professors banding together altruistically to give aid to the full professors. Similarly, since those in the future will be better off than we are now, why should anyone look favorably upon a redistribution of wealth toward the future? Tullock (and Baumol) seem fully to share the feeling of the

Preacher in Ecclesiastes 2:18 quoted in Marglin's article: "Yea, I hated all my labour which I had taken under the sun: because I should leave it unto the man that shall be after me."[11]

All this disagreement has been uncovered without even considering the factor of risk. Investment involves surrendering present resources for the chance of receiving greater resources in the future. Since the future is less certain than the present there is some risk in every investment. When a private investor puts his capital into a project he normally bears this risk himself; however, he may purchase some sort of insurance against components of it.

Many economists assert that the individual wishes to avoid risk, or is "risk-averse." The standard example of this concept is a man confronted with a choice between a sure $50 on the one hand, and on the other $100 or nothing with equal probabilities of either. He would opt for the $50. This is so even though the second alternative is a "fair bet" in the sense that if it were taken over and over there would be an average payoff of $50. The question is more complex than this, of course, for it is quite possible that the rational man's choice between the sure thing and the fair bet will depend on the stakes and on his initial wealth. For example, where a poor man would almost certainly take the sure $50, a millionaire might well take the fair bet. Indeed, there is experimental evidence to suggest that if the stakes are "small" to an individual, he is likely to be a "risk-preferrer."

It is worth noticing that the rational man with declining marginal utility of income would consider taking such a gamble only where the stakes are very small to him relative to his initial wealth. Technically, the possible outcomes of the bet must be spread over such a small range of possible income positions that his marginal wealth valuation does not decline over this range. Indeed, if the marginal utility of income were steadily declining over the whole range of possible incomes, then the rational man would never take a fair bet. In the economists' language, each man would be a "risk-averter."

Now suppose that an individual is confronted with an opportunity to make the following bet. He is asked, "How much would you *pay* to gamble on getting $100 or nothing with probabilities equal to one-half?" If the individual responds honestly, he will generally pay less than $50. Let us suppose he would pay up to $40 and no more for the gamble. Then we can say that $40 is the *certainty equivalent* of the gamble to this person. We might also expect the millionaire to be willing to pay somewhat more for the gamble than the pauper.

Now we will expand this situation to include two possible gambles. One is the example above, and the other is the opportunity to get $75 or $25 with probabilities equal to one-half. People would generally pay more for the second gamble than for the first, so it can be seen that as the spread of the outcomes (the uncertainty) is reduced, the certainty equivalent goes up. Again, this spread or uncertainty is a relative concept and depends on the spread of the stakes relative to the initial wealth of the bet-taker. Consequently, the poor man might pay $40 for the first bet and $48 for the second, whereas the rich man might pay $49 and $49.50, respectively.

Given these elementary concepts, it is evident that the government will voluntarily take riskier gambles than a private investor, since if the gamble does not pay off the government's loss is spread out over all the taxpayers. For any particular investment project, the spread of outcomes for a given taxpayer is going to be a minute part of his income; consequently, for the citizen, the marginal utility of income is not declining in this range. But if the individual investor considered the same project, its failure would mean a relatively large loss to him. Thus, in the terminology introduced above, the certainty equivalent of a given project is higher to the government than it is to the private investor.

Now let us suppose that the government sells bonds at some rate r, and that the purchaser of a bond bears no risk at all. Then the private market rate of interest where private investments are risky might be $r_1 = r + c$, with c representing the *risk premium*. If the private securities markets were in equilibrium, r would be the certainty equivalent of r_1. The policy question, then, revolves around which rate the government should use to discount investments. Should it be (1) the riskless bond rate r, (2) the market rate of interest r_1, or (3) the social rate of time preference introduced above, ignoring considerations of risk altogether?

Baumol and Hirschleifer argue that the government should generally employ the market rate (r_1) to discount projects. They contend that in situations where resources are fully employed an extra unit of capital in government investment will come out of private investment; and, if the government is using a discount rate lower than the market rate, this will mean shifting resources from uses that are highly productive to those that are of lower productivity. From society's point of view this is an improper allocation decision (assuming that everybody desires an increase in the GNP) since it will lower the GNP.

Arrow and Lind[12] believe that the government ought to use the riskless rate of return. Hirschleifer, they say, fails to consider the distribution of risk-bearing. "When risks are publicly borne, the costs of risk-bearing are negligible; therefore, a public investment with an expected return which is less than that of a given private investment may nevertheless be superior to the private alternative."[13] Their position is that society as a whole is better off only if at least one individual is better off, and no individual is worse off, than before. Therefore, since taking a dollar away from a private investment with a certainty equivalent to the investor of less than r and putting that dollar into a government project makes the investor better off and does not hurt anyone, it is a socially better use of the dollar.

The author inclines toward the Arrow-Lind view because it rests on the easily defensible standard of efficiency; on the other hand, the Baumol-Hirschleifer position appears to involve a defense of arbitrary redistributions because their argument rests on the Kaldor-Hicks criterion. The third position, the one put forth by Marglin above, is of an entirely different character. It rests on intergenerational efficiency criteria in the presence of altruism. Arrow and Lind, Baumol, and Hirschleifer all deal with intersectoral efficiency among self-seeking investors.

The three positions described above are all predicated on a uniform discount rate for benefits and costs that applies to all investment projects. In practice, government agencies all employ such uniform rates, though different agencies use different rates. Some economists maintain that there is no reason for such procedures. For example, when irreversible production processes are in use, such as those that lead to the extinction of a species or to the exhaustion of a natural resource, then Marglin's intergenerational rate of time preference might be very low and ought to be used. On the other hand, where no irreparable damage is done to the environment in terms of its utility for future generations, the market rate (with or without a risk premium) might be more appropriate. Costs and benefits can be discounted according to different rates. As an example we can use the building of dams on the Russian River in California. The costs included the more or less irreversible destruction of the steelhead fishery; however, there were recreational, flood control, and irrigation benefits. Perhaps the cost stream should have been discounted at a lower rate (since it involved the permanent removal of a resource from the use of future generations) and the benefit stream discounted at a higher rate (reflecting the true opportunity cost of capital). Also, as Arrow and Lind point out, benefits from projects frequently accrue to individuals (as with improved flood control, irrigation, and navigation), whereas costs are largely borne by the public. Therefore benefits should be discounted at the market rate of interest and costs should be discounted at the riskless bond rate.

This exposition has sought to show that the choice of a discount rate is a controversial question among economists because it is largely a political question. The choice of one rate over another inevitably involves the dispossession of one group in favor of another through some form of coercion, although this is not always explicitly realized. The agencies that employ benefit-cost analysis have chosen discount rates which are generally far below market interest rates (with or without risk premiums); these rates are applied uniformly across projects and equally to benefits and to costs.

The benefit-cost theory developed thus far may be simply summarized. When one finds the "correct" discount rate, one simply invests in all projects with a benefit-cost ratio greater than one. It is irrelevant whether this is paid for by raising taxes or by borrowing through government bonds. In fact, however, the decision-makers in government face a very different situation. For political and bureaucratic reasons each agency has a fixed budget ceiling on available funds at any time. It can be shown that the political and bureaucratic device of giving each agency a budget and having the agency choose its best investment package is a shibboleth.[14] Society could theoretically do better by pooling all public investment opportunities in a central authority. Lindblom[15] argues that the synoptic (or centralized) method is unfeasible, and he might argue that incentives operate under a fixed-agency-budget (F.A.B.) system to make it economically better than it would appear to be theoretically.

The optimal investment rule for the agencies operating under the F.A.B. system is to rank projects according to their benefit-cost ratios and then choose from the top until they either exhaust the budget or come to a project with a benefit-cost ratio less than one. The inefficiency of the F.A.B. system is evident in a government of even as few as two agencies with fixed budgets and separate pools of possible projects. For only by accident will the last projects each agency chooses have the same benefit-cost ratios. If Agency 1's last project has ratio B_1, and Agency 2's last project ratio is B_2, with $B_1 > B_2$, then if there is a project left in Agency 1's pool with benefit-cost ratio B_3 so that $B_1 > B_3 > B_2$, society would have been better off if Agency 1's budget had been expanded and Agency 2's budget shrunk so that project B_3 would have been chosen rather than B_2. Although Lindblom might argue that congressmen, in reviewing agency budgets and making marginal changes in them, have incentives to find and correct gross distortions introduced by the F.A.B. system, his argument is in principle subject to empirical examination. On the face of it, however, it is not all clear that congressional or bureaucratic incentives will work in favor of reducing the budgets of agencies whose last-choice projects have lower benefit-cost ratios than the last-choice projects of other agencies. In any event, until such incentives are demonstrated, we can hardly be content with the assertion that synoptic methods are impossible to apply. There may be new methods (economists interested in economic planning are discovering some), requiring only slightly more information than the F.A.B. method requires, that can approximate a synoptic method through different bargaining structures.

This optimal method of project choice is predicated on the use of the "correct" discount rate. If the rate used is "too low," then agencies using either a strict benefit-cost rule (investing in each project with benefit-cost ratio greater than one) or an F.A.B. benefit-cost rule will always have too much investment. The Herfindahl and Fox paper cited earlier in this chapter indicates that the extent of such over-investment is likely to be quite large.

The analysis so far has proceeded in what economists sometimes consider the "classical world," where productive resources are scarce, there is no unemployment, and there is no idle capacity in the economy. Since these conditions are only rarely approached in the American economic system, the benefit-cost rules must be reformulated to make them applicable to our imperfect world.

The key concept now turns out to be opportunity cost. In the classical full-employment setting, putting resources into public investment removes them from private investment, with the result that the income they would have earned through such private use is lost. Where there is unemployment and excess capacity, though, some resources employed in public investment might otherwise have remained idle if the public project did not exist. If this is true for a unit of productive resource, then its opportunity cost should properly be equal to zero—it should be considered a *free factor of production*. Consequently, when unemployment is high labor should have a lower opportunity cost than its market price; when an industry has excess capacity, use of the products of that industry should have a lower opportunity cost than when it is operating at full capacity.

Things are not quite this simple, for labor is not just a homogeneous pool of man-hours to be put to one use or another. Labor consists of specialized pools—occupations—with limited mobility from one pool to another, at least in the short run. Unions and skill requirements are frictional forces that make it possible (even usual) for some occupations to be at full employment while others have high unemployment rates.

Geographical distance is another source of friction because it leads to situations where there can be full employment in an occupation in one region and high unemployment in the same occupation elsewhere. Similar restrictions on labor mobility retard movement between industries as well: machinists in the aerospace industry are not perfectly mobile to automobile manufacturers, repair shops, and similar industries.

Thus we have to accept the dictum that the *costs* in the benefit-cost ratio will vary with aggregate unemployment and excess capacity for the whole economy, as they will by region, occupation, and industry.

Robert Haveman recently published an empirical analysis of five types of water projects in ten regions of the United States. He estimated opportunity costs as a percentage of dollar costs under economic conditions in 1960.[16] The national unemployment rate then was 5.64 percent, and there was considerable variation by region, occupation, and industry. His results are presented in Table 2.1.

Since the table entries are less than 100 percent, dollar costs overestimate opportunity costs and project benefit-cost ratios are uniformly underestimated. Despite considerable regional variation, we see that for all project types except dredging relative opportunity costs are highest in the Southeast. If decision-making were to proceed on

TABLE 2.1

Opportunity Cost as a Percentage of Dollar Cost for Five Project-types

Region	Large earth-fill dams	Local flood protection	Medium-size concrete dams	Large multiple-purpose projects	Dredging	Median percentage
New England	89%	84%	88%	87%	84%	86.5%
Mid-Atlantic	82	77	84	82	78	80.5
East North-Central	91	90	92	92	90	91.0
West North-Central	88	85	90	89	89	87.5
Southeast	93	93	94	94	88	91.5
Lower Atlantic	78	69	77	76	75	73.5
Kentucky-Tennessee	83	78	83	81	79	80.5
West South-Central	92	92	93	93	87	90.0
Mountain	92	92	93	93	94	93.0
West Coast	86	84	87	87	76	81.5
Median percentage	88.5%	84.5%	89%	88%	85.5%	

SOURCE: Haveman, "Evaluating Public Expenditures Under Conditions of Unemployment," p. 341.

economic grounds alone, there would be a relative shift of investment away from the Southeast and toward the Lower Atlantic (Virginia, West Virginia, Maryland, Delaware, District of Columbia), the Kentucky-Tennessee, and the Mid-Atlantic regions since the benefit-cost ratios in these regions are more seriously underestimated. Overall, public investment should rise in slack years in every region. Two separate phenomena should occur: first, the agency budget should expand when the economy has more slack resources; second, the relative proportions of investment should shift away from the Southeast.

It should also be noted that some projects require large immediate capital outlays and have low continuing operating costs, whereas other projects have higher operating costs and require less in initial outlays. The type of project with very large initial costs and low continuing costs will be the most sensitive to economic conditions. The reasons for this are evident: projects with large immediate capital requirements will exhibit sharp dips in opportunity costs as economic conditions worsen. If immediate capital needs are small relative to total project costs, there is little responsiveness to short-term economic fluctuations.

In summary, although many of the important considerations underlying the use of benefit-cost analysis have been introduced, the exposition has avoided the genuinely technical issues of imputing economic values to nonmarketable goods and services. The actual behavior of decision-makers has been ignored in favor of an examination of how they should behave if they want to achieve efficient public investment (under the assumptions made here). Observably, this normative theory constitutes a poor predictive theory—decision-makers in practice deviate substantially from what they should do. To ascribe all such deviation to "politics" is too easy, just as it is too easy to ascribe all behavior consistent with the efficiency model to economics alone. Efficiency is in fact a political goal for some actors; thus such a simple partition must be avoided.

For convenience, some propositions follow that would be true if efficiency were the only goal of policy-makers. It must be reemphasized beforehand that the efficiency goal is ambiguous "at the edges," so to speak. These propositions refer to a simple world of two governmental agencies and a private economy. This merely simplifies exposition, for these propositions apply equally to the complicated array of governmental institutions.

1. If the correct discount rate is used, all projects with benefit-cost ratios greater than one should be undertaken.

2. If there is unemployment or idle capacity in the economy, the

benefit-cost ratios should be recomputed and all projects with benefit-cost ratios greater than one should be undertaken. If these ratios are *not* recomputed, then it will be efficient to undertake some projects with benefit-cost ratios less than one.

3. If agencies are operating under a fixed-agency-budget constraint, then projects should be undertaken in descending order of their benefit-cost ratios.

4. Under the F.A.B. system, if Agency 1 consistently has a lower last-project benefit-cost ratio than Agency 2, then Agency 2's budget should grow faster than Agency 1's.

5. If there is unemployment and idle capacity in the economy, then the budget constraints should be shifted upward for both agencies through expansion of the public debt.

6. If there is unemployment and/or idle capacity, and if their extent varies regionally, then there should be a relative regional shift in projects selected.

7. If the rate of discount is increased under an unconstrained budget, the total public investment will decline.

8. Under the F.A.B. system a "large enough" rise in the rate of discount will bring a decline in public investment.

We have assumed throughout this chapter that benefit-cost analysis, if properly carried out, would constitute a desirable method of screening proposed projects. In other words, if a project had a true benefit-cost ratio of less than one, then since it would cost society more to build and operate than it would return to society, all of the beneficial effects of the project could be achieved at less cost by a direct cash transfer from the taxpayers to the beneficiaries. In short, the project ought not to be built.

The idea of "pork" or the "pork barrel" has been in the vocabulary of political observers for many years. It is taken to mean a project that is inefficient in the Kaldor-Hicks sense, or, equivalently, one that has a true benefit-cost ratio of less than one. The true benefit-cost ratio of a project is the one obtained if project benefits and costs are properly estimated* and if the correct discounting procedures are applied. The reader will therefore note that this definition of the true benefit-cost ratio cannot be applied to yield a particular benefit-cost ratio for a particular project until the fundamental disagreements over these notions within the economics profession are resolved.

---

* The notion of proper estimation is an *ex ante* one. All that is required is that the estimation procedures be free of systematic bias in one direction or another. The estimates need not turn out to have been true in every case, for that would be impossible.

However, by using the various acceptable definitions for the discount rate outlined earlier and some actual empirical studies of project-benefit estimation, a probable range for the true benefit-cost ratio can be bracketed. Using this technique the following two points will be argued: (1) the discount rate currently in use is too low; (2) project benefits are systematically overestimated by the Corps of Engineers. By themselves these two propositions suffice to show that the benefit-cost ratio of a project is systematically biased upwards. Therefore projects with benefit-cost ratios near one are likely to be inefficient. All that remains in order to complete the argument is to observe that many such projects are actually built.

Some dissent exists over the propriety of utilizing technical efficiency as a defining concept of the public good. There are economists and political scientists who maintain that certain projects with benefit-cost ratios lower than one ought to be undertaken on redistributive grounds. Proponents of this view observe that there is a trade-off between efficiency and redistribution and that policy-makers may reasonably choose to give up a little efficiency for a little redistribution. They also hold that unless redistribution occurs through public investment projects it is unlikely to take place at all.[17] Thus the particular configuration of political institutions makes what might seem to be inefficient projects justifiable since they distribute wealth to poor areas of the country.* In order to defend this view, its proponents would have to show that projects which are not judged efficient by the benefit-cost ratio have some redeeming merit—for example, redistributing wealth or providing opportunities to the poor. The test must be applied on a project-by-project basis, and where an inefficient project would help to further some socially justifiable goal it might wisely be recommended for construction. If this line of reasoning is accepted, there appears to be no simple way to define the pork barrel since, depending on which nonefficiency goals society wants furthered, all sorts of seemingly inefficient projects might actually be socially desirable.

This entire argument may be tentatively rejected on several prac-

* This point of view is similar to that of the economists who insist that to make policy recommendations economists must have some idea of society's "social welfare function." Without such knowledge the economists' recommendations are either trivial or misleading, since they all emphasize that society should end up with an efficient allocation of goods. If some allocations are politically unfeasible though technically achievable, the insistence that society choose an efficient allocation may actually make society worse off in terms of its (unknown) social welfare function.

tical grounds. First, there is no evidence that inefficient projects do further socially desirable goals. Project beneficiaries, even in poor parts of the country, tend to be well off. Construction unions have rigid entry barriers, and the provisions of the Davis-Bacon Act* tend to make work on federal projects attractive to laborers outside the immediate locality. These two last-mentioned factors minimize the direct effects of projects on local unemployment. Second, even if some inefficient projects have socially desirable consequences there is no evidence that the presence of these consequences is what enables the projects to pass congressional review. The argument, advanced seriously by some economists,[18] that the explanation for why inefficient projects are chosen is that they must have other beneficial consequences is tautological and naïve. Third, the concept of political feasibility is an ambiguous one. An economist may decide to testify in favor of an inefficient project which he believes will deliver some benefits to slum-dwellers because he thinks Congress incapable of passing a law to make direct income transfers to such people. The basis of his estimation of what Congress is or is not capable of passing must be regarded as dubious and possibly self-fulfilling.

While it may be true that certain inefficient projects ought to be built since they do result in a redistribution toward poor people, the burden of proof must rest on those who desire an exception to the efficiency criteria. It seems absurd to argue as some do that the congressional process as presently constituted does in fact make these social calculations, and that when Congress decides to construct an inefficient project it does so for good reason. This argument cuts away all possible grounds for criticism of policy-making.† For these reasons the efficiency criteria are considered a rough but acceptable guide to determine which projects are pork and which are not.

There are two principal arguments that the discount rate currently

---

* This act, originally passed in 1931, requires contractors and subcontractors working on federal construction projects budgeted at $2,000 or more to pay workers no less than the locally prevailing wages for similar work. Local prevailing wages are determined by the Secretary of Labor.

† Some congressional partisans of navigation projects have made their case on redistributive grounds. They argue that even though a particular navigation project has an unfavorable benefit-cost ratio it is desirable, since it will force the railroads to lower their rates to bulk shippers. This argument is strongest when the shippers are low-income farmers. Its weakness is that the effect of lowering transportation costs will aid shippers in proportion to the amount of goods they ship. Thus, the large-scale farmer will obtain more benefits from the project than the small-scale farmer. Ordinarily this is not the sort of redistribution that is considered desirable by social critics, though some would agree that the transfer of wealth away from the railroads is a good consequence of the project.

in use is too low. The first has been given in an earlier section of this chapter. Briefly it is that the correct rate of discount is the opportunity cost of capital, which is by most accounts around 8 percent or higher. However, the current discount rate for newly authorized projects is around 5.125 percent. The second argument is that a "grandfather clause" has been in effect that allows projects already authorized to retain the discount rate of their original authorization, despite the fact that the federal government has raised the discount rate several times throughout the last decade. In other words, a project that has a Corps-computed benefit-cost ratio of 1.1 under a discount rate of 2.625 percent (the rate in effect during the 1950's) is still considered to have that benefit-cost ratio and is thus eligible for construction funds, even though if it were evaluated under a 5.125 percent rate it would have an unfavorable benefit-cost ratio. Most projects in the active authorized list were authorized under previous (and lower) discount rates. Therefore, those with low benefit-cost ratios are inefficient and by definition a part of the pork barrel.

To demonstrate overestimation of project benefits would require more technical argument. Fortunately there is available an excellent study that evaluates realized benefits from several Corps projects.[19] Robert Haveman has evaluated the actual benefits as compared with the Corps' estimates of benefits from a flood-control project (the John H. Kerr Reservoir), a navigation project (the Illinois Waterway), and several hydroelectric projects. He found that in each case the Corps overestimated project benefits by a wide margin. Though generalization from these case studies to other projects must be made with caution, it is safe to say that existing evidence indicates that the Corps routinely overestimates project benefits. Haveman points out that the Corps does not simply make rosy guesses about project benefits; rather, their standard estimation procedures contain built-in biases that lead to overestimation.

We can conclude from these arguments that there most certainly is a pork barrel. The size of the pork barrel is difficult to estimate, and we shall not attempt to do so here. Little confidence could be placed in any estimate that did not carefully evaluate each source of bias in benefit estimation, examine the local opportunity cost of capital to obtain a discount rate unique to the project, and explore the possibility that any particular project furthered other desirable social ends. We proceed in the next chapter to analyze some qualitative features of the political processes of project approval that support and sustain the biases in project choice mentioned here.

3

Political Benefits and Political Costs

If there is a widely accepted theory of democracy* it is probably that put forth by Schumpeter and Dahl,[1] which identifies as the key feature of democracy the competition among elites for votes in order to obtain or retain public office. Competition for office is presumed, in itself, to call forth policy proposals (or platforms) from the competitors that are capable of winning the popular test (obtaining a majority of votes). The requirement of competing for votes is supposed to instill in office-seekers accountability or responsibility to the voters. If incumbents wish to retain their positions, then they are bound to act in such a manner as to enable them to win reelection.

The actual accountability of an officeholder to his constituents rests on two factors: his desire to retain office and the presence of a genuine competitor for the office. Dahl and Lindblom maintain that this theory of democracy corresponds closely to reality.[2]

The responsiveness of leaders in polyarchies is a good deal more complicated than a simple function of their expectation of votes in the next election. But there can be no doubt that this expectation keeps them highly re-

---

* The notion of a "theory of democracy" may be ambiguous. The authors of the theories discussed here intend a theory of democracy to provide some conditions that must be satisfied for a government to be considered a democracy. There seems to be a scholarly consensus that in a democratic government the preferences of all citizens must bear some relation to the public choices made by the government. There have been disagreements over the years, though, between theorists who, with Rousseau, believe that individual preferences when expressed in political action must be "educated" or distilled in order to express the "general will" as distinct from the "will of all," and theorists who believe that individual preferences must be taken as given and that a set of institutions must be designed to translate these preferences into public policy. The theorists dealt with here belong to the latter school.

sponsive, sometimes astonishingly so. The fear that a bloc of voters will support the opposition in the next election if not given at least some of what it wants; the desire to forestall criticism; the realization that a legislative alliance might crumble if a leader chooses one policy rather than another; the willingness to listen to pressure groups; the abruptness with which some obscure matter suddenly becomes high policy because some group or other is making a row over it; the sensitivity to charges and countercharges—are all clearly evident in the behavior of polyarchal leaders and all are testimony to the need such leaders feel to respond to ordinary citizens and subleaders.

In practice there is a crucial difference between the situation of the current officeholders and that of their competitors for office in the next election. Incumbents are vested with the power (or more frequently, a part of the power) to make policy. Where Congress is concerned, however, this fact may appear at first glance to give the individual member, especially of the House, no great advantage. After all, a congressman is but one of 435 representatives, each endowed with a single vote. Nonetheless, the institutions of Congress are so structured that the individual congressman can in effect make certain policy decisions by himself or with a small (generally like-minded) group. For example, if some agency is considering building a project in a congressman's constituency, his announced support, opposition, or indifference will have a great effect on whether or not the project is built. It is the committee system that is designed to facilitate the decentralization of decision-making from the whole House or Senate to an individual or small group. Most decisions made in committee survive substantially unaltered during the remainder of the congressional process. In short, the requirements of the division of labor and the practice of reciprocity on constituency matters serve to "privatize" many congressional decisions, that is, to leave them up to individual congressmen.

The first part of this chapter will focus on the individual congressman, presumably seeking reelection (or perhaps advancement to a higher office), who is faced with the decision of whether to support, oppose, or remain neutral on a proposed project within his constituency. The conclusions reached in the previous chapter may seem to make the solution to the congressman's dilemma obvious. We might be tempted to argue that if a project has a benefit-cost ratio greater than one, and if the local district pays about 1/435 of the total cost of the project while retaining nearly all of the benefits (both assumptions hold approximately), then the benefit-cost ratio to the district will be in excess of 400 to 1. Surely the congressman could not afford to oppose or remain neutral on a project of such great profitability to his district. Yet sometimes congressmen do oppose projects with such favorable ratios for their districts, and we shall try to discover why.

The second section of this chapter will investigate the conditions under which House members will favor or oppose projects outside their constituencies. One might think that, if project benefits are generally concentrated within single congressional districts while costs are spread out, congressmen would tend to oppose projects outside their own districts or remain neutral toward them. In general, however, they do not. On occasion congressmen actively favor some projects outside their districts, and they rarely oppose others. The motivations behind this phenomenon will also be explored.

Political Benefits and Costs of Projects Within the District

In the literature about Congress it is generally assumed that local projects are always desired. Bailey and Samuel, in *Congress at Work*, describe the genesis of a project as follows. "After a local group has become interested in a project, the next step is for its members to make a trip to their representative or senator, who normally is happy to fill their request."[3] But this description does not take into account the philosophy behind the adage that "for each political appointment you make nine enemies and one ingrate." Local projects can help a congressman, but they can hurt him, too, especially if they are controversial or poorly handled.

Congressmen generally agree that constituency-oriented expenditure can be valuable to them. There appear to be three separate reasons why congressmen value projects in their districts. First, projects are valuable in a reelection campaign as part of an incumbent's record in office. Second, they maximize discretion over other legislative issues. Third, they ensure that a project issue will not be held against the congressman by groups who could enter or back an opposition candidate in the next election.

Water projects in particular are something that congressmen generally believe can help them get reelected. Basically, the process can work in two ways. In the first place, getting the projects can be symbolically important in a reelection campaign, since it shows voters that their congressman can do things for them in Washington. Examples of this sort of election appeal can be found in campaign literature. In Senator Mundt's (Republican–South Dakota) 1966 reelection campaign, one of his flyers claimed that when the Budget Bureau cut funds for the Oahe Dam in 1954, Mundt got them restored. Perhaps even more important is the fact that projects provide benefits for a few well-organized groups in the district. Construction workers, contractors, and local businessmen receive economic rewards from nearly any sort of construction project; these groups frequently contain important potential contributors to, or workers in, a particular congressman's campaign. Clapp quotes a congressman in this regard:[4]

> Wouldn't everyone agree that if you can get something done that you can't justify on merit, but which goes into your district, the so-called pork-barrel project, that you find it is effective. I agree there are a sophisticated few very substantial opinion molders who get the implications of this, perhaps even before you bring home the bacon. And I think the sophisticated few are pretty important.

It is clear that many congressmen feel that local projects are a relatively cheap way to ensure reelection.

In the second place, a congressman who successfully "brings home the bacon" may be able to ensure himself more freedom in voting on other issues of greater interest to him. The most famous example of this was Frank Smith, a former Mississippi congressman. Of course, no amount of federal expenditure in his district would have allowed him to vote for a civil rights bill, since his constituency had very intense feelings against such legislation. However, by bringing a lot of projects into his district, Smith felt that he could afford to go along with the legislative desires of the Democratic leadership fairly often. He remarked, "In my twelve years in the House I voted with the Democratic leadership three-fourths of the time."[5]

One issue on which he was able to vote with the leadership consistently was free trade. "Speaker Rayburn asked me if I would be interested in going on the Ways and Means Committee in 1955, but I couldn't even afford to think of the change. My one hope of keeping a Delta district together was the importance of my position on the Public Works Committee." Smith summed up his position in the following way: "When I came to the House of Representatives I wanted to be a responsible member. If my constituents were to give me this freedom, I felt I had to render them special service in areas of major concern to the district. This called for specialization in flood-control and water-resource developments."[6]

The third motivation, that of inhibiting potential opposition, is somewhat mingled with the desire to ensure reelection. Not all congressmen fear that defeat awaits them at the next election. For some, although there is still some uncertainty about being returned, reelection campaigns are a bothersome ritual made necessary only if the opposing party puts up a candidate or if the opposing candidate has serious backing. Sometimes careful attention to projects in the district can help forestall opposition. Frank Smith, for example, was opposed by the powerful Delta Council in his district in his initial run for a House seat. By 1962, however, after he had worked for 12 years on the Public Works Committee, the majority of the Delta Council business leaders supported him in his campaign against Jamie Whitten (Democrat–Mississippi), with whose district his had been merged.[7]

Even though a project may be useful to a congressman in the ways listed above, it may also be dangerous in other ways. Joe Martin (Republican–Massachusetts) gives two examples of dangers in his autobiography:[8]

When I was first elected to Congress . . . I fell heir to the old Taunton River issue. For a hundred years my district had been interested in having the river widened and deepened to make it navigable for steamers.

Where my predecessors had failed I got the necessary legislation through Congress, only to find it the biggest issue raised against me in the next election. The railroads were angry because it threatened them with new competition. The gas company people were furious because they feared that they would be put to great expense removing their pipes from the river bed. The owners of a large stove company at Taunton were frantic lest the widening of the river weaken the foundation of their factory. And to top it off many of the voters were suspicious that I, who was to become a veritable symbol of economy in government, was a big spender.

Many people suppose that rivers-and-harbors legislation and the pork barrel are a congressman's surest means of keeping a hold on his district. Before going to Congress I may or may not have shared this belief, but once there it did not take me long to discover the fallacy.

In 1928 a fire destroyed a large part of the Fall River business section. It occurred to me that it might inspire private owners to rebuild quickly if the federal government would step in and put up a new post office, even though the old one had not been damaged. I went to see President Coolidge about it . . . [and] Coolidge penned a note to Secretary of the Treasury Andrew Mellon: "please see what you can do to give Joseph a post office." In no time I had the funds, which I might reasonably have concluded would make everyone in Fall River happy and, therefore, well disposed toward me on the next election day. The first thing I knew I was in the middle of a sizzling fight in Fall River over the location of the post office.

These are disturbing anecdotes for those who believe in the truth of the conventional wisdom about the pork barrel. Why does one project help a congressman and another hurt him? What can he do to prevent making mistakes and miscalculations?

One of the common explanations for the existence of pork-barrel expenditure is that the costs are spread thinly over all districts and the benefits are highly concentrated in one or a few districts. The costs of organizing opposition to a congressman whose district must bear only 1/435 of the costs of a project are so great relative to the potential benefits that it is not worth the trouble to get other congressmen together to oppose the project. If a congressman tries to oppose a project without previously having organized opposition, he will gain only the enmity of the project's sponsors; as a result, they may try, more successfully, to oppose his projects. The few congressmen whose districts gain heavily from the project have lots of incentive to organize support for it at the critical points of decision. The basic theory is that when costs are spread out and benefits concentrated, the project eventually ought to work its way through the whole formal procedure.

This theory presumably applies to economic costs and benefits, and it is stated in a way that ignores the distribution of benefits and costs within the district. The Corps' evaluation of project benefits generally measures the following kinds of benefits, among others: flood control, navigation, recreation, water supply, water-quality control—low-flow augmentation, fish and natural wildlife enhancement, electric power, irrigation, and beach erosion. All benefits are measured in dollars according to certain specified rules of thumb.

Certain of these benefit categories plainly entail a cost to particular concentrated economic groups. For example, the presence of navigation benefits in a project indicates that the project will make water transportation available over certain routes at marginal costs low enough to be competitive with other modes. If these alternative modes have economies of scale in operation, as railroads do (ton-mile costs decline as more tons are shipped), the marginal costs to the railroad increase since tonnage is directed to the waterway while the rates are forced to decline (all of this is subject to I.C.C. regulations, of course). Thus building a project with navigation benefits imposes a severe tax on railroads shipping over the same routes.

Another example is power benefits. Building a project with power benefits will generally act to lower local rates and at the same time raise average costs to local private power companies.* In addition, dams built to provide power must be taller than flood-control dams so that more upstream land is flooded. As a result, coalitions between power companies and upstream landowners often form to oppose

---

* Costs will increase because there are economies of scale in electricity generation and supply too.

TABLE 3.1
Classification of Projects

		WINNERS: Concentrated and organized	WINNERS: Dispersed
LOSERS	Concentrated and organized	I Strong pressure both ways	II Local opposition to project
LOSERS	Dispersed	III Local support for project	IV Little controversy —congressmen can safely choose sides

such projects, although power company opposition has lessened somewhat since the late 1940's as the federal government has sold more and more of the power it generates to private companies for distribution.

Flood control generally can be accomplished in two ways: the first is to build dikes and levees to keep the river in its stream bed in case of high water not exceeding the height of the structures; the second is to build dams to hold the water during flood stages. The building of dams involves the flooding of upstream areas in order to provide flood protection downstream. Consequently, upstream landowners can usually be counted on to oppose the building of dams.* This provides a more or less constant source of opposition to building dams for flood-control purposes.

Some benefits in the benefit-cost ratio are widely dispersed over large population groups. In particular, recreation, wildlife, water-supply, and water-quality-control aspects of projects provide small benefits to large numbers of people. Sometimes organized groups such as the Sierra Club or Friends of the Earth will participate in the debates about a project, but most often these dispersed-benefit recipients are unorganized and exert little pressure one way or the other.

Table 3.1 indicates the kinds of forces the local congressman will generally be subjected to. If the project is built there will be two groups: winners and losers. This figure treats characteristics of these

* "Eminent domain" is frequently employed to procure the land that will be used for the project. This generally has the effect of forcing upstream people to sell land at a price lower than they might voluntarily take on the open market. Thus upstream landowners will frequently oppose such projects.

groups as independent variables. The entries describe the local pressures. The various types of benefits from projects arrange themselves very approximately into the figure in the following way.

I. Navigation (railroads lose; barge operators, construction operators, construction workers, and shippers gain). Flood control where land upstream is privately owned. Electric power when there are power cooperatives.

II. Power if there are no cooperatives. Flood control when downstream land is owned by poor people or the government.

III. Most flood control (especially dikes and levees), beach erosion (hotel owners gain), water supply (local water companies can buy the water).

IV. Recreation, water-quality control, or fish and wildlife enhancement when land to be flooded is not valuable or is owned by the government.

The benefit categories are not an infallible guide to the local response to the building of a project. Consequently, over the years very elaborate and time-consuming formal procedures have been evolved to allow the localities affected by the project ample time to develop opposition and support. The congressman need not commit himself to any great degree until fairly late in the process, and then only when he is fairly sure of local opinion on the matter.

Arthur Maass provides an excellent discussion of the Corps' activities in adjusting group interests. He says:[9]

Engineers have encouraged participation by local interests for the purposes of (1) protecting and safeguarding the respective interests; (2) obtaining information desired and necessary for the planning of projects; (3) making possible an adjustment of diverse viewpoints and the winning of consent for proposed action based on such an adjustment.

This quotation makes clear the obvious fact that projects do not just spring forth from some Zeus's head complete with a particular configuration of benefits. In the planning process the Corps may choose to design a project to include water-supply benefits but not power benefits, for example, because of a desire to maximize local support for the project. Bailey and Samuel state it concisely:[10]

In the field, working with various local groups interested in flood control, canals, drainage, and a host of other projects, they have learned to "maximize the total desires of the community." Translated this means adjusting local differences and uniting local pressures behind the most feasible method of accomplishing the project. And being extremely politically conscious, the Corps has learned how to "maximize" its congressional relations as well.

Project planning is inevitably a political process; it determines whose land will be taken and whose protected, what shipping costs certain firms will pay, who will be employed locally, and who will make financial contributions. In short, planning helps to shape the future of the local community; therefore, in making up plans for improvement of the water resources of a community, the Corps must and does try to build a coalition broad enough and stable enough to see the project through. Local opposition and controversy constitute an invitation to congressional opposition, or at least reluctance. Projects with strong local opposition are put off until most opponents can be mollified.

The observer might wonder why there are projects with opposition at all. The Corps can move a dam (for example) up or down the river, change its height, remove power-generating facilities, and make other variations until all major groups are contented with the project. There are, however, some constraints on the process of adjustment to group interests. The chief one appears to be the requirement that the benefit-cost ratio exceed one. A low flood-control dam could be favored by the local community, but its benefit-cost ratio might be below one. The addition of electric-power-generation facilities may raise the ratio over one but, at the same time, may generate the opposition of local private power companies.

For an example of such a situation we can take the Roanoke River Basin Project. The Corps report issued in 1944 (House Document 650) concluded that "comprehensive development of reservoirs for flood control only was not justified economically on a basin-wide program."[11] However, the Corps found that if electric-power-generation capability were to be built into the basin projects, there was an economically feasible plan to provide flood protection and power. Wallace sums up the report in the following manner.[12]

The economic balance sheets make it perfectly clear that the Buggs Island project [one of the separable parts of the basin project] could not be built economically for flood-control purposes only. Furthermore, the facts also make it plain that flood control for the basin could not be achieved except by use of multi-purpose reservoirs with sale of hydroelectric power to provide a favorable economic ratio.

After the issuance of the report, the House Flood Control Committee held hearings for the 1944 Flood Control Act. The major power companies, the Virginia Electric Power Company (VEPCO) and the Carolina Power and Light Company, led the coalition against the project. The power companies contacted members of Congress who were known to be ideologically opposed to federal power projects and hired a public relations firm to arouse local opposition. The opposition aroused by the companies was sufficient to turn one local congressman, Harold Cooley (Democrat–North Carolina), against the project. He argued, procedurally, that there had been inadequate hearings and that as a result the project should not receive funding.

The planning process engaged in by the Corps is likely to help determine the electoral impact of a project for affected congressmen as well as the project's engineering features. Even so, there are constraints placed on the Corps' discretion not only by the benefit-cost ratio but also by geography. If a river runs between two states (as does the Savannah River between Georgia and South Carolina) or between two congressional districts, the political benefits and costs of a project may fall unevenly among the affected senators and representatives. There are plenty of examples of conflicts between states or districts on matters of this sort: Georgia and South Carolina over the Savannah River, North Carolina and Virginia over the Roanoke River basin, and Illinois and Indiana over the Wabash River are only a few. This last conflict is illustrated in the following testimony before the Senate Appropriations Committee's Subcommittee on Public Works.[13] Senator Douglas (Democrat–Illinois) is testifying in favor of a levee system on the Illinois side of the Wabash River at Mount Carmel and an upstream reservoir (Lincoln Reservoir).

Senator Douglas. Mr. Chairman, I feel deeply indebted to you for the way you recognize the merit of claims of those on the Illinois side of the river. I do not want to exacerbate the cleavage between Illinois and Indiana which I want to have healed at the earliest possible moment. But our Hoosier friends slipped things over on us in the past in having levees built on the Indiana side which do protect their lands—and we are very glad to do that—but it throws the water over on the Illinois side. This having been done in connection with a project at Vincennes, the same crime was about to be perpetrated on us at Mount Carmel. But at my insistence, and with your help, Mr. Chairman, we are instituting parallel construction on the Illinois side which will save Mount Carmel in all probability from being flooded, and which will protect agricultural land south of Mount Carmel.

We are very glad to join in a levee program—although we think it is not the ultimate solution—provided that the levees are built on both sides of the river, are of an equal height, and are constructed more or less simultaneously. We could not construct them simultaneously this time, because our Hoosier friends got theirs first. But they have reformed, and it is all over now. And we hope that they will move in the paths of virtue in the future. If they do not, we will properly defend our interests.

So I hope that this work on the Illinois side of the river may proceed.

Now, Mr. Chairman, I also hope that we may start work on the upstream reservoirs on the Illinois side of the river. I want to say frankly that I think our Indiana friends showed greater alertness in this matter than we have on the Illinois side. They started a reservoir system before we did. We lost one authorization on the so-called Lincoln Reservoir south of Charleston when it was withdrawn by popular vote.

But I want to thank you, Mr. Chairman, for last year, both for authorizing this, and for supporting it in your other capacity as a member of the Appropriations Committee. I am not betraying anything when I say that the Lincoln Reservoir was something unique in congressional history, in that the money was appropriated a few days before the authorization was given. And I want to thank you, Mr. Chairman, for making this possible. I use it to show to our Hoosier colleagues that we are not quite as dumb as they once thought us to be.

Senator Hartke. Will the Senator yield?

Senator Douglas. It is hard to keep up with these country boys.

Senator Hartke. Will the Senator yield?

Senator Douglas. Yes.

Senator Hartke. I might call attention to one very important fact that the State of Illinois, rich as it is, is able to take care of most of their problems themselves. We are poor people over in Indiana. We appreciate the help that you have given us. But let me point out the fact that the Indiana territory used to include the State of Illinois, and that they were so capable of taking care of themselves that we have let them go by themselves. We have disentangled ourselves from their properties. They have never repaid us for that. We want you to know that we did not relinquish it in fee simple, that we only gave them a life estate. If they feel that they are neglected too much, if they want to join us, we know it will be to their benefit. If they want to join the State of Indiana, we will be glad to have them back.

Senator Douglas. I am very glad this offer is made, but I don't think we should accept it, because then Illinois would control Indiana again.

Senator Hartke. Some people think that this has happened already.

Senator Ellender. I want to say that I have always been very sympathetic with the situation in Illinois and Indiana. I need not repeat this too often, but I thought it was a bad thing for us to have constructed the levees on the Indiana side and not on the Illinois side. Of course, the reason why I suggested that we build the levees on both sides of the river is that we had the same situation in my area years ago when Congressman Whittington was chairman of the Flood Control Committee of the House. He always saw to it that the levees on the Mississippi side were about three feet higher than the ones on the Louisiana side, so that Louisiana would get flooded before Mississippi would. So it is because of that experience that I sympathize with the problem in Illinois and Indiana.

Senator Douglas. We are very grateful to you.

Senator Ellender. I hope to continue with the construction proceeding on both sides of the river, because I certainly believe that it ought to be handled that way. I don't believe in drowning out some people to take care of others.

Senator Douglas. I will say that in recent years there has been an improvement in the behavior of the Senators from Indiana, partially due to the change in the composition of the delegation, and partially due to an inner state of grace, too.

Senator Ellender. I am glad to have a little help in my efforts to have these levees built concurrently.

Senator Douglas. You have been of tremendous assistance.

The economic theory developed in Chapter 2 indicated that the economically optimal package of projects for a given budget would consist of the group of projects with the highest benefit-cost ratios. This chapter has shown, though, that in large part the benefit-cost ratio is determined by the essentially political nature of the processes of project choice. The requirements of local support—and especially local congressional support—make it imperative on occasion to trade off a higher benefit-cost ratio for more local support. In addition, there are categories of benefits, particularly in the areas of recreation and water supply, that are evaluated according to rules of thumb that have little relation to the real benefits received by the people living near the project. The addition of recreation benefits, for example, has allowed many previously unfeasible projects to display favorable benefit-cost ratios.

When a congressman or an aspiring opponent faces the decision of whether to support or oppose a proposed project, or of whether to ask the Corps to modify it so that it becomes more acceptable to him, he must evaluate the benefits and costs to himself of building the project or some variant of it. The political benefits and costs of a project to a congressman depend first on who stands to gain and who to lose if the project is built, and second on how these people or groups will reward or punish the congressman for his decision. In many cases his decision is simple, but in others he faces uncertainty. In such situations the rule of thumb available to the congressman is that only those people who stand to gain or lose large amounts if the project is built (or not built) might change their political behavior as a consequence of the congressman's decision. It may pay them to find out his position on the project and then to try to change or to reward it. Typically, certain people stand to gain substantially from the construction of any local project: contractors, construction trade unions, and local merchants. In addition, these groups are often deeply involved in local politics. If a congressman must rely on these segments of the local population for political support, then he is likely to favor construction of many projects that produce few benefits in a benefit-cost analysis, even in the local district.

There are also strategic considerations behind the congressman's choice. If his opponent already has taken one position on the project, or is likely to, the congressman may take the same position out of fear of losing votes on the issue if he guesses wrong. An interesting example of this phenomenon occurred in the race for the congressional seat representing the newly redistricted 21st district of Illinois for the 93d Congress. This district had previously been the 22d district represented by William Springer (Republican–Illinois), who announced his retirement as of the end of the 92d Congress. The Democratic nominee for the seat was Lawrence Johnson, Champaign County State's Attorney, while the Republican candidate was Edward Madigan, a representative in the Illinois state legislature.

The project under consideration was the controversial proposal by the Corps of Engineers to build Oakley Dam on the Sangamon River above Decatur, Illinois. The principal benefits of the dam would be water supply (for Decatur), flood control, and recreation. If it was built, the flooding pattern of the Sangamon upstream of the reservoir would be substantially altered so that some of the forest in Allerton Park, which is owned by the University of Illinois, would occasionally be subject to severe flooding. Environmentalists contended that many trees would be destroyed* and that the project, properly evaluated, was not economically feasible.† Many upstream farmers opposed the project since it might have raised the water table sufficiently to cause serious drainage problems.‡

---

* Most of the forest is second-growth, although according to the Committee to Save Allerton Park, one of the major groups opposing the Oakley Dam project, there are some virgin stands. Allerton Park has been used by the University of Illinois as a field experiment area for more than 30 years. The park is one of the very few forested areas in the state in approximately presettlement ecological condition; it is considered valuable for recreational and research purposes.

† Professor A. J. Heins of the Economics Department of the University of Illinois has analyzed the benefits and costs of the Oakley Dam project and has demonstrated, employing the Corps' techniques, that the Corps committed several errors in its original analysis. He shows that the benefit-cost ratio is actually .97 rather than the 1.15 the Corps reports. If the Corps were required to employ the discount rate in effect in 1971—5.125 percent instead of 3.25 percent—the benefit-cost ratio would drop to .69. See Heins, "A Reconsideration of the Economic Aspects of the Oakley Reservoir Project."

‡ Central Illinois was originally marshland, and settlers in the area have always had drainage problems. Most of the farms in the area have been "tiled," or provided with underground drainage channels leading to drainage ditches. The state is organized into drainage districts which levy local assessments for this work. Farmers in the area are very conscious of the drainage problem since they have had to combat it all their lives. Some farms around the Carlyle Reservoir, a nearby Corps project on the Kaskaskia River, have been subjected to severe problems of this type during the spring planting season.

Congressman Springer was a strong supporter of the Oakley Dam project, but the two congressional candidates for his vacated seat had not formally announced positions on the project prior to May of 1972. Environmentalists, who are well organized in Champaign County, had hoped that Johnson, the Democratic candidate from Champaign, would come out against the project. The principal benefits of the project, those relating to water supply, would go to traditionally Democratic Macon County, where Decatur is located.

Terry Michael, a staff writer for the *Champaign-Urbana News Gazette*, argued that Johnson would have to run very well in Macon County if he hoped to defeat the Republican Madigan, who was expected to do well in his home area of McLean, DeWitt, and Piatt Counties as well as in traditionally Republican Champaign County.[14] The environmental opposition was centered in Champaign-Urbana. Johnson expected to do well in the university community in these cities regardless of his announced position on Oakley Dam. Therefore, it came as no surprise to environmentalists when both Madigan and Johnson endorsed Oakley Dam on May 7, 1972. Both felt that there were votes to be gained in Macon County but none to be lost in Champaign County. Johnson remarked: "If there is a feeling I am taking a politically popular position (in support of Oakley) I don't recognize one. I regret that some people in Champaign County will be upset with my position. I would point out that there are many other issues to consider."[15] Johnson's staff was very sensitive to the environmental groups in the area, and environmental group leaders believed that Johnson was sympathetic to their arguments.* They felt that he had to announce the position he did for fear of losing too many votes in Macon County.

This example serves as a partial illustration of the very complicated relationship between a proposed project's political benefits to a candidate for office and its economic benefits. One of the complicating factors is the fact that congressmen do not know who cares enough to switch votes on a project issue. Madigan and Johnson both apparently felt that most Champaign County voters were traditionally of either one party or another, or that they would make their voting decisions on the basis of other issues.† When there is significant

* This statement is based on private interviews with a director of the Committee on Allerton Park. Although Madigan did not endorse the Oakley Dam until May, there seems to have been little doubt in anyone's mind that he would do so.

† The matter was complicated by the fact that the Lindsay-Schaub newspaper chain, which owns the only Decatur newspaper and one of the two Champaign-

local opposition to a project, considerations of this sort would seem to make the decision of whether or not to favor a project a difficult one for candidates.*

Political Benefits and Costs of Projects
Outside the Constituency

The simplified model offered in this chapter establishes an image of a congressman supporting certain projects in his district, staying neutral on others, and even opposing a few. On projects outside his own constituency one might expect his mild opposition or neutrality. However, the observer of public works decision-making is struck by the fact that congressmen regularly express support for projects that do not have a direct and positive effect on their constituency. Why does a representative from Los Angeles lend enthusiastic support to a project in the 1st district of California, located more than 400 miles away? Why does a congressman from the Delta region of Mississippi come out strongly in favor of a navigation project in Ohio or Florida?

Partial answers to these questions can be found in the formal and informal institutions of the House of Representatives. Two well-documented phenomena provide explanations: first, members of the same state delegation cooperate with each other to a great extent; second, members of the same committee cooperate with each other. The second phenomenon is easy to understand, since the committees are decision-making entities. Cooperation among members is likely to be exhibited since committee decision-making is the major channel for exercising influence over policy for most representatives. Representatives frequently join the Public Works Committee or choose to stay on it because they desire a particular kind of decision on some project from their peers. It is not surprising, then, that committee members support each other's projects.

Urbana newspapers, was strongly in favor of the Oakley Dam. A director of the Committee on Allerton Park said that the chain would certainly try to make an issue of Oakley Dam in Decatur if one of the candidates failed to endorse it.

* Corps of Engineers projects in central Illinois are facing more and more local opposition in part owing to the fact that environmental groups are forming alliances with local farmers and drainage districts. In addition, environmentalists have informed the author that the Illinois Central Railroad is showing interest in financing some of their efforts to combat navigation projects in the state. These alliances have formed the backbone for opposition to several projects in the central and southern part of the state. For example, a coalition of a drainage district and an environmental group recently obtained an injunction enjoining the State of Illinois from continuing work on a project in central Illinois. This sort of thing seems to be becoming more common throughout the nation.

State delegations seem not to play as critical a role in House decision-making as committees do, for they have no formal part in the ordinary course of policy-making. However, several scholars have found that certain delegations meet regularly, tend to vote en bloc on many issues, and favor each other's pet projects.* Why should this occur? It has been argued that by voting in roll calls as a group whenever possible, state delegation members can maximize their bargaining advantage and hence their ability to get projects for their districts. This argument would seem to apply with equal force to any arbitrary group of congressmen though.

Another argument has been advanced to the effect that congressmen from the same state tend to have "similar" districts, and that hence their interests will tend to converge on a broad range of policy issues. This is surely an empirical question. There are many projects that, if built in one district, actually harm adjacent districts. In other cases, there are projects that could reasonably be built in any of several districts in a state, but that when built in one district cannot be built in another. It is evident that with regard to some projects, congressmen from the same state will tend to have more conflicting than parallel interests.

There are certain mechanisms that link the interests of congressmen from the same state. The democratic theory outlined by Dahl, Schumpeter, and Downs[16] is characterized by basing the link between popular demands and policy-making on the desire of political decision-makers to retain office. This theory has been extended by Joseph Schlesinger[17] to include a mechanism (ambition for higher office) that encourages certain political decision-makers to respond to broader constituencies than if they were only seeking reelection. Many representatives seek the opportunity to run for senator, governor, or some other statewide or even national office.

Another mechanism is more technical in character. The growth of economic activity in one section of a state is likely to have certain indirect effects on economic activity in other sections of the state. These mechanisms depend heavily on the structure of transportation networks and of the economy in the particular state and region. This explanation is viable only where a relatively integrated intrastate economic structure exists, or where a project built in one district

* There is an extensive literature on the influence of the state delegation on the behavior of the individual congressman. In the following analysis, Barbara Deckard's "State Party Delegations in the House of Representatives" will be heavily relied on because of its richness in interview material and breadth of scope.

actually has *direct* spill-overs into other districts (this would hardly account for state delegation *units*, however).

Still another source of incentive for cooperation within the delegation is the fact that the state delegation chairman has some control over committee assignments. The delegation chairman, at least, would seem likely to have a clear preference for a cohesive delegation over which he would have some influence through his control of committee assignments.

In certain issue areas in which the location of projects or the distribution of federal funds is a major payoff to the congressman, local interest groups have formed statewide alliances. Chambers of commerce, river basin associations, and various associations of mayors, city managers, farmers, and others are frequently organized at the state level. Consequently, in many policy environments the influences of local interests are coordinated by state-level organizations.*

There are, of course, additional incentives for cooperation within the delegation which are peculiar to various states. The Chicago delegation (which happens to include most of the Illinois Democrats in the House) is cohesive in part because the reelection of its members is largely controlled by a strong centralized political party organization which believes that a cohesive party delegation from the city advances its interests. Each state probably generates forces for or against delegation cooperation that are unique to it.

Whether all of the relevant forces have been catalogued or not, it can be stated with certainty that the state delegation structures much important congressional behavior. Roll-call research[18] has established that the state delegation is an important source of cues for the representative's voting decision. Matthews and Stimson, in their analysis of roll calls in the 85th through 88th Congresses, found that the state party delegation was the most important "cue-giver." Clausen, analyzing roll calls on five issues in the 85th and 86th Congresses, found that state delegations are an important explanatory variable.

There is more to congressional behavior than roll calls, of course. Recently there has been some interesting work done on state delega-

---

* Daniel Elazar has written extensively on this subject. He argues that certain states are very successful in obtaining federal funds because the state government, local groups, and congressional delegation have learned to work together on matters of interest to the state. Such states function as what Elazar calls "civil societies." He says that "the key to the acquisition of federal benefits is intensive state and local activity to secure those benefits. The better a state is able to function as a coordinated civil society, the more likely it is to obtain a large share of federal expenditures" (Elazar, pp. 74–75).

tion cooperation over a wider range of behavior than roll calls. Barbara Deckard's dissertation attempted to find out just how members of state delegations cooperate with one another. Not surprisingly, she found a good deal of variation. In some states, the members of the same party met frequently, talked over a wide range of topics, and expected to give and to get help from other delegation members in achieving policy goals. In other states, members of both parties expected regular cooperation across party lines on certain types of issues. In still others, members of the same party never met as a group, and considerable acrimony reigned among delegation members.

Matthews and Stimson, in the work already cited, interviewed a large sample of congressmen in an attempt to explore to what extent state delegations work together. As in Deckard's interviews, we find in Matthews and Stimson the same great diversity in the expectations of congressmen and and in their behavior.[19] Some state delegations meet regularly. For example, the California and Texas Democratic delegations meet once a week, the Tennessee Democratic delegation once a month. Large delegations speak of having a "spread" of members on committees. A 15- or 20-man state party delegation might have members on all of the House committees. This enables the members to get together to review committee work with each other, arrange testimony, and keep track of projects important to them in other committees. Deckard says that the Texas members see the delegation as a good source of information about what is going on in committees because they have a good spread.

Other state party delegations meet only when issues of special interest to someone in the state come up. Matthews and Stimson cite the response of a Florida Republican in one of their interviews: "As far as delegation meetings go that's pretty much left to the discretion of the ranking member. . . . The entire delegation gets together on his call when a subject matter comes up that he feels we need to discuss. It's more in the form of matters of interest to Florida, rather than national policy." On certain kinds of issues, members of one party delegation help out members of the other party in their state. A Washington Republican said, "If I can get a bill through for one of the Democrats I do so." The Pennsylvania representatives have a steering committee made up of senior members of both parties. Deckard summarized references to some of their activities in her interviews. "Flood control, highways, a proposed canal, an oceanographic lab, problems affecting the Port of Philadelphia, and the closing of the Air Force base near Harrisburg were given as examples of the problems and projects upon which the steering committee had taken action."[20]

Deckard ventured two hypotheses to explain the fact that some state party delegations act together on a broad variety of issues while others do not. First, the greater the number of delegation members interested in a career in Congress, the more cooperation; second, the more stable the delegation, the more it should act as a group. She also argued that large delegations had the additional resource of broad committee coverage. It is evident that among those delegations that occasionally work together the following two propositions are true: (1) cooperation is most likely on divisible or distributive policies (highways, dams, buidings, and so on); (2) there is an expectation that the member of the relevant committee will help out a delegation member, and this expectation crosses party lines in some delegations.

Some delegations are unable to cooperate even on constituency matters. The best known of these is the New York Democratic delegation. Its members claim that the senior delegation members could be very effective in getting projects for colleagues if they wanted to, but that they do not. A New York Democrat complained, "Many of the senior men are barely polite.... They wouldn't go out of their way to help you with anything." Deckard quotes an administrative assistant to an upstate New York congressman: "It's like two states. The city congressmen ... don't even know where upstate is.... New York didn't get reimbursed for the Thomas F. Dewey thruway and Buckley was chairman of Public Works at the time. He couldn't care less."

Among delegations that do work together on projects, various types of activity are possible. The simplest and probably the most common type is watching out for one another's bills and projects in committee. A second type of activity is co-sponsorship of bills. In a third activity frequently mentioned, members of the same delegation utilize their access to agenices or to other congressmen to help each other out. A Massachusetts Democrat said of McCormick during his tenure as Speaker: "If you are having trouble with an agency, you can have him call over and that has more effect than if any one of the rest of us called, and he has been very helpful on constituency matters." A New York Republican is quoted, "I needed something from an agency. One of our members is on the Appropriations Subcommittee that handles that. I got him to help. They heard him fine while they seemed to have some trouble hearing me."

The most cohesive delegations will sometimes work together as a group on projects. Certain state delegations testify together as delegations at the hearings on Public Works Appropriations. The same states will also have their delegation testify informally before the Budget Bureau. The most effective of these state delegations work out in consultation with the district engineer of the Army Corps and with local interest groups an agreed-upon set of projects to support. They then go before the Budget Bureau and the Appropriations Committees unified behind a single construction program. Clem Miller has described the Budget Bureau hearings: "Witness after witness files by—governors, senators, congressmen, county engineers, state water directors—an endless procession. . . . Our state delegation (California) irons out its differences in advance. Our people then go in with a united front, agreed on our askings, agreed on our non-budgeted requests."[21] A Pennsylvania Democrat had this to say: "We work together on state matters. Appalachia, highways, public works projects. We all support anything that's for Pennsylvania no matter where it goes. You have to in this place with its logrolling. You have to convince the delegation of need, then we'll all support you."[22] Congressmen seem to agree that committees take testimony from a united group more seriously than requests from individual congressmen. One congressman is quoted by Deckard as follows: "I'm getting people together to talk about a dam, the North River dam. There's no money in the budget for it, and Jordan and I decided to get together and see if we couldn't get some money for it. . . . I'm going to get the other people in on that. It always helps to have more people, . . . the committee takes it more seriously if you have a number of people involved."[23] Matthews and Stimson's interviews contain these remarks by a Virginia Republican in response to question 17: "I think it tends to help the state when you have the whole delegation working. For example, if there is a project pending in the state and you get the force of a whole delegation behind you on the [sic] bipartisan basis—it helps—rather than piecemeal."

The evidence from interviews suggests that in some delegations members are willing to exercise their political resources (their time, their access to agencies and committees, their committee membership, their expertise, and their advocacy) to advance the interests of their colleagues from the same state. Of course they expect reciprocity; and from the satisfied tone of most of the members of cohesive delegations interviewed by Deckard and others they think they receive it. The completely uncooperative delegation (the New York Democrats seem to be an extreme case) appears to be untypical; in particular, its lack of cohesion was referred to frequently in interviews with members from other states.

The phenomenon of cooperation within delegations broadens the concept of political benefits and costs considerably. It makes it necessary to say that if a project is seen as beneficial to one district, it is seen as beneficial to the whole state. The whole concept of political benefit must be interpreted as negotiated within the delegation. If, for example, a project is desired by one congressman in a state but is opposed by another (perhaps the second congressman represents the upstream people adversely affected by a proposed dam), the only way to tell if its political benefits exceed its costs is to see if the delegation comes out in favor of it. The fact is that negotiation and compromise within the delegation prevent the observer from seeing if a project is politically desirable to a congressman when it is considered by itself. All that can be observed is the congressman's negotiated support for or opposition to a project after having dealt with his state delegation.

The importance of the state delegation as an institution within which a significant amount of exchange on certain issues takes place has serious implications for the testing of the hypotheses of this study. Congressmen have well-established expectations that they can convert their influence over some issue area (let us say agriculture or defense) into indirect influence in another issue area (public works or H.E.W.) within their state delegation. This means, to some extent, that if a member of a state delegation has great influence over a particular issue his whole state will reap the benefits. What is more, if his district is not in a position to benefit directly from his influence over a particular agency or program, his state will receive benefits from the program although his district will not.

This situation is not particularly unusual. For one thing, state party delegations have established prerogatives over seats on certain committees.[24] When a seat becomes available on a committee and a particular state has a claim on it, the state will usually have a very limited number of congressmen who will (or can) take the assignment. Thus to hold its claim it may have to put on a committee a congressman who has no constituency interest in the jurisdiction area of the committee. If this congressman must wait a long time before a desirable assignment becomes available for him, his state delegation colleagues will frequently try to get him to stay on the committee where he has built up some seniority and, correspondingly, some expertise and influence. Thus a congressman with no constituency interest in a committee's jurisdiction will frequently stay long enough to become powerful on the committee; part of his motivation will have been the opportunities for cooperation open to him within the state delegation.

The preceding statements indicate that the hypotheses of this study must be examined at the state level. We should not expect to observe a particularly strong relationship between influence in the House and benefits from the agency at the individual district level, except by chance. A member's increased influence on a committee raises the ability of each congressman in that member's state to get projects from the agencies under that committee's jurisdiction; in turn, it raises the influential member's ability to obtain other kinds of projects outside his committee's jurisdiction for his own district. Since this study focuses on a single agency, this latter statement cannot be proved. All that can be measured is the first effect, and a district-level model would underpredict the projects received by the state delegation colleagues of an influential congressman on the Public Works Committee and would overpredict the projects received by the congressman himself. The overprediction will result from the fact that he can obtain a maximum of n new starts in a given year through his influence with the House Appropriations Committee's Subcommittee for Public Works; however, if he gets one project for a state delegation colleague, he cannot also put it in his district.

This effect is evident in the data discussed in Chapters 8 and 9. The benefits from projects authorized in the Omnibus Rivers and Harbors and Flood Control Bill of 1968 were allocated (in whole or in part) to congressional districts. A certain number of these projects were new starts in the 1969 Public Works Appropriations Bill. An attempt was made to estimate the effects of various variables that were hypothesized to have a relationship with influence on public works decision-making (membership on the Public Works Committee, seniority, and so on). All of the relationships were of inconsequential size and frequently went in the "wrong" direction. Yet the state-level data reported in later chapters reveal very strong and intuitively appealing relationships. This result suggests the importance of the state delegation as an institution for mediating exchange among certain policy areas. A thorough treatment of this topic from the point of view of its effects on policy outputs and distributions would require a book-length effort. For the present it is sufficient to point out its importance in identifying the concepts of the political benefits and costs of constituency-oriented policy decisions.

PART TWO

The Appropriations Process for the Corps of Engineers

4

The Making of the Corps of Engineers' Budget

In this chapter we turn from the legislative branch to identify and discuss the principal factors operating within the executive branch in determining the budget for the Corps of Engineers. The three groups of actors within the executive branch making decisions that help determine the size of the Corps' budget are the Corps of Engineers itself, the Budget Bureau, and the President and his staff. Although each of these groups can affect the size of the budget request for the Corps of Engineers, each operates under various physical, political, and legal constraints. The decision problem for each of these groups has quite limited possibilities if the various constraints are taken as given (which they are during the budgeting process).

The chronology of the budgeting process within the executive branch is as follows. First, the Corps of Engineers prepares an estimate of its "capability" of carrying out construction work for each of the projects currently under construction as well as for each proposed new construction project. In addition, similar estimates are made of planning capability. The total of these estimates constitutes the Corps' budget request, which is sent to the Budget Bureau generally around the end of the summer or the beginning of the fall each year.

Next, the Budget Bureau analyzes the Corps' budget request, usually reducing requested funding for projects already under construction (or in the planning stage) and removing many proposed new starts. During this process the Budget Bureau holds hearings at which congressmen and local interest groups appeal for the retention of the funding level recommended by the Corps of Engineers. The Budget Bureau, though, applies its own criteria in deciding which new projects are acceptable and sometimes does independent economic analyses of projects.

At a point during this period of Budget Bureau consideration, the President or the President's staff is shown the "suggested" budget requests recommended by the Bureau. Some Presidents have taken a deep interest in which new starts are approved, while others have not. The President's role in the process allows for the explicit introduction of some political goals of the Administration into the calculus of budget-making. President Johnson, in particular, allegedly took great interest in making sure that congressmen or senators who opposed him on issues he felt were important did not get new starts in the budget.

Once the President's recommended changes are incorporated, the Budget Bureau makes up its official estimates and the result becomes part of the President's budget submitted to Congress early in the congressional session.

Both the Corps and the Budget Bureau are bureaucratic organizations which utilize routinized procedures to arrive at budgetary decisions. The Presidency is also a bureaucracy, but its operating procedures vary substantially with the personality and interests of the President. In addition, the total dollar impact of presidential modifications of a particular Corps of Engineers' budget (as distinct from the long-run impact of a presidential policy decision on public works projects) appears to be small relative to the impact of the two other organizations. Because of these factors, and because less is known about the strategic calculations of the President and his staff in getting his legislative program approved, this chapter will focus principally on the constraints surrounding the decisions of the Corps of Engineers and the Budget Bureau in determining the budget.

Constraints on Corps of Engineers' Budget Decisions

The Corps' budget has several components, among which are administrative expenses, Army cemetery expenses, general investigations of proposed water projects, and planning and construction of water projects. The planning and construction section, which dominates the Corps' budget, is the component that concerns us in this study. The engineers in the Corps plan and design projects, but most construction is contracted out to private firms.

Construction projects undertaken by the federal government are funded in two distinct ways. The first method is called "full funding," which means that when a project receives its first appropriation its whole federal cost is put into the budget. For example, if a project's total federal cost was ten million dollars, of which only one million was to be spent in the first year, the whole ten million would appear in the budget. The second method, year-by-year funding, would put only the first year's one-million-dollar figure in the budget. The Corps of Engineers, significantly, is the only major federal agency that utilizes year-by-year funding.

The Budget Bureau has long opposed year-by-year funding on the grounds that it conceals the long-term financial commitments of the government from the public. There are difficulties inherent in both funding systems. Full funding, combined with the executive authority to re-program funds, allows the executive to make expenditure decisions independently of congressional intent. For example, the Secretary of Defense has the authority to take money "in the pipeline" (already appropriated for some long term project) and re-program it for use on some other project. The total of "pipeline" funds in the defense budget in 1972 was about forty-five billion dollars and the re-programming authority of the Secretary of Defense extended to about one billion dollars. This executive discretion removes a sizable part of the congressional authority over the initiating and funding of projects. Consequently, there is considerable congressional reluctance to convert the Corps' budget to a full-funding basis. It is worth pointing out that as the size of the "pipeline" has grown, especially in the Defense Department, the Armed Services Committees and other congressional committees have been moving toward requiring yearly authorizations (as distinct from yearly appropriations) for large segments of the budget.

The chief characteristic of year-by-year funding is that it tends to conceal the long-run effects of apparently minor current budgetary decisions. For example, in 1968 there were fifty-one new construction starts in the Corps' budget with a total federal cost of $822 million. In the first year, appropriations for these projects amounted to $33.5 million, less than 5 percent of the total federal construction costs. The following exchange between the Chief of Engineers and a senator during the Senate Appropriations Committee hearings illustrates one basis of congressional support for year-by-year funding.

General Itschner [Corps of Engineers]. What I am proposing is that for construction projects we would come to you just once for a single appropriation.

If we needed more money later, if we could not do the job for the amount that we originally said we would require, then we would have to come before you to explain why, and obtain an additional appropriation.

But we would still appear before you every year anyway, both for the new starts and for operation and maintenance and any other expenses.

Senator X. Are you suggesting a lump-sum appropriation for a project such as John Day Dam, that cost how much?

General Itschner. $418 million or something like that.

Senator X. Talk about shouting pork barrel, you would really get it there, I guess. That would make the initiation of a large project almost impossible.

General Itschner. This is just a suggestion. I recognize that disadvantage.

Senator X. We would consider it a disadvantage.

General Itschner. There are many disadvantages to it, but in the end I think it would save money. I recognize there are problems in doing it. But after the first year or two, after the system was put into effect, the overall bill should be no greater than it is now.

Senator X. I understand that, but without having studied the matter too deeply, I feel that the public reaction to a request for say a tenth or a fifth of the total cost of a project is bad enough, without going into this.

The first thing opponents of resource development would say is "Look at the money that is being appropriated over the budget this year," when as a matter of fact under the present system, if you were to provide funds to start the John Day Dam, which would probably take six or seven years to build, you would provide only that amount of money required for the first year.

Senator Y. If we asked for the total amount we wouldn't get it.

Senator X. This is the point. I believe that it would be much more difficult to obtain the funds for new starts under that system than under the present method.[1]

The fact that the Corps operates under year-by-year funding means that decisions made over the past ten or fifteen years create current spending obligations. Approximately 95 percent of the Corps' budget represents this cumulative spending obligation. Once a project has received initial funding it is put on a construction schedule by the Corps. One motivation behind establishing a rigid schedule is the physical characteristics of the structures built by the Engineers.

Many projects must be built in relatively large indivisible components or else the weather may jeopardize the partially completed structures. Although the schedule of construction is partly governed by physical features surrounding the project, the Engineers have a good deal of discretion in determining the pace of construction. Since the Public Works Appropriations Bill is customarily one of the last appropriations measures to receive congressional approval, so that generally the Engineers must wait until October to receive their appropriations from Congress, the Corps operates under concurrent resolutions for from three to five months of the year. Under its operating procedures, the Corps lets most construction contracts to private contractors during the third and fourth quarters of the calendar year, while it is operating under a concurrent resolution. By the terms of the concurrent resolution, the agency may spend at the same level as the year before. This is interpreted to mean that it may spend either at the rate of last year's quarterly average or at the rate of the same quarter last year. Thus if the Corps lets contracts in the third quarter each year, the third-quarter spending rate will be very high. By the time the appropriations bill is passed the Corps has effectively determined on its own what will be spent on each ongoing construction project, since once a contract is let the government must live up to it. The result is that to a great extent the rate of expenditure on ongoing projects is determined by technical factors and by the Corps. Of course, the Engineers try to take into account the desires of local groups and local congressmen, and to some extent Congress can and does change allocations for ongoing projects. However, the hearings convey the very strong impression that these changes have been extensively negotiated and concurred in by the affected parties. The large changes in funds for ongoing projects made by Congress are most frequently requested by the Corps for technical reasons (the weather, problems with contractor specifications, local labor shortages, and so on).

Year-by-year funding, combined with the Corps' procedures for letting contracts, occasionally produces a situation in which the authorization for a project has been spent but the project is not completed. The House rules specifically exempt the Corps from the necessity of obtaining a new authorization in this situation. Customarily, however, a new authorization will be sought from the Public Works Committees. The following citation is from Galloway. "House Rule XXI, clause 2, provides that 'No appropriation shall be reported in any general appropriation bill, or be in order as an amendment thereto, for expenditure not previously authorized by law, unless in continuation of appropriations for such public works and objects as are already in progress.' "[2]

These legal and technical considerations give the Corps of Engineers a floor below which their current budget cannot fall. It would be exceptional to witness a 5 percent drop in the budget between one year and the next.* The Corps has substantial motivation to use

* The following exchange between the chairman of the Public Works Subcommittee of the House Appropriations Committee, Michael Kirwan (Democrat–Ohio), and the Chief of Engineers, General Cassidy, illustrates the limited congressional

its discretion to expand its budget. The political support of the Engineers in the Congress rests on the Corps' local alliances with contractors, the building trades, and local chambers of commerce. These groups usually advocate increased expenditures in their own particular geographic area; thus there is always considerable demand in Congress to expand the program of the Engineers. The Corps can best maintain its congressional support through a steady expansion of its program. The Engineers therefore generally advocate a large budget, which is severely cut by the Budget Bureau. The Congress is then put in the position of playing an "appeals court" role, and it restores many of the slashes made by the Budget Bureau.

Although it is evident that the Engineers' budget request does not decline except in unusual circumstances, its rate of expansion remains to be explained. To begin with, the Corps' budget does not expand at the same rate from year to year. However, there appear to be periods during which the rate of expansion is relatively constant. It is not obvious whether the rate of expansion is governed by internal factors (for example, the supply of authorized projects) or by external factors (war, inflation, congressional support for the agency) or, as is more likely, by both. Wildavsky has argued that over a period of time agencies negotiate with the Budget Bureau a "fair share" of the total

---

discretion over the Corps' budget. (From U.S. Congress, House, House Appropriations Committee. *Public Works Subcommittee on the Public Works Appropriations Bill for Fiscal Year 1969, Hearings*, before the House Appropriations Committee, 90th Cong., 2d sess., 1968, p. 37.)

"*Mr. Kirwan.* Of the $940 million requested for planning and construction in fiscal year 1969, only $26,702,000 is for new construction and planning starts, including the carry-overs from 1968. This leaves about $877.3 million in new appropriations for work on ongoing projects.

"To what extent are these funds considered uncontrollable ... needed to finance going contracts or to let associated new contracts essential to prevent disruption of project construction?

"*General Cassidy.* The area of large expenditures is in the construction, general appropriation. Of the total of $923 million estimated expenditures in fiscal year 1969, approximately $665 million is for continuing requirements on contracts that will be under way by the end of fiscal year 1968. To this we must add associated land acquisition, government costs, and new contracts, which must be follow-on work for the going contracts. We estimate that this will amount to about $125 million. This leaves $133 million for new contracts, ongoing projects, continuation of land acquisition on an orderly basis, engineering and design and supervision administration, and the initiation of deferred 1968 new starts and 1969 new starts. We estimate that expenditures on this latter category of new and deferred construction starts and the new planning starts will be only about $23.7 million. Considering that the other appropriations are already at minimum levels—that is, general investigations, operation and maintenance, general expenses, Mississippi River and tributaries—the amount which is controllable in our program is actually very small, probably less than $100 million."

federal budget. During the relevant period the agency's budget should be growing at roughly the same rate as the total budget (if it has an established fair share). Of course, it is possible for external factors to affect different agencies in different ways so that the fair-share rule may not always correspond to proportional growth. This possibility is ignored here, and only a proportional growth model will be examined.

Since the Corps is primarily a construction agency, its budget can expand in the short run either by increasing expenditures for current projects or by adding new projects. In the long run, however, expansion can be achieved only by adding new projects to the budget. A project cannot receive construction money unless it has been authorized and planned (which requires a specific appropriation). The Corps' budget cannot expand unless a steady stream of new projects are made eligible to receive construction funds. In order for a fair-share rule to be observed in a construction agency, the public works committees and the appropriations committees of the Congress, as well as the various offices in the Presidency, must at least tacitly cooperate in moving projects along until they become eligible for construction funds. The set of projects eligible for construction or planning appropriations, sometimes called the "shelf," is maintained and expanded by the Corps and the relevant committees and thus constitutes a source of constant demand for construction and planning money. This list of projects must grow constantly to support a fair-share expansion of the Corps of Engineers' budget.

In order to get an idea of the magnitude of the fair-share effect, the presidential request for the Corps was plotted against the size of the total budget. Figure 4.1 shows the results.

By the definition given here, a strict fair-share rule would imply that the Corps' budget would be a constant proportion of the total budget and that the Corps' share would remain relatively stable from year to year. If this were the case, the correlation between the Corps' budget request and the total budget would be 1.0. In fact, over the period 1948 to 1967, the correlation between these variables was .61. The presence of other influences accounts for the relatively low correlation.

The hypothesis that the deviations from a simple fair-share model are purely random can be examined. The residuals from the regression of the Corps' budget request on total budget were obtained; now if the deviations from the fair-share model are random, they should scatter in an unpredictable fashion about the regression line. Fig-

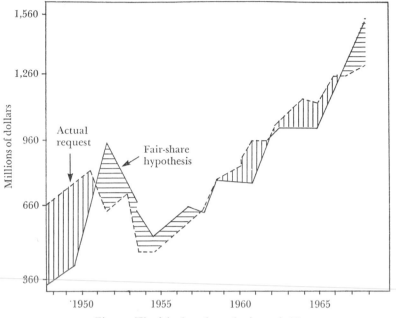

Fig. 4.1 The fair-share hypothesis, 1948–68

ure 4.1 graphs the expected Corps' request (this is the request the Corps would have made if it were just going to obtain a fixed share of the total budget) and the observed request over time.

Deviations of expected requests (under the fair-share rules) from observed requests tend to fall neatly into three periods. The first period is 1948–50: observed requests regularly exceeded expected requests under the fair-share rule. In the second period, 1951–56, observed requests fell short of the fair share. Finally, in the third period, 1959–67, observed requests exceeded the fair-share requests.

The vertically hatched area in Figure 4.1 indicates that the Corps received more than it would have under a strict fair-share rule; the horizontally hatched area indicates that the Corps' request was less than under a fair-share rule. The peculiarly nonrandom appearance of the data (since the periods for different rules do seem to be consecutive) leads us to suspect either that there were different sharing rules working for different periods or that other forces were operating during these periods to produce systematic deviance from the fair-share rule. In the first case one must search for the reason that different sharing rules were adopted; in the second case one must determine the forces producing deviance. In any event, the use of a single sharing rule for the whole period is unsatisfactory. This result confirms the finding by Davis, Dempster, and Wildavsky. The results of the fair-share hypothesis

are inferior to those reported in Tables A and B; indeed, the simple correlations between (the agency budget) and (the total nondefense budget) are usually poorer than those between (the agency budget) and (the budget request). Moreover, the *d*-statistics are usually highly significant and the residual patterns are either increasing or decreasing over time. . . . Thus it would appear that in practice the notion of "fair shares" serves, at the very best, as only a rough guide to decision-making.[3]

It would appear that the fair-share principle may be operative but, if so, that it is filtered through other influences not randomly distributed, or that the choice of the fair share shifts over time.

The Budget Bureau

The Budget Bureau has different goals from the Corps of Engineers. In the first place, its decisions about the federal budget have fiscal significance; their total impact may promote inflation or recession, depending on the current economic climate. Second, the Budget Bureau tries to coordinate the public works program as a whole, and it has established its own priorities for different kinds of projects. There are three principal continuing areas of disagreement between the Corps and the Budget Bureau: (1) the Budget Bureau prefers a high discount rate while the Corps prefers a low one; (2) the Budget Bureau evaluates proposed navigation projects differently than the Corps does; (3) the Budget Bureau prefers to judge projects solely on their net contribution to the national income while the Corps would like to expand the bases for project evaluation. These disagreements, in practice, lead the Budget Bureau to cut the Corps' budget in a very selective way.

The Budget Bureau has argued for increasing the discount rate for many years, contending that it is so low that it does not accurately reflect the cost of removing resources from the private sector and utilizing them for public-sector construction. The discount rate was raised several times during the 1960's, as a result of prodding from the Budget Bureau, the Joint Economic Committee, and almost all professional economists. The principal effect of raising the discount rate is to decrease the number of projects with favorable benefit-cost ratios (see Chapter 2). In reviewing the Corps' budget requests, the Budget Bureau strikes many projects with benefit-cost ratios barely

greater than one that would become economically undesirable should
the discount rate be revised upward.

The Budget Bureau differs with the Corps on the valuation of
many different kinds of benefits and costs. The major disagreement
has always been over navigation benefits. In order to evaluate the
contribution a navigation project would make to the national income, one must estimate first the current ton-mile shipping costs between points to be served by the proposed project, second the projected ton-mile shipping costs if the project is built, and third the
number of tons that will be shipped under the new costs. The estimated contribution to the annual national income is simply the difference between current costs and future costs if the project is built
times the amount of ton-miles shipped. The Corps and the Budget
Bureau differ in their estimates of current ton-mile costs. The Corps
uses current rates charged to shippers, but these may well be monopoly rates charged by the railroads and so may have little relation
to actual costs. The Budget Bureau advocates estimating the real
costs of shipping. The Budget Bureau's method would greatly reduce
estimated navigation benefits in cases where the railroads are charging
monopoly rates (which would of course be higher than marginal
costs). The Corps' benefit estimate will be the contribution to national
income plus the railroad's monopoly profit; this last factor is not a
net national benefit of the project, since the project would merely
distribute this profit away from the railroads to shippers and consumers. At one point the Budget Bureau ordered the Corps to use
its evaluation method, but a severe congressional reaction ensured
that the Corps would stay with its previous method. Congress wrote
the prevailing-rate method (the Corps' preferred method) into law
in the Department of Transportation Act of 1966.

In addition, the Budget Bureau advocates utilizing the net contribution to national income (i.e. not counting redistributions of wealth
toward one group or another) as the major basis of project evaluation.
According to the Budget Bureau, a project must increase the net
wealth of the country in order to be a "good" project. The Corps, on
the other hand, would prefer to use multiple objectives in evaluating
projects, so that those projects which do not have favorable benefit-
cost ratios might still stand some chance of approval. The debate
over these issues is still raging in Washington, and although currently the Budget Bureau's method is still being practiced, a powerful
coalition of local interest groups and congressmen is at work trying
to allow the incorporation of additional objectives.

The Budget Bureau has independent standards which it applies to recommended new starts. Briefly, these standards can be listed as follows.

1. The benefit-cost ratio must be fairly high.
2. Navigation projects are seldom acceptable.
3. There is a preference for urban flood-control projects.
4. Small-boat harbors have low priority.
5. Rural flood control has low priority.
6. Power projects are acceptable if they are "good" power projects.*

Each of these standards rests on fairly elaborate justifications within the Budget Bureau, and together they are the basis for much of the project-by-project decision-making that takes place in the Budget Bureau with respect to the Corps' budget.

The Corps' spending is part of the federal government's fiscal policies, as noted above. The difficulty with relating budget-making to fiscal policy is that fiscal policy is made on the basis of the actual rate of spending whereas budget-making is done in terms of requests and appropriations. The connection between these two phenomena is often quite remote. We saw earlier that the Corps is able to spend money under concurrent resolutions more or less independently of the outcome of the appropriations process. Similarly, the President can and frequently does impound funds duly appropriated for projects. In the past, Presidents have done so without regard for what economists might consider to be sound fiscal reasons: for example, Eisenhower impounded construction funds at the start of the 1957 recession because Congress had added many new starts to his budget. Some economists have argued that this helped intensify a recession that was just getting under way. Thus it is possible that the government's fiscal policy may obscure the relationship between the Corps' appropriations and the state of the economy. Still, one might expect that political pressures for the government to counter unemployment with additional construction spending would be strong enough to withstand attenuating influences and to show up in the data. It was felt that the most powerful economic variable would probably be unemployment; thus, for the present, we will confine our attention to examining the impact of unemployment on the difference between presidential budget requests and the previous year's actual appropria-

* The Budget Bureau has internally defined standards as to what constitutes a "good" power project. These standards relate to the environmental damage the project will cause, the amount of the power that will actually be utilized immediately, the availability of alternative power sources, and other criteria.

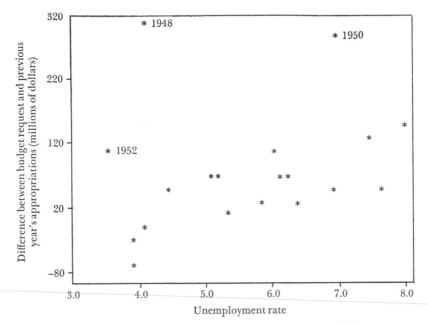

Fig. 4.2 The effect of unemployment on budget size, 1948–66

tions. The correlation between the variables was .26, and Figure 4.2 shows the relationship. The time period was 1948–66.

As indicated in Figure 4.2, several factors are at work that mitigate the effect of the economic state of affairs on the Corps' budget. Public works has always been recognized as a crude fiscal instrument, if an unavoidable one. Some reasons for this have already been given. Wilfred Lewis adds, "Actions that might be more difficult to reverse, such as new public works starts (as distinguished from speeding work in progress), generally have been avoided."[4] Because public works is regarded as an inflexible fiscal instrument at best, other spending programs tend to be used in response to unemployment, and we would expect a fairly weak relationship between unemployment and budget size. Thus for good reason the correlation here is of a low order of magnitude.

The same sort of analysis was done using a price index for the nonresidential construction industry. We would expect that in years when construction costs exhibit sharp rises governmental construction expenditures should be held down, since they are inflationary in such situations. Figure 4.3 examines these effects. The time period was 1948–69; the correlation was −.24. However, 1948 was the end of the

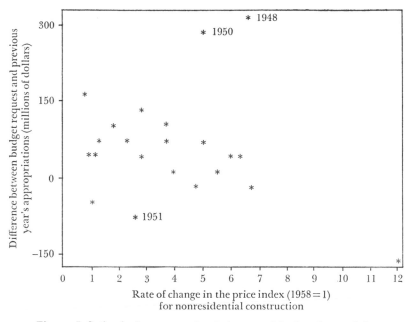

Fig. 4.3 Inflation in the construction industry and budget size, 1948–69

postwar inflation and the first year of the 1948–50 recession; if 1948 is dropped, the correlation is −.43.

It appears that the economic situation does exert a modest degree of influence on the Corps' requests. There is no reason to look more deeply into these fiscal effects, since it is enough to show that there is a relationship here and that it is not terribly strong.

The Budget Bureau makes its decisions on the Corps' budget in the knowledge that the Engineers enjoy considerable political support in the Congress. Congress acts as a court of appeals for the Budget Bureau's decisions, as we have already mentioned. Budget officials are quite aware of this and attempt to anticipate congressional reaction to their decisions. The mechanism, as perceived by a Budget Bureau official, is the following one.

If the President's budget has no or few new starts, the appropriations committees respond by adding a whole bunch since they resent the policy by the B.O.B. If there are already a lot of new starts the appropriations committees are more willing to accept the administration recommendation as it stands and defend it on the floor (since it is more defensible there, as a number of congressmen are receiving new starts and therefore have a stake in the budget).

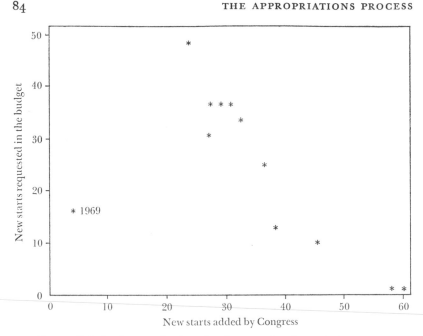

Fig. 4.4 Relation between budgeted and congressional new starts, 1959–70

This amounts to saying that there will be a negative relation between budgeted new starts and new starts added by Congress. Data were used for the period 1959–70, and the correlation was observed to be −.56, as expected. Figure 4.4 shows the relation in graphic form. The outlying year is 1969. An interview with a former Budget Bureau official throws some light on why 1969 was an exception.

In 1968, the Vietnam War and accelerating inflation led the Budget Bureau to propose very few new starts for the Corps in 1969, fewer in fact than had been requested since the Eisenhower "no new start" years. Budget Bureau officials felt that the congressional response was predictable, especially since the seriousness of the inflation was not yet apparent. The expected response materialized and the final budget contained five times as many new starts as were budgeted. The following year the Budget Bureau asked for more projects (14 rather than ten); inflation was more severe, and Congress was more cooperative. Only three new starts were added by the Congress in 1969, even though the number asked for in the budget was lower than usual. The impact of the economic environment appeared to be quite telling during that year. This example indicates that the Budget Bureau operates in an environment, at least with respect to the number of

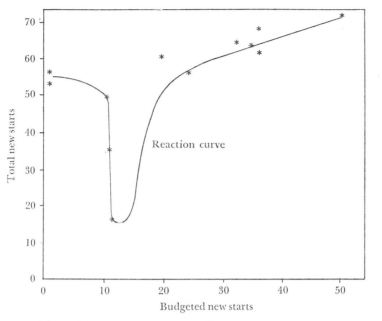

Fig. 4.5 Total new starts as a function of budgeted new starts

new starts, in which congressional response is highly predictable in any but the most unusual economic circumstances. Its ability to recommend any desired number of new starts is severely constrained by the anticipated congressional response. Budget Bureau officials realize that recommending too few construction starts can have precisely the opposite of the desired effect. Consequently, the Budget Bureau will tend to come in higher than it might were it not operating in a situation dominated by a law of anticipated reaction. Figure 4.5 shows the policy choice that faces the Budget Bureau as it anticipates congressional reaction. The reaction curve that appears on the graph gives the total number of new starts as a function of the number that the Bureau recommends to Congress. Apparently, if the Bureau wants to minimize the number of new starts in a given year, it should recommend about 14 or 15 projects rather than none.

The figure also illustrates a part of the decision problem facing the Budget Bureau. The Bureau tries to achieve its objectives (building only "good" projects, producing desired fiscal effects) in a political or strategic milieu. It cannot perfectly control the behavior of the Corps or the response of the Congress. It recognizes that the Corps' initial requests will be reported to the appropriations committees and that many of its cuts in the budget will be restored. If it has the support of the President, it can use the threat of veto (the Public Works Appropriations Bill of 1959 was vetoed) or impoundment. These weapons, however, are not sufficient to give the Budget Bureau very much control over the budget of the Corps of Engineers in comparison to the control it exercises over other agencies (since the use of these weapons is costly to the President). About half the new projects and about half the budget in a given year originate in congressional new starts, that is in projects initiated by Congress according to its own diverse criteria. If the Budget Bureau initiates fewer projects the Congress will initiate more.

The Corps of Engineers correctly considers itself to be a congressional agency, and the proof lies in the fact that the political executive—the Presidency and its administrative extensions—has comparatively little control over its program or its budget. In the next two chapters we will analyze the way the House and the Senate deal with the budget requests for the Corps—"their" agency.

5

The House Response to the Budget Request

THE MOST POWERFUL CONGRESSMAN

Years ago a colleague who had been trying to get some planning funds
for the ———— floodwall, talked to me and asked me to help him out.
I said "————, if you could arrange for a little flood or something it
would improve the chances." As it turned out, that April there was
the flood of record, and so we put the money in the bill during markup.
   —Interview with a member of the Public Works
      Subcommittee of the House Appropriations Committee

The fact that the Corps is by its own claim a congressional agency
and the widely held expectation that Congress will act as an appeals
court for Budget Bureau decisions make the House's reaction to the
Corps' budget qualitatively different from its response to the budget
requests of other agencies. This chapter explores the contrast between
the way the appropriations process "normally" works—utilizing Fenno's *The Power of the Purse* as a comparative base—and the way it
works where the Corps' budget is concerned. Some explanations are
ventured here, among the most important of which is the idea that
members of the Public Works Subcommittee of the House Appropriations Committee have constituency interests in the Corps' budget.
This contention will receive support in Chapter 9. For now it is
merely a hypothesis that, if true, explains some observed behavior.

In his study of the appropriations process, *The Power of the Purse*,
Richard Fenno lists four goals of the members of the House Appropriations Committee (hereafter referred to as the H.A.C.). They are
(1) to protect the power of the purse, (2) to guard the federal treasury,
(3) to reduce budget estimates, and (4) to serve member constituency
interests. The pursuit of these four objectives is supposed to maximize
the power, or influence, of H.A.C. members. For the purposes of this
chapter, we shall restrict our attention to the third and fourth objectives. In what follows, these latter two goals will be explicated with
the aid of Fenno's treatment, and his results will be compared with
those found in this study.

Fenno shows that a dominant value of committee members is cut-

TABLE 5.1

*H.A.C. Budget Decisions: Fenno's 36 Bureaus and the
Corps of Engineers Compared*

Committee decisions	Fenno's bureaus (percent)	Corps of Engineers (percent)
Increases over budget estimates	8.0%	22.7%
Same as budget estimates	18.4	—
Decreases below budget estimates	73.6	77.3
TOTAL	100.0% (N = 576)	100.0% (N = 22)

SOURCE: Fenno, p. 371.

ting the budget. Committee members feel that congressmen both within and outside the committee expect this sort of behavior from them. One member said, "When you're on the Committee people expect you to cut."[1] A former chairman of the H.A.C., Clarence Cannon (Democrat–Missouri), put it best. "It has long been an unwritten rule of the Committee on Appropriations that the budget estimate is taken as the maximum and the efficiency of the subcommittee has been judged—and the chairman of each subcommittee has prided himself—on the amount . . . cut below the budget estimate."[2]

Table 5.1 was constructed from Fenno's results for the 36 bureaus studied in his book, and from committee behavior on the Corps' budget estimates from 1948 to 1969.[3] Apparently the committee increases the Corps' budget estimates more frequently than it increases those of the 36 agencies that Fenno studied. This result should be interpreted in light of the fact that Cannon, the chairman of the H.A.C. until 1964, was also chairman from 1955 to 1964 of the subcommittee that reviews the Corps' budget. During his tenure, 30 percent of the committee decisions were increases over the budget estimates.*

Fenno categorized the 36 bureaus in his study and showed that the client-oriented bureaus appeared to be more successful in defending their budget requests than other agencies. He remarked: "The appropriations success for the top 12 bureaus would seem to be associated either with the combination of a noncontroversial function and a well-defined work load or with constituency-oriented clientele support." But why did Cannon, while he was subcommittee chairman, go against his own unwritten rule and actually increase the Corps' budget on 30 percent of the occasions that he had to review it?

---

* Note, though, that the Corps' budget is cut below what is recommended more frequently than are the budgets of Fenno's 36 bureaus.

One obvious factor is that on public works bills members of the subcommittee are themselves cross-pressured. A senior leader said, "Cannon wants to cut, cut, cut—unless Missouri is involved. He fights hard for Missouri."[4] A member from Texas said, "I am for economy in Idaho and perhaps in Maine and a considerable amount down in Oklahoma. Then in the districts of some of my Texas colleagues I am for economy over there unless it would injure and hurt my colleagues; but when you come into my district I am for economy but."[5] Chapter 9 presents evidence of the extent to which H.A.C. subcommittee members get more Corps projects in their districts than other congressmen get. The cross-pressure theory can be broken into several independent mechanisms. First, there are the mechanisms relating to recruitment onto the Public Works Subcommittee. Members with district interests in projects tend to want to join the subcommittee. "Service on [Interior and Public Works subcommittees] and success in getting projects authorized may make these members especially desirous of a place on the money-granting committee—still for constituency service reasons." Members wanting to maximize their influence in the House may desire service on the Public Works Subcommittee. As Fenno says, "Committee members know that power in the House rests at bottom on their perceived capacity to affect the electoral fortunes of fellow members by granting or withholding funds for pet projects." A member of the committee said, "They are very polite to us. They've all got pet projects in over here and they know what we can do to them."[6] Second, once on the subcommittee, for whatever initial reason, there are several pressures not to cut too deeply. After all, subcommittee members want to maintain good relations with the legislative committee. The Public Works Subcommittee authorizes projects and has a programmatic commitment to increase the Corps' expenditures. If the Appropriations Subcommittee cuts too deeply, the distributive nature of the public works budget makes it possible for the authorizing committee to mobilize against the Public Works Subcommittee on the floor. Also, if members of the subcommittee want to get any particular thing accomplished in the House, their membership on this subcommittee will tend to make it easier since other members have to come before them to ask for projects; but there has to be some reward in it for the other members. Cannon, John Taber (Republican–New York), and Ben Jensen (Republican–Iowa) were all high-ranking members of this subcommittee, and all reportedly used their power over projects to protect appropriations bills on the floor.[7]

Members of Congress not on the Public Works Subcommittee press those on it for pet projects. The way that projects are budgeted makes the subcommittee members particularly susceptible to pressure. In particular, the fact that there is no full funding for Corps projects means that the first year's construction costs of a new start are but a small proportion of the total cost of the project. In addition, members of the House know that "if you can get a survey, your project will probably push along to completion."[8] The survey amounts are small—$25,000 to $35,000 or so—and congressmen are not willing to say no to a colleague when the amount in question is of this order of magnitude. "We keep an eye out for the fellow who needs something in his campaign. If he can bring back a little something and we can help him in his campaign, we naturally go along."[9]

The Public Works Appropriations Hearings are structured so as to be responsive to member demands of this sort. Fenno states that in 1963, 172 House members testified in the House hearings. The following remarks by Representative Samuel Devine of Ohio in behalf of the Alum Creek Reservoir are illustrative.

> Gentlemen, I have either written or talked to all of you personally about the Alum Creek Reservoir project in Ohio. . . . Last year you very properly approved the sum of $225,000 for preconstruction planning, and this proceeded in orderly and normal fashion. Thereafter, the U.S. Army Corps of Engineers established a capability for fiscal 1968 of $2,400,000 to initiate construction.
> The Bureau of the Budget deleted this figure. . . . Although the Corps of Engineers has already demonstrated a capability of $2,400,000 for fiscal year 1968, and the figure can be justified and should be approved, construction can and will get underway if you men will approve a token amount, and I would suggest only $75,000 to $100,000.[10]

This is not an untypical presentation by a congressman. In his statement Devine tries to establish two basic things: the project is justified, and the amount of money being asked for is very small. He knows that once the project is under construction, the committee will not (and will not really be able to) alter the pace of construction.

Fenno also remarks that demands for budget reductions tend to be amorphous and general, whereas demands for budget increases are likely to be specific. The hearings process in the public works appropriations area facilitates the raising of these specific demands to the committee. These hearings are the longest and most detailed, and receive the most testimony, of any of the appropriations hearings.

Explicit cooperation between members of the subcommittee and other members is common, especially within state delegations. For example, many states have members on both the Public Works Committee and the subcommittee. Fenno quotes an Iowa Republican as follows.

Fred and I have had to work closely together since he came to Congress, and so I have become aware of this ability his constituents respect so much. He is on the Public Works Committee; I am on Appropriations as a member of the flood control projects, etc., which clear through his committee ... [and] come up to the Appropriations Committee for the necessary funds.[11]

Arrangements like this are not unusual, especially where the state delegation is cohesive and has a tradition of working together. We have already explored the state delegation's influence in public works decision-making in Chapter 3.

Another form of cooperation is that between subcommittees of the House Appropriations Committee. Among members of the H.A.C., influence depends on the friends one has on the other subcommittees. A member reports.

There's the fellow who asked me about a hospital he's got coming up. Then when I want something done, I will go and see him. They pay more attention to me when I'm a member of the committee. You trade back and forth across subcommittees that way. It's a matter of scratching each other's backs, I suppose. But that's the only way you get any specific project accomplished around here.[10]

The factors presented thus far describe several sources of upward pressure on the House recommendations for the Corps of Engineers' construction budget. First, members of the Public Works Subcommittee want pet projects themselves. Second, the subcommittee member's influence in the House rests partly on not suffering defeat on the House floor in the form of successful amendments to the subcommittee bill. The way to hedge against this possibility is not to cut deeply and to add popular projects while the bill is in committee. Third, cooperation within state delegations and within the whole H.A.C. guarantees a favorable hearing for a large proportion of projects in any given year.

These pressures, together with the norm to serve member constituency needs (insofar as it is separate in the minds of subcommittee members from the factors which support it as a norm), work to counter the norm of reducing budget requests. If these two norms were in direct conflict over the time period being studied, one might conclude that the norm to reduce the budget is generally the stronger one. However, because of the way budgeting decisions are made in the area of public works, the two norms are not directly in conflict:

it is possible to serve both at the same time. The way that the law governs the funding of public works projects gives the appropriations subcommittee some slack and makes its work much easier than it might otherwise be.

As explained in Chapter 4, there is no full funding for Corps projects. When a new construction start is put into the budget only the first year's construction money appears. Thus it is possible for the subcommittee to reduce funding for ongoing construction projects while simultaneously adding new starts. The total obligation on the treasury can therefore increase while the appropriations bill is before the subcommittee at the same time that the current appropriation for the Corps decreases. Not only is this possible, but it occurs with great regularity. A former Director of the Bureau of the Budget, Charles Schultze, commented on this situation:

> Each year the Congress appropriates to start more new public works projects than the President has recommended. Yet each year the Congress reduces the public works appropriations recommended by the President. This sleight of hand is made possible by the way in which public works projects are financed.[13]

Schultze went on to assess the impact of this phenomenon.

> During the past ten years, administration budgets have recommended 282 new starts on Corps of Engineers construction projects costing an estimated total of $4.1 billion. To these recommendations the Congress added 270 new starts with a total estimated cost of $4.5 billion. But because the first year costs are typically so small, the Congress had to add only $144 million to administration appropriation requests to get the $4.5 billion of new work under way.[14]

Unfortunately, these figures are not broken down by stage in the appropriations process. However, they have been computed for this study and are reported in the next chapter in Table 6.3. In 1959, one of the years when Eisenhower's "no new starts" policy was in effect, the House added 38 new starts and the Senate 71. Only one or two of the House new starts were added on the floor, so that the House subcommittee was responsible for adding a substantial fraction of the unbudgeted new starts. In 1966, the House subcommittee added 59 new starts as compared with 29 Senate additions.

This is normal subcommittee behavior in the public works area. The way in which the yearly appropriations requests for the Corps are considered is very different from the way other appropriations requests are considered. For other agencies, the appropriations subcommittee receives the budget requests from the Budget Bureau and the agency witnesses are expected to support the figures the Budget Bureau has sent to the Hill. Fenno and Wildavsky both discuss how the Budget Bureau tries to discourage "end runs" by the agencies. This occurs when an agency tells the subcommittee what figure they actually requested before the Budget Bureau cut it to fit with the President's budget. Wildavsky describes the phenomenon: "the Bureau of the Budget . . . lays down the rule that members of the Executive Branch are not to challenge the Executive Budget. But everyone knows that the administration officials want more for their agencies."[15] With most agencies, witnesses have to be very tactful in communicating to the subcommittee how much they really want as opposed to how much the Budget Bureau has recommended. This is not the case with the Corps of Engineers. It is true that when Corps officials come before the subcommittee they display the customary reticence before disclosing how much they asked the Budget Bureau for. However, the subcommittee also takes testimony from outside witnesses on a state-by-state basis. These witnesses generally include a sizable part of the state's congressional delegation as well as many members of the Appropriations and Public Works committees. The testimony of these outside witnesses frequently amounts to over 1,200 pages. The following passage illustrates the flavor of this testimony.

Mr. Price [Congressman Melvin Price from Illinois]. Mr. Chairman, I am pleased to have the opportunity to support Congressman Shipley and also to point out that yesterday, in testimony with regard to the Wabash River, Congressman Kenneth Gray also appeared here in support of the Kaskaskia River navigation project. That is a project that was approved in a report from the Corps of Engineers last year. It went back to the district and to the division for further study and review, and has been returned in an even more favorable light than the original report; it has been submitted and is now before the Bureau of the Budget. The Corps of Engineers have informed me, unofficially, of course, that they see no reason why it would not obtain budget approval.

The favorable situation is such that they have this confidence. The cost-benefit ratio is so much in favor the project.

Now, the District Office of the Corps of Engineers informs us that they could begin construction work, initiate construction work on this project, with $1.5 million. We are appearing here this afternoon urging this item to be approved by the committee, even though it has not yet been submitted to you by the Bureau of the Budget.[16]

Accompanying Price's testimony was support from Governor Kerner of Illinois, from a representative of the Mississippi Valley Associa-

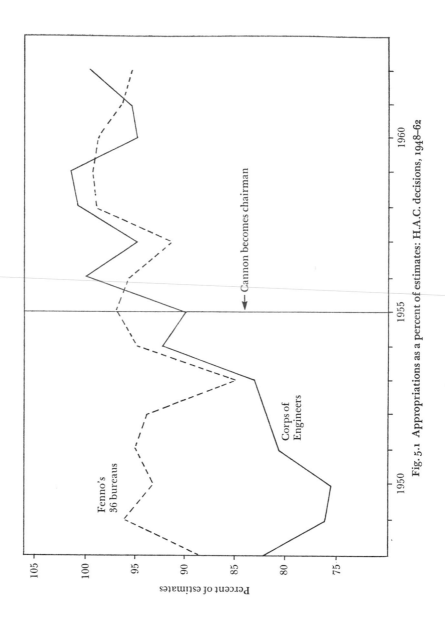

Fig. 5.1 Appropriations as a percent of estimates, 1948–62

tion, from members of several local groups, as well as from several other Illinois congressmen. This sort of thing is not unusual. Much of the testimony the subcommittee hears from outside witnesses, including that of most congressmen, is in favor of unbudgeted requests either to speed up construction or, as above, to put in a new start. Almost inevitably the witness will present assurances from the Corps in favor of the unbudgeted project. In the area of public works the end-run strategy seems to be institutionalized more than in any other area. There is no reason for agency officials to be coy and circumspect —their local congressmen will carry out the strategy themselves. That the H.A.C. has manifested occasional concern over this phenomenon is evident from the following caveat from the House Report that accompanied the Civil Functions Appropriations Bill for the Fiscal Year 1954.

It should also be pointed out that the Budget and Accounting Act and Executive regulations require agencies to support the President's Budget. These letters to congressmen are not technically requests for more funds than requested in the Budget. It is well known, however, that they are considered to be tantamount to such a request. The Committee is intrigued by the Executive Branch's apparent lack of attention to this situation in the Corps when these regulations are so assiduously enforced with respect to other agencies.[17]

The factors introduced so far serve to explain the static differences between appropriations committee behavior on public works and its behavior in other areas. The differences can be traced to two distinct sources. The first is motivational: subcommittee members individually profit by acting the way they do with respect to public works appropriations. The second is situational: the method of funding in public works permits subcommittee members to avoid the conflicting norms of reducing the budget estimate and serving member constituency interests. The situation is structured so that they are able to do what they want to do. Subcommittee behavior will now be examined over time, so that we can attempt to explain changes in that behavior.

It is instructive to compare the H.A.C.'s actions on the Corps' budget with its actions on the budgets of Fenno's 36 bureaus. Figure 5.1 shows agency appropriations as a percentage of requests from 1948 to 1962, and reveals that prior to 1956 the committee was consistently less favorable to the Corps than it was to Fenno's 36 bureaus (on the average). What would explain this difference in behavior?

A number of events occurred in 1955 that might help to explain this observed shift. To begin with, 1955 was the first year of existence of the Public Works Subcommittee of the H.A.C. Fenno documents this change:

In 1955, with the acquiescence of Mr. Taber, Chairman Cannon created a new Public Works Subcommittee and gathered under its jurisdiction the budget for the Army Corps of Engineers, the Bureau of Reclamation, the Atomic Energy Commission, plus all of the agencies dealing with public power. . . . He then assumed the chairmanship of the Subcommittee. Representative Taber, too, designated himself as a minority member of the Subcommittee and remained on it until he retired in 1962.[18]

In addition, the size of the subcommittee reviewing the Corps' budget went from seven in 1954 to 16 in 1955. On the Republican side, three of the four members of the former Civil Functions Subcommittee were on the new Public Works Subcommittee. For the Democrats, all three of the members were carried over. The Republicans added a member each from the Interior Subcommittee and the Independent Offices Subcommittee, both of which subcommittees gave up parts of their jurisdictions to the new Public Works Subcommittee. The Democrats added Michael Kirwan (Democrat–Ohio) from the Interior Subcommittee, four new members of the H.A.C., and John Fogarty (Democrat–Rhode Island) and Fred Marshall (Democrat–Minnesota).

There was also a change of party control of the House in 1955. This may have led the subcommittee to expect a different sort of reaction to the Corps' budget on the floor and, conversely, it may have led interested House members to expect the newly Democratic subcommittee to treat the budget request in a particular manner. Naturally, the change of party control gave the Democrats the chairmanship of the House Appropriations Committee. Fenno claims that Cannon took the chairmanship of the Public Works Subcommittee himself as a protection against House pressure for increased public works spending.[19]

Which of these events was most crucial to the switch in subcommittee behavior? Evidently they were all closely interrelated. Had the Democrats not taken control of the House, Cannon would not have resumed his chairmanship of the H.A.C. and thus could not have restructured the subcommittees and taken over the Subcommittee on Public Works. If, in fact, the reason that Cannon took over the Public Works Subcommittee and added four new members on the Democratic side was to hold down public works spending, then

TABLE 5.2
Floor Reception of H.A.C. Recommendations

House action	Fenno's bureaus (percent)	Corps of Engineers (percent)
Accept recommendation	89.9%	50.0%
Decrease	5.2	18.0
Increase	4.9	32.0
TOTAL	100.0% (N = 576)	100.0% (N = 22)

one would expect him to have cut Corps requests deeply in his initial budget. A former member of the House Public Works Committee commented on the outcome of the committee consideration in 1955. "The budget that year was sharply limited in its allowances for natural resources items, and the Appropriations Committee carried the reductions even further."[20] So severe were the committee reductions that a floor revolt was begun with broad support. It has been argued that because Cannon suffered such a resounding defeat on the floor with his first Public Works Appropriations Bill, he was forced to change his behavior (and therefore the behavior of his subcommittee) thereafter on such bills. This hypothesis explains the observed major change in subcommittee behavior in 1956, which is precisely what we wanted to explain. Figure 5.2 shows presidential requests and H.A.C. recommendations for the Corps from 1948 to 1969. Again, we can see the change after 1955 in committee recommendations.

Returning to the four goals that Fenno attributes to the H.A.C., we can see that in practice the committee has adopted a form of behavior which allows it to make the third (reduce the budget estimates) and fourth (serve member constituency interests) goals compatible. This is accomplished only at the cost of nearly completely discarding both the goal of guarding the federal treasury and the spirit behind the economy norm. An examination of the response of the House to committee recommendations will show that protecting the power of the purse is also neglected in practice. The prerogatives of the committee are not effectively guarded against changes on the floor.

It is illustrative to begin comparing the floor reception of the Corps' budget to the floor response to the 36 bureaus that Fenno analyzes in his book. Table 5.2 gives the results. The committee's recommendations for the Corps appear to receive much less favorable treatment

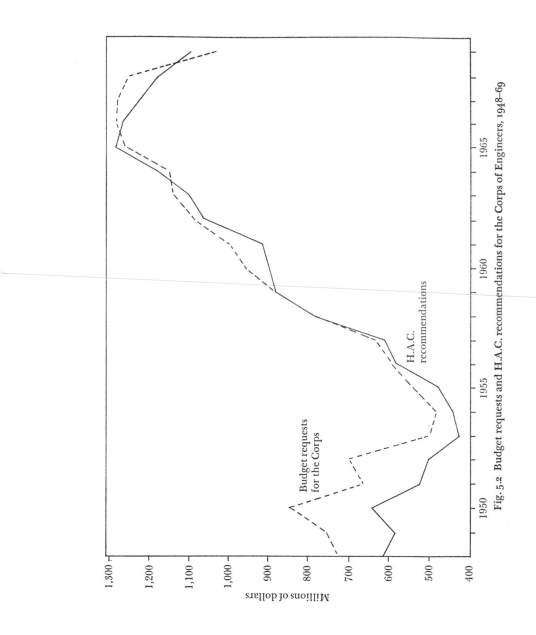

Fig. 5.2 Budget requests and H.A.C. recommendations for the Corps of Engineers, 1948–69

TABLE 5.3
Amendments to Appropriations Bills

Department	Amendments proposed			Amendments passed		
	Number	Increase	Decrease	Number	Increase	Decrease
Public Works	159	143	16	23	22	1
Interior	96	61	35	40	22	18
Agriculture	73	37	36	25	17	8
State	53	6	47	10	0	10
H.E.W.	52	32	20	19	11	8
Labor	36	20	16	13	3	10
Commerce	30	25	5	10	8	2
Treasury	20	6	14	15	4	11
Justice	8	3	5	3	1	2
Other	20	7	13	5	3	2
TOTAL	547	340	207	163	91	72

SOURCE: Fenno, p. 458.
NOTE: Amendments that covered several departments at once and could not be allocated to one department were left in the residual category "Other."

from the House than do the recommendations for Fenno's bureaus.*

Certainly much of this difference has to do with the constituency orientation of Corps spending. Table 5.3 (from Fenno) shows proposed and passed amendments for eight departments plus Public Works. The three departments that might be considered most constituency-oriented (Public Works, Interior, Agriculture) receive the bulk of floor amendments and the bulk of successful amendments as well. Floor managers for the Public Works Bill seem to feel that they are vulnerable on this sort of bill and so feel called upon to defend their generosity. Cannon was quoted in 1962 as saying that that year's bill "included every state and practically every congressional district. There is something here for everybody and no project of merit has been omitted."[21] Representative Kirwan argued in 1963 that "About 350 members of this Congress made requests of our committee to either raise a budget item or include an unbudgeted item."[22] That

---

* The floor reception of H.A.C. action on the Corps' budget seems contrary to Theodore Lowi's theory of congressional policy-making. He argues in his review article "American Business, Public Policy, Case Studies, and Political Theory," *World Politics*, XVI (July 1964), p. 677, that policy-making in a distributive policy arena (he explicitly identifies rivers and harbors decisions as distributive) should be primarily committee-centered. Evidently, when compared to the floor reception of H.A.C. action on Fenno's 36 bureaus, the House floor's response to H.A.C. recommendations for the Corps is to question an abnormally high proportion of committee decisions.

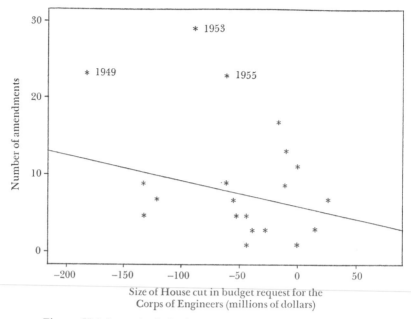

Fig. 5.3 H.A.C. cuts in the budget and number of floor amendments

year the committee added 19 new construction starts, 30 unbudgeted surveys, and 17 unbudgeted planning studies. The House made no change on the floor.

One reason why floor managers of public works appropriations bills are defensive is that the whole House acts as an appeals board for the subcommittee's decision. Whenever the subcommittee slashes deeply there is a rash of floor amendments. Figure 5.3 shows the relationship between subcommittee cuts in the Corps' budget and number of floor amendments (which is taken to be a measure of floor dissatisfaction with the subcommittee's proposal).

The correlation between the two variables is −.31. This shows that the more the House Appropriations Committee cuts the Corps' budget the more amendments are offered on the floor. The regression line is drawn in the figure for convenience. Of course, the fact that a lot of amendments were offered on the floor does not mean that many of them succeeded. Therefore, the dollar change that the House makes in the H.A.C. recommendations will not necessarily be highly correlated with H.A.C. cuts in the budget. The relationship between these two variables is in fact only −.07. The reason for this attenuation is the intervening factor of "floor success." When the H.A.C.

reports out a bill with large reductions in the Corps' budget, the floor manager is aware of his weakness and works hard to hold together a coalition on the floor. There are several methods of doing this, one of which is to add new starts to compensate for the cuts. The strategic advantages enjoyed by the H.A.C. are employed as well: (1) it will obtain great committee cohesion on floor votes; (2) it may be able to get leadership help on the floor if needed; (3) the fact that most members have projects before the committee means that they will be reluctant to go against it on the floor; (4) the H.A.C. will exploit its advantages in the timing of the floor consideration of the bill.

Even with the aforementioned advantages, the committee does occasionally run into trouble on the floor that it cannot contain. There are times when amendments will carry despite the opposition of the subcommittee. Generally, the explanation for such an occurrence is that one or more of the committee's strategic advantages has broken down. For example, during the successful floor revolt against the committee on the Public Works Appropriations Bill in 1955, the leadership gave its support to the opponents of the committee. Fenno reports the remarks of a member of the Democratic leadership:

> The President sent down a public works budget and they cut it by about $78 million. But they cut more projects of Democrats than Republicans.... The money was in the budget and the projects had been authorized.... The members were upset. They came here and yacked and yacked and yacked. I said to them, "What's the matter with you? Are you so afraid of the Appropriations Committee?... Why don't you go out and round up some support?... Get yourselves a coalition. I'll be helping you."[23]

Another interesting situation occurred in 1959 when Otto Passman (Democrat–Louisiana), a member of the House Appropriations Committee, offered an amendment to add $500,000 for water-hyacinth eradication. Fenno describes how the fact that the H.A.C. did not vote together on the floor accounted for Passman's success.[24] Although it is often difficult to assess the influence of Fenno's third and fourth factors directly, his book offers a wealth of support for their existence and importance.

If the relations between the House floor and the H.A.C. are examined over time (see Figure 5.4), we see once again that there is a decided change in 1955. The material presented above with respect to the floor revolt against the H.A.C. on the Public Works Appropriations Bill of 1955 should give the reader some indication of what to expect in the way of an explanation. A high-ranking member of

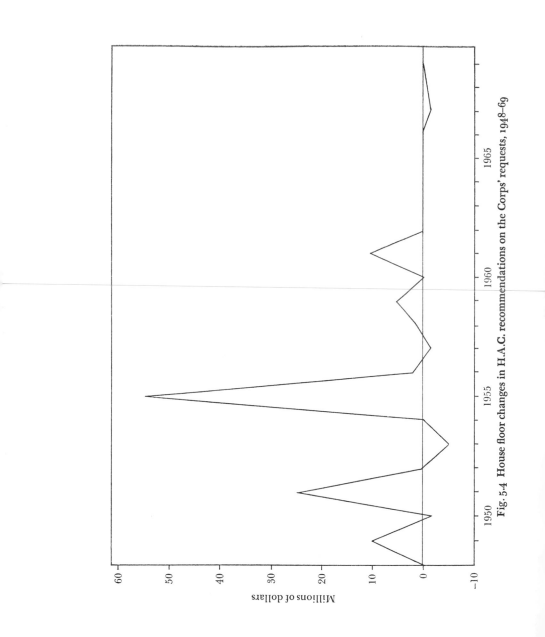

Fig. 5.4 House floor changes in H.A.C. recommendations on the Corps' requests, 1948–69

the Public Works Committee reported, "Cannon was trying to run a one man show. He didn't care whether or not a project was budgeted.... He'd strike it out anyway. He wanted you to go over and bow and scrape for him."[25]

To some extent the floor revolt was an intercommittee fight. Frank Smith (Democrat–Mississippi), a member of the Public Works Committee, was the floor manager for the opponents of the bill, and the debate was dominated by members of the Public Works and Interior committees. However, some members of Appropriations took advantage of the situation to add amendments of their own. The most important factor behind the revolt appeared to be that many members thought Cannon arbitrary in his behavior; in addition, he refused to follow the accepted rule that if a project is in the budget request, it receives funds. There were, of course, other reasons, and they are spelled out in more detail in Frank Smith's autobiography. One thing that appears to be clear is that there were long-lasting effects: "No more fights were necessary in succeeding years because the committee refashioned its tactics to meet the mood of the House."[26]

After 1955, the behavior of the committee with respect to presidential requests became more liberal, and success on the floor increased, as Figure 5.4 shows. It is from this date that the H.A.C. departed from a rigid adherence to the budget-cutting norm and adopted a mode of behavior more in line with the constituency service norm. There are at least two reasons why the adverse floor response in 1955 changed subcommittee behavior: first, because the committee had to change or surrender much of its authority over public works appropriations to the floor of the House; second, because the Public Works Appropriations Bill could be used by H.A.C. leaders to enforce floor compliance with committee expectations on other appropriations bills, so that it had to make sure that few floor amendments were offered and succeeded.

Fenno reports that since 1955 the Public Works Appropriations Bill has been among the last to come to the floor, and he argues that the reason Cannon took over the subcommitee was to have more control over the House's behavior on appropriations bills. Figure 5.5 graphs the number of proposed amendments to Fenno's 36 bureaus and eight departments plus Public Works. Admittedly, the number of amendments on the floor is a crude sort of measure of noncompliance with committee expectations, since some amendments may be unopposed by the H.A.C. The data are also not complete, but

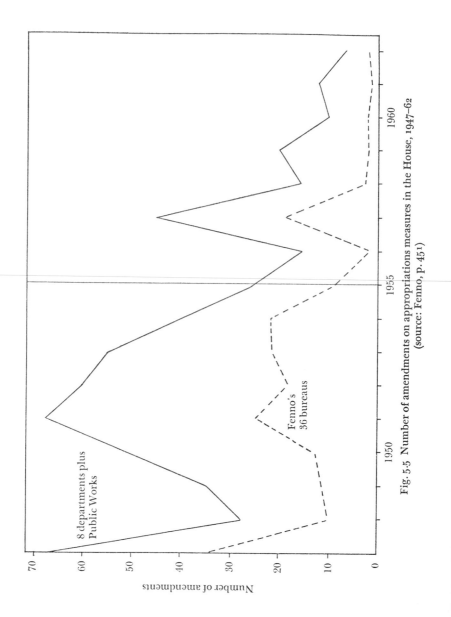

Fig. 5.5 Number of amendments on appropriations measures in the House, 1947–62 (source: Fenno, p. 451)

there are enough to give tentative support to Fenno's assertion. A complete analysis of this provocative hypothesis lies outside the scope of this study. The data presented here are included only to give some credibility to the notion beyond that found in Fenno's book.

This chapter introduced the broad configurations of House behavior on the budget of the Corps of Engineers. It produced several hypotheses along the way, one of which warrants examination in a later chapter. That hypothesis is that the change in subcommittee behavior observed in 1955 is related to a change in the constituency interests of subcommittee members in the Corps of Engineers' projects. Of further theoretical interest are the observations indicating that, in the long run, the H.A.C. must behave differently with respect to the budgets of clientele-oriented agencies or those that promulgate distributive policies. This idea will be further developed and explored in Chapter 9.

6

The Senate's Response to the Corps' Budget

One day when Adams was pleading with a Cabinet officer for patience
and tact in dealing with Representatives, the Secretary impatiently
broke out: "You can't use tact with a Congressman! A Congressman is
a hog! You must take a stick and hit him on the snout!" . . . He knew
a way of silencing criticism. He had but to ask: "If a Congressman
is a hog, what is a Senator?"   —*Henry Adams*

The literature on the appropriations process is filled with observations attesting to the differences between the Senate and the House.
The Senate is frequently called the "upper" body because it usually
raises the appropriations recommended by the House. In addition,
the Senate is alleged to hold less thorough hearings, and senators are
not considered to have as intimate and fine a knowledge as their
House counterparts of the federal agencies whose budgets they must
review. The Senate is sometimes said to function as an appeals board
before which the agencies, having had their budgets severely pared
in the House, come with appeals for restoration of cuts.

Generally speaking, the House is considered by congressional scholars to be more influential in the appropriations process than the
Senate. Fenno remarked that the House "dominates appropriations
politics in Congress."[1] The Senate exerts some independent effect but
it generally operates within the broad limits set by the agencies and
the House Appropriations Committee.

Fenno has tried to provide an explanation of these differences between the two appropriations committees. Constituency pressures in
the Senate incline senators toward greater program support than is
displayed by members of the House Appropriations Committee.
Many members of the House "represent fairly homogeneous constituencies. In some of them—particularly rural ones—the ideology of
minimal government, small budgets, and frugality remains strong."[2]
The economy norm which dominates the appropriations politics of
the House is far weaker in the Senate because of the relatively more
heterogeneous constituencies of senators.

The Senate also comes second in the process by long-standing tradition. The House has the first crack at the federal budget. Agency testimony will therefore naturally attempt to convince the Senate to resurrect treasured programs just whittled down in the House. Senate hearings are thus focused on the cuts made in the House whenever agency personnel are permitted to guide the direction of these hearings.

The Senate Appropriations Committee (S.A.C.) members have several committee assignments; work on the S.A.C. is only one of their committee tasks. As a result, since their time is very limited, senators will not be able to specialize as much as House members in the work of a few agencies. They will employ time-economizing devices that reduce their work load. One of these devices is a division of labor between the House and Senate committees whereby the House looks deeply and critically into agency activities and programs (especially new programs) and the Senate focuses its attention on reviewing decisions made by the House.

The Senate Appropriations Committee is less insulated from the Senate legislative committees than the H.A.C. is from the House legislative committees. The House maintains two separate committee systems, and membership in one or the other is based on fundamentally divergent recruitment processes. Program advocates tend to dominate the legislative committees while members interested in economy are more likely to get onto the H.A.C. Conflict between these two committee systems is institutionalized to a large extent. In the Senate, however, recruitment to the two committee systems is not dominated by two separate and conflicting values. Program-oriented members tend to dominate both the legislative and the appropriations committees.*

What is more, through the device of ex officio membership the leadership of the authorizing committee takes part in the meetings of the appropriations subcommittee. For example, on public works appropriations three members of the Public Works Committee— usually the chairman and ranking Democrat as well as the ranking Republican—sit with the appropriations subcommittee. According to Fenno, the conflict between the two committee systems is "kept to a minimum and well below the level reached in the House."[3]

Another reason why the Senate subcommittee fails to cut funds is

---

* One reason for this is that within the S.A.C. senators choose their own subcommittee assignments. There is a seniority system by which senators with the longest service on the S.A.C. choose their subcommittees first, and so on down the line.

TABLE 6.1

S.A.C. Budget Decisions: Fenno's 36 Bureaus and the Corps of Engineers Compared

Committee decisions	Fenno's bureaus (percent)	Corps of Engineers (percent)
Increases	18.9%	68.0%
Same	18.4	—
Decreases	62.7	32.0
TOTAL	100.0% ($N = 576$)	100.0% ($N = 22$)

that the Senate is a smaller body than the House and one with fewer formal rules and conventions. As a result, reciprocity and mutual agreement play a larger part in legislation in the Senate. The smallness of the body and the lack of insulation of the S.A.C. make it likely that severe budget cuts will adversely affect the fortunes of a close colleague and consequently transgress the reciprocity norm.

Our examination of the H.A.C.'s behavior on Corps of Engineers' appropriations indicated that many of the usual generalizations about the H.A.C. were incorrect or misleading when applied to this area. Those generalizations that appeared to be supported—the H.A.C. did usually cut the budget—evaporated upon closer examination (the apparent cuts were replaced many times over by added new starts). We may expect as a consequence that many of the theories about the Senate and its relationship to the House will similarly require modification. The difficulty may run even deeper, for Fenno's description of the appropriations process may not be accurate for the area of public works and, more generally, for distributive issue areas.

The Senate Appropriations Subcommittee for Public Works does not cut below the budget estimate very frequently. For comparative purposes the table above (Table 6.1) places Fenno's data for his 36 bureaus next to committee decisions on the Corps' budget. This table must be interpreted with some caution. The Senate committee always increases the House committee's recommendation; thus if the House committee recommends more than the budget figure, so will the Senate committee. The amount the Senate committee adds to the House's recommendation depends directly on the amount by which the House has changed the budget request. The equation is written below. (For this regression equation, and for subsequent ones in this form, the bracketed terms represent variables. The numbers that appear in parentheses beneath coefficients are t-values. All variables are measured in millions of current dollars.)

$$[\text{Senate addition}] = 55.7 + .442 \text{ [House cut in budget]}$$
$$\qquad\qquad\quad (9.9) \quad (7.0)$$
$$\bar{R}^2 = .70.^*$$

According to this equation, if the House cut the President's budget by $10 million, the Senate figure would be above the budget by approximately $60 million. If the House cut the budget request by $100 million, then the Senate figure would be just about equal to the budget request. A House cut of $200 million would produce a Senate addition of about $140 million, so that the ultimate Senate figure would end up below the President's budget request. Using this equation it is evident that, on the average, the House would have to cut at least $100 million for the Senate figure to end up below the budget estimate. The House has cut this deeply only six times out of 22 budgets, and these six occasions account for all but one of the times that the Senate committee recommended an amount lower than the budget figure.

Table 6.1 also fails to indicate important changes in the behavior of the Senate and House committees. Six of the seven times that the Senate recommendation was below the budget request occurred in the consecutive years 1948–53. This was closely related to the fact that in those years the House cut the President's requests for the Corps very deeply. A most striking indication of change in behavior during this period is the fact that from 1948 to 1954 the Senate increases in the House requests ranged from 12.3 to 35.4 percent, and that after 1955 the range was from 1.6 to 10.8 percent.

This change in behavior is documented in the speeches and statements of Senate Appropriations Committee members in the *Congressional Record*. Senator McKellar (Democrat–Tennessee), the floor manager for the Appropriations Bill for Army Civil Functions for Fiscal Year 1953, argued on the Senate floor as follows:

Yes. During the last 128 years—a very long period of time—the appropriations for the civil functions of the Corps of Engineers have amounted to a total of approximately $8,000,000,000 including $680,900,000 in the approved budget items for the fiscal year 1953. Of this amount, $5,911,000,000 has been for construction. The expenditure of money has built up our country and has aided tremendously in making the United States the greatest country in all the world.

Yet under the bill as it has come to us from the House of Representatives,

---

* The data for this equation are the number of dollars the House cut from the budget and the number of dollars the Senate added for each year from 1948 to 1969. The $\bar{R}^2$ is the proportion of variation in the dependent variable accounted for by the independent variable adjusted for degrees of freedom.

the House has provided for stopping these projects; the House would not even allow the appropriation of planning money for such projects.

The bill as passed by the House provided no appropriation for the planning of river-and-harbor and flood-control projects. The budget estimate for this function was $2,300,000; the Senate committee recommendations are $2,285,000 for this function.

The committee feels very strongly that planning funds should be provided.[4]

Even the Republicans who were attacking the Senate bill conceded that the House figure represented much too severe a cut. Since the 1955 floor revolt, however, the House committee has not cut the budget deeply. The Senate floor manager seldom makes accusatory references to the House any more, for the range of disagreement between the chambers has narrowed substantially both in relative and in absolute terms.

More light can be thrown on the change in behavior of the House and the Senate by examining the Senate's response to House cuts in individual line items in the construction budget requests. Table 6.2 indicates that after 1955 there were two separate shifts in behavior, one by the Senate and one by the House. Evidently, the House subjected a much smaller proportion of line items to cuts after 1955 than had been the case in earlier years. At the same time, the Senate revised a more substantial percentage of House cuts than it had prior to 1955. The Senate would seem to have been exercising a more extensive review of House cutting decisions than it had done previously.

The Senate response to the Public Works Appropriations Bill has changed in another way since 1955. The Senate subcommittee now holds much more detailed hearings on the Corps' budget. The growth in the Senate hearings has been fairly continuous since 1946. In 1946 the Senate hearings on Army Civil Functions Appropriations formed a modest volume of 556 pages. By 1955 the same hearings made up two

TABLE 6.2

Percentage of Line Items in the Corps' Construction Budget Changed in the House and Revised in the Senate

	1951–55	1956–69
Percentage of line items cut by the House	43%	12%
Percentage of line items cut by the House but restored or partly restored in the Senate	72%	90%

books and totaled 2,008 pages. Since then there has been a gradual increase to perhaps 3,400 pages a year, a number comparable to that produced in the House. The rapid proportional growth occurred, not surprisingly, during the years 1948–54, when the House cut the Corps' budgets deeply. The change in House behavior in 1955 did not cause the Senate subcommittee to revert to its former ways since the habit of project-by-project consideration of the appropriations bill had become well ingrained.

The growth of Senate scrutiny of the Corps' budget is part of a larger pattern in which the Senate appropriations subcommittees have generally been taking a more activist role in reviewing the budget. The Senate subcommittees increasingly are studying budgets *de novo* rather than as appeals courts.

Stephen Horn[5] has tried to measure this tendency by counting the number of days from final passage of the House bill until the first Senate hearing was held. For the Corps' budget the figures are as follows: 1946–49, an average lapse of 11 days; 1952–55, an average lapse of −57.8 days; 1962–65, an average lapse of −125 days. The negative averages reflect the fact that the Senate hearings now run concurrently with those in the House. After the House report is issued, the Senate schedules a hearing on the House-recommended changes in the budget. Horn indicates that several other Senate appropriations subcommittees have switched to concurrent consideration of the budget with the House.

Horn makes no attempt to actually assess the differences in policy this change has induced—if any. For this purpose, we can compare the years 1949 and 1967 on a project-by-project basis. In 1949 there were 359 projects in the Corps' budget. The House subcommittee cut appropriations on 213 of them, and the Senate restored or partially restored 174 of these cuts. In 1967, of 445 projects, the House cut 14 and the Senate restored funds on eight of these. The primary kinds of decisions made by the subcommittees changed entirely between these years. The Senate added 42 new starts in 1949 compared with 39 in 1967. The House added seven new starts in 1949 compared with 32 in 1967. In both years new starts by one body were generally concurred in by the other.

The difference that Horn found in Senate consideration over time is related to the sorts of decisions that are made. The budget estimates are now accepted by both the House and Senate as the basic eventual allocations. In the late 1940's and early 1950's, though, the budget figures were considered to be a ceiling by the House. The Senate was

TABLE 6.3

Planning and Construction New Starts Initiated by the House and
Senate from 1951 to 1969

Year	House	Senate	Number of projects in the bill
1951	—	7	120
1952	—	12	93
1953	1	14	81
1954	—	19	143
1955	20	54	205
1956	27	66	267
1957	1	27	265
1958	43	75	220
1959	38	71	278
1960	23	75	300
1961	14	31	365
1962	18	46	418
1963	33	50	401
1964	32	25	415
1965	18	45	416
1966	59	29	399
1967	40	27	379
1968	—	5	367
1969	37	44	347

forced to spend much of its time restoring funds cut by the House. This led the Senate subcommittee to expand the scope of its hearings, since the House cut just about everything. Now both bodies focus on adding new starts. Table 6.3 presents data on this phenomenon.

The Senate and House hearings are similarly structured. The strategies and patterns described for the House hearings are approximately the same for the Senate ones. The major difference is that the Senate subcommittee holds additional hearings after the House report is published to give the agency an opportunity to present reclamas and to officially support House increases on projects.

The types of logrolling or cooperation among senators are much less structured by formal institutions than is the case in the House. In the House there is coordination on seeking projects among members of the same state delegation or the same committee. The Senate, being a smaller and less hierarchical body, is characterized by wider and less ordered kinds of cooperation in project-seeking. Members of the Senate belong to several committees and tend to know a high proportion of the other senators. One member of the Senate Appropriations Committee who had also been on the House Appropriations

Committee commented, "Over here it's much looser. It's much easier for the individual senator to get his project in the bill."[6]

The behavior of the Senate committee can be summarized briefly: the Senate seldom cuts funds for projects. It did not do so, to any significant extent, at any time from 1948 to 1969. This fact is reflected in the observation that the Senate budget is always larger than the House budget. The Senate did act as an appeals court before 1955. It could do this *only* because the House slashed budget recommendations very deeply and for many projects. After 1955 the House refrained from cutting funds for many projects, and so the Senate's role as a court of appeals for restoring House cuts became less important, since there was less to appeal. The Senate merely accepted the House's recommended new starts virtually as they stood, revised whatever House cuts there were, and spent its time making up a list of its own. The relations between the two bodies became decidedly less conflictual after 1955. The Senate subcommittee's behavior has indeed shown a dramatic change but only in response to an even larger change in the budget recommendations received from the House. The institutional barriers between the Senate Appropriations Committee and the Senate as a body are low compared to those in the House. Fenno argues that since the S.A.C.'s consideration of the bill is more open than the H.A.C.'s consideration, one would expect fewer amendments on the floor. The permeability of the Senate committee acts to diffuse dissatisfaction among senators. On the other hand, Fenno also recognized that the open bargaining process in the Senate would likely carry over to the floor. Normally, when amendments pass in the Senate, they increase the budget, typically adding a project or increasing funds on a project. The best summary of Senate floor action is a table comparing the floor reception of Fenno's 36 bureaus with that of the Corps' budget. See Table 6.4. Committee recommendations appear, in both the Senate and the House, to be more vulnerable

TABLE 6.4

Senate Action on Fenno's 36 Bureaus Compared with Senate Action on the Corps' Budget

Senate action	Fenno's bureaus (percent)	Corps (percent)
Accept committee recommendation	88.5%	63.6%
Decrease	2.6	—
Increase	8.9	36.4
TOTAL	100.0% ($N = 576$)	100.0% ($N = 22$)

to floor amendment in the case of the Corps' budget than in that of other appropriations bills. The permeability of the S.A.C.'s subcommittee does not seem to increase the Senate's acceptance of committee figures.

Three typical sorts of amendments are made on the Senate floor. The first two to be discussed are cutting amendments. In the early 1950's, Senator Douglas would frequently ask for an across-the-board percentage cut in the Corps' budget. This kind of amendment has been introduced occasionally in recent years as well. A second kind of amendment is one that attempts to strike a project. Senator Proxmire (Democrat–Wisconsin) often has tried to focus on a few projects that seem to him to be particularly unjustified in an attempt to get them stricken from the bill. This poses a built-in dilemma for senators who wish to reduce the public works budget. If they push amendments for across-the-board cuts they virtually ensure that there will be a majority against them, since a majority of senators usually have projects in their states. Former Senator Douglas would advocate these cuts on fiscal grounds, but for any particular senator the weight of political benefits is usually on the side of building the projects, his own included. On the other hand, if a senator tries to strike a particular project outside of his state, he violates the norm of reciprocity and invites retaliation. He is also forced to argue his case on the merits of the particular project, and consequently the debate tends to become very technical. Senators will generally go along with the Corps of Engineers in a technical debate.

Stephen Horn provides an illustration of this last sort of problem.

In March 1963, for example, a few months before William Proxmire became a member of Senate Appropriations, he successfully implored the Interior Appropriations Subcommittee to add $3.8 million to the Interior bill for fiscal 1964 for a wood chemistry and pulp and paper laboratory at Madison, Wisconsin. When the bill was before the Senate, Republican leader Dirksen sought to illustrate what he regarded as the spending proclivities of the Kennedy administration. The Interior bill exceeded the previous year's appropriations by over $43 million and Dirksen moved to recommit it with instructions not to exceed the total for fiscal 1963. The primarily partisan motion was defeated by a vote of 56 to 22. But among the twenty-two economy minded Senators there were five Democrats, including Senator Proxmire.

The next economy vote was on an amendment by Democratic Senator Frank J. Lausche of Ohio to strike $310,000 in funds for a National Fisheries Center and Aquarium. This was merely seed money to finance the preliminary plans of what was estimated to be a $10 million project. It was dear to Democratic Congressman Mike Kirwan of Ohio, a long-time member of the House Committee on Appropriations, who was chairman of its Interior

Subcommittee and second-ranking member of its Public Works Subcommittee. The Lausche amendment was rejected 58 to 22. Five Democrats also supported that motion, among them Senator Proxmire.

The Interior bill passed the same day and eventually a conference was held with the House to resolve differences between the House and Senate versions. The conferees had hardly sat down when Congressman Kirwan indicated that since Senator Proxmire wanted to save money on the Interior appropriations bill, a good way to start would be to eliminate the $3.8 million forest products laboratory at Madison, Wisconsin. Out went the project with the concurrence of the Senate conferees.[7]

The third type of amendment that is usually offered is that designed to add projects. This is generally the most successful of the three. Though frequently defeated, the attempt to add a project is looked upon as a reasonable request. Even if it is defeated, the floor manager might assure the senator that his project will receive consideration the next year. There is little risk in offering this kind of amendment even if it stands little chance, and consequently this is far and away the most frequently offered.

The Senate floor is not an appeals court for decisions made in the subcommittee in the same way that the House floor is a court of appeals. In the House, if the committee cuts deeply, there are many amendments to restore funds. In the Senate, if the committee adds funds, so does the floor. The correlation between Senate Appropriations Committee additions to the House figure and Senate floor additions to the Senate figure is .50. It will be remembered that the relation in the House is negative. This indicates that the Senate floor is subject to the same general forces as the Senate subcommittee, whereas the House floor seems to be subject to forces opposite those felt in the committee. This supports Fenno's contention that the Senate Appropriations Committee is more permeable and open to the rest of its parent body than is the House Appropriations Committee.

7

The Conference Committee

In general, the appropriations bills containing funds for the Corps of Engineers as passed by the House and by the Senate are different from each other. There are sometimes more than a hundred projects on which the two houses of Congress disagree. Each chamber appoints a delegation to go into a joint conference with the intention of coming up with a compromise bill acceptable to both bodies.

The membership of the Conference Committee is determined in the following way. Formally, the presiding officer of the Senate picks the Senate conferees. In practice, though, the floor manager, usually the chairman of the Subcommittee on Public Works, submits a list of suggested conferees. The Senate conferees must include at least one member of the Authorization Committee—usually one of the ex officio members of the Appropriations Subcommittee.

In the House, the Speaker has the formal authority to appoint conferees, although this authority is exercised in practice by the chairman of the Appropriations Committee. The conference delegations vote under a unit rule, and the conferees of both chambers must concur for the conference report to be signed.

The Senate and the House send different numbers of members to the Conference Committee. Generally the Senate sends more than the House. From 1947 to 1969, on the appropriations bill containing the Corps of Engineers' funds, the House has sent fewer conferees than the Senate 20 times and more than that only twice. The number of House conferees ranged from a low of four (in 1959) to a high of 14 (in 1956). From 1958 to 1964 the House sent four or five conferees. The Senate's number ranged from six (in 1947) to 16 (in 1955, 1956, 1958, and 1967).

The conferees from the House generally include the chairman and ranking minority member of the H.A.C. Public Works Subcommittee. However, this rule is not without exceptions. For example, in 1951 the House conferees were all Democrats. In 1958, when the Republicans were in the minority, only Representative Taber attended the conference even though he was not the ranking minority member of the subcommittee. The Senate delegation has always included at least one member of the Authorization Committee.

The number of conferees from each of the chambers might appear to be of little consequence, since the delegations each have only one vote. On the other hand, when a senator or representative is present in the room it makes it difficult to cut projects in his state or district. A ranking minority member of a House subcommittee complained, "Someone on the other side will say, 'Senator so-and-so wants this project or Senator so-and-so is interested in this item.' That Senator isn't even on the committee and hasn't attended the hearings, but he wants something and the rest look out for him."[1] When there are 15 or 16 senators on the Conference Committee, nearly everyone in the Senate is represented—everyone's interests are being looked out for. The House delegation, on the other hand, is a small part of the whole House, so that House members with favored projects are likely to receive much less consideration than is the case on the Senate side. The House delegation, after all, is made up in part of the Appropriations Committee and consequently has certain goals that are at variance with the program-oriented goals of many House members.

There is perhaps no segment of congressional decision-making about which there is such little academic consensus as the conference. Three major studies by Steiner,[2] Fenno, and Vogler[3] come to disparate conclusions about the relative influences of the two chambers, about the measures of such influence, and about the explanations for their measured outcomes. Steiner's study found that the House was generally dominant in conference. Fenno acknowledged that House conferees were better prepared, more organized, and more determined than their Senate counterparts, but he found that conference outcomes tended overwhelmingly to favor the Senate over the House. Vogler's results tend to correspond closely with Fenno's over a much wider sample, which includes the legislative as well as the appropriations committees.

Fenno explained Senate dominance in conference by two closely related factors: first, the Senate conferees' goals were more congruent with the goals of the whole Senate than were the goals of the House conferees with those of the whole House; second, many House members were prepared to accept the Senate position in preference to that of the House. Vogler attempts to explain variable House success rates in conference by committee prestige, and he finds that the less prestigious the House committee, the more successful it is in conference. However, he offers little in the way of an explanation for this finding, apparently feeling that he has left the question in a less puzzling state than he found it in.*

The three studies all proceeded as follows. For each conference, the author identified the House position and the Senate position. He then identified the conference outcome as being closer to one than to the other. In the case of appropriations legislation the procedure is deceptively simple, since dollars appear to give an unambiguous guide to the three positions. There are some difficulties, however. The Senate is generally the "upper" body, and always is the second body to act on an appropriations bill. Fenno wisely controlled for the fact that the Senate is usually defending a figure higher than the House's by demonstrating that the Senate prevails even more frequently when it defends a figure lower than the House's. This removed the alternative theory—that the higher figure wins—from contention.

Fenno's procedure does not deal with the just as obvious possibility that the second body usually wins. There appear to be sound reasons for his failure to test this alternative. Since the House always comes first in considering appropriations bills, it would appear to be impossible to consider empirically the possibility that if the House were second it would prevail in conference. The fact that this possibility cannot be empirically tested does not mean that it is not the correct explanation for Senate dominance.

The image of the process conveyed in Fenno's study is that each committee deliberately chooses its preferred position and goes to conference to do battle for it. There are frequent references to "staying until the snow flies," walking out of the conference, and so forth. But there is another possibility, namely, that the Senate and the House may have worked out an interchamber division of labor on appropriations bills. There are some items that House members care about and others that Senate members care about. Therefore this would

* One avenue of explanation that Vogler fails to explore is similar in spirit to Fenno's reasoning: the less prestigious House committees may be more permeable to influence from the House as a whole than the prestige committees, which are expected to control some natural excesses of the House. Thus conferees from low-prestige House committees enjoy more floor support than do conferees of the prestige committees.

imply that first the House would work over the budget and change the items it was interested in, and next the Senate committee would receive the bill, accept most of the House changes, and then focus on the items that the interested senators were concerned with. The bills each chamber sent to conference would differ, but only on items where the Senate members showed interest. If the two sets of items were separate, conflicts between the two bodies could be avoided simply and consistently with a reciprocity norm, by the House deferring to Senate changes just as the Senate deferred to the House changes. Under this theory the Senate would generally prevail; however, it would not indicate that the Senate was more powerful, only that it was second.

This image seems reasonable for bills that have a lot of line items and separable features. The chances for head-on conflict between chambers are reduced in inverse proportion to the number of small independent decisions to be made on a bill. The Public Works Appropriations Bill has hundreds and hundreds of separate lines. Each project, being geographically defined, is more or less independent of the others, and members of the committees have natural interest over largely separate sets of projects.

The general practice recently has been for the House to put in a number of new starts and unbudgeted raises in funding and to make a few reductions. The Senate generally accepts all of the House additions, and acts as an appeals court in the few instances where the House has cut funds for a project. The Senate committee adds its own new starts and additions to projects, and it restores some project funds the House has cut.

The conference results were examined from 1951 to 1967 on a project-by-project basis. Figure 7.1 shows the number of items in disagreement and the number of Senate "victories" (either the Senate figure prevails or the final figure is closer to the Senate recommendation).

This figure shows the same picture of Senate dominance in conference that is found in the other studies. For the 17 years there were 1,309 disagreements, and the Senate prevailed in 859 of the conference decisions (65.5 percent). This is almost exactly the percentage reported independently by Fenno and by Vogler on different sets of data.

Under the alternative theory proposed above the data must be broken down in a different way altogether. Let H_t be the total number of changes in the budget figure made by the House. H_t can be

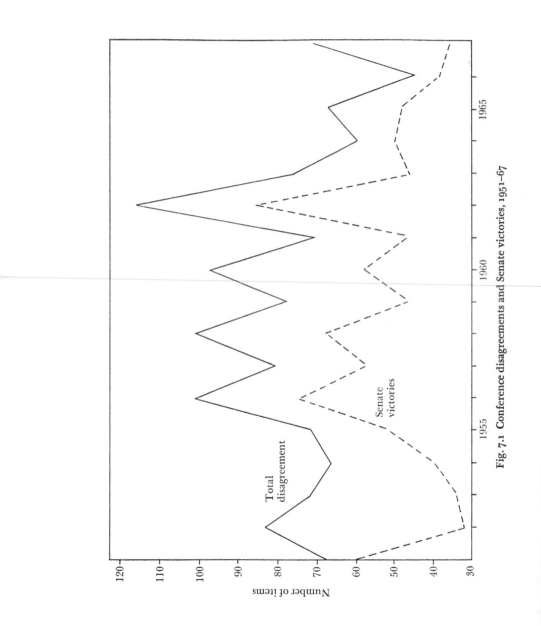

Fig. 7.1 Conference disagreements and Senate victories, 1951–67

decomposed into the number of upward changes (U^H_t) and the number of downward changes (D_t). The number of Senate changes in the budget request is composed of all the upward changes by the House (U^H_t), all the upward changes by the Senate (U^S_t), plus the proportion (a) of the downward changes made by the House which the Senate did *not* restore ($[1 - a]D_t$). The number of disagreements between the bills is the sum

$$U^S_t + aD_t .$$

The conference, according to the proposed decision rule, accepts nearly all of the Senate changes and (let us say) half of the real disagreements (aD_t). Thus the conference outcome is

$$bU^S_t + \tfrac{1}{2}aD_t ,$$

and b is very close to 1, indicating that the House accepts nearly all of the Senate's proposed upward changes just as the Senate accepted all of the House's. Under this model, the House is slightly more influential than the Senate in conference if b is less than 1.0; but the Fenno-Vogler method of measuring victories would give

$$bU^S_t + \tfrac{1}{2}aD_t \text{ Senate victories.}$$

In percentages the Senate success would be

$$\frac{bU^S_t + \tfrac{1}{2}aD_t}{U^S_t + aD_t} .$$

Here are some reasonable estimates for each of these parameters:

$U^S_t = 40\text{--}100$ approximate number of upward changes in the budget by the Senate,

$D_t = 10\text{--}40$ approximate number of downward changes by the House,

$a = \tfrac{2}{3}$ proportion of Senate revisions of House downward changes,

$b = .9$ House acceptance of Senate upward changes in conference.

These ranges of estimates were obtained by consideration of the stage-by-stage budget data. Under the model postulated here, the estimates for the Senate success ratio used by Fenno and Vogler range from .74 to .84, despite the fact that the way the model is set up the House would seem to be slightly more influential, since it does not accept all the upward changes the Senate recommends although the Senate accepts all the upward changes the House allows.

We can take the figures for 1967 as an example:

$$U^S{}_{1967} = 59, \qquad D_{1967} = 13.$$

Assuming that the parameters a and b are correct, the general estimated Senate success ratio is .85. If a and b are computed from the 1967 data, then the Senate success ratio would be .63, even though under these assumptions the House is in fact more influential in conference than the Senate.

In estimating a and b it was noticed that the a parameter (the proportion of House deletions that the Senate restores) seems very stable. The b parameter (the proportion of Senate upward changes that the House accepts in conference) appears to vary a good deal from year to year. The 1967 estimate of a is .46, and the 1967 estimate of b is .575. If we wanted to explain the observed results of Fenno and Vogler —that the Senate wins 65 percent of the time—by using this model, it would be most plausible to permit b to vary. It should be remembered that as b gets smaller the House in effect gets more powerful. Estimates of b in the range .5 to .7 would seem to give outcomes of Senate "wins" around 65 percent of the time depending on $U^S{}_t$ and D_t in each year. The "real" estimates of influence in this model are reflected in parameter b, in which the House is always the more persuasive body.

The data utilized here are at the project level, unlike the data employed by Fenno and Vogler. The same model may work for bills rather than for projects with little modification by allowing U^H, U^S, and D to refer to dollar amounts while leaving a and b with their original interpretation. The point here is that the results obtained by Fenno—which clash with his own observations and interview data, and which he successfully "explained"—may be erroneous and the result of a purely procedural phenomenon and logrolling between the House and Senate conferees.

The data used in this section can be used to demonstrate clear House dominance in the conference. The parameter of interest will be the probability that a new-start project gets accepted by the conference after having been initiated by the House or by the Senate. For 1967, if a project was initiated by the House, it had a .95 probability of getting in the budget. For the same year, if the Senate initiated a project, it had only a .70 chance of being included in the budget. On the other hand, if the House wished to cut a budget figure, it was successful with probability .85. Clearly the House is the more potent body; yet the Senate success ratio for the year is .495, reflecting only slight House dominance.

TABLE 7.1

Proportion of New Starts Initiated by the House and Senate
and Funded in the Conference Budget

Year	Probability for a House new start to be funded	Probability for a Senate new start to be funded	Year	Probability for a House new start to be funded	Probability for a Senate new start to be funded
1951	*a*	1.00	1961	1.00	.77
1952	*a*	.33	1962	.94	*b*
1953	1.00	.64	1963	1.00	.80
1954	*a*	.58	1964	.97	.84
1955	1.00	.91	1965	1.00	.82
1956	1.00	.91	1966	1.00	.83
1957	1.00	.65	1967	.98	.70
1958	.98	.79	1968	*a*	.80
1959	1.00	.63	1969	1.00	.73
1960	.96	.72			

a No new starts were initiated.
b None of the Senate starts were accepted in conference.

The conference outcomes generally follow the pattern of House dominance. The data presented in Table 7.1 illustrate this. If the House adds a new start to the Corps' budget it almost always is funded in the final budget. A Senate-initiated new start usually has a much smaller chance of being in the conference budget. The House's superiority in the conference and in the appropriations process generally stems from the fact that it is a bottleneck. House approval generally implies Senate approval, but the converse is not true. In Appendix A a simple model of the appropriations process is presented which produces conclusions similar to the ones reached in the four chapters of this section. The results obtained here may extend to other areas of appropriations politics, and the puzzling results indicating Senate dominance can be corrected through consideration of the simple model presented here.

The modes of decision-making used in conference have undergone a secular change over the period of study. This is not surprising, since the two previous chapters have revealed secular changes in both the House and the Senate appropriations processes on the Corps' appropriations requests. The literature on conferences indicates two primary methods of reaching agreements: first, accepting the figure of the House on one line item or project and accepting the Senate's figure on another item (we shall call this "logrolling" in conference); second, splitting the difference. There are, of course, thousands of possible splits on each item, only one of which is an "even" split.

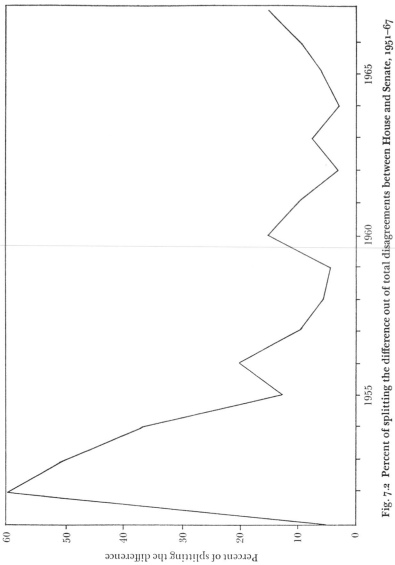

Fig. 7.2 Percent of splitting the difference out of total disagreements between House and Senate, 1951–67

Percent of splitting the difference

Dollars may or may not be a good measure of which body prevailed in a split. For example, the Senate may initiate a new construction project and put a million dollars in the budget for it. In the conference, the House may only accept $100,000, and so it may appear that the House has prevailed. However, the House has accepted the new start; as a result, the project will have contracts let on it and be put on a construction timetable, and with near certainty it will be built at a rapid pace after the initial year. Actually, in this case, the Senate has "won" by getting the new start in the conference bill at all.

Chapters 5 through 7 have documented a shift in the behavior of the House Appropriations Committee's Subcommittee for Public Works. Before 1955, the subcommittee would customarily reduce budget requests on more than half of all projects and would add very few new starts. Since then, the subcommittee annually has reduced budget requests for a handful of projects and has started from 20 to 70 projects (either planning or construction). We might expect that conference decision-making would tend toward logrolling and away from splitting the difference since both bodies are currently interested in adding new starts and not in reducing budget requests. Figure 7.2 graphs the percentage of splitting the difference in conference decisions from 1951 to 1967. Evidently, beginning in 1955, logrolling became the primary mode of decision-making in the conferences. Only once after 1955 did the number of splits go above 20 percent. This is taken as a rough indicator of the general shift since 1955 away from conflict between House and Senate on public works matters. This shift was possibly the result of a change in the nature of the House Appropriations Committee's Subcommittee for Public Works to a constituency service committee. This change was itself triggered by the floor revolt of 1955 (see Chapter 5).

Part Two has outlined in aggregate the appropriations process for the Army Corps of Engineers' construction budget. The chapters in this section contain an indication of how the gross monetary magnitudes are determined—what external factors and internal norms and expectations act to make the budget a little bigger (or smaller) than it might otherwise have been.

The appropriations process in this area seems to have been in two separate equilibria: the period before 1955 and the period that followed. The change in the relationship between the H.A.C. Public Works Subcommittee and the House was touched off by unmet member expectations and was backed up by widespread support in the House for enlarged public works expenditures. When the subcommittee changed its role conception from defender of the "economy norm" to constituency service paying lip service to economy, the rest of the appropriations system in public works changed as well. The Senate no longer acted as an appeals court and the conferences became more accommodating. However, the one constant that remains in both the pre-1955 and post-1955 systems is that of general House dominance. To a very great extent in both periods, the House's behavior has determined the limits of the Senate and conference outcomes. This is why a single event, the House floor revolt of 1955, could lead to such a major change in the behavior and expectations of participants in the appropriations process in public works.

PART THREE

The Distribution of the Corps of Engineers' Construction Projects

8

Committee Effects on Project Choice:
The House Public Works Committee

Any project over a certain size must receive legislative authorization in order to be eligible for construction appropriation. This means that the House Committee on Public Works,[1] which reports out the Omnibus Rivers and Harbors and Flood Control Bill, must have at some time approved the project. Project authorizations once made do not lapse. Consequently, there is a long list of projects that have received authorization but that are not yet under construction.

The decision on whether or not to start a particular project "this" year is made, or at least ratified, by the appropriations committees of both houses of Congress (see Chapters 5 and 6). Formally, the House Public Works Committee (H.P.W.C.) has no jurisdiction at this stage. All that the H.P.W.C. can do is to add projects to the list of those authorized; it cannot force the appropriations committees to fund them. One might expect, therefore, that membership on the H.P.W.C. would have little direct or immediate impact on the number or size of projects in a congressman's state.

Nevertheless, students of Congress and of the H.P.W.C. have observed that members seek to join the committee because they expect to be able to help their districts obtain more projects. James Murphy observed that of the 34 committee members, 25 thought that membership was valuable for meeting constituency needs. In addition, "of the 25 members who thought a public works seat was valuable for meeting constituency needs, 13 were specifically asked if meeting those needs benefited them electorally and all 13 responded affirmatively."[2] A senior committee member who was asked whether most members of the committee were on for constituency reasons responded, "Yes. I'd say at least 90 percent of the guys are on the committee for that reason."[3] This testimony indicates that membership on the H.P.W.C. might have some effect on projects chosen, since apparently members expect that they will be able to help their constituents while on the committee.

Though lacking formal jurisdiction over the funding of projects, the members of the H.P.W.C. would seem to be able to help their constituents in two different ways. First, as members of the H.P.W.C. they can work to get authorizations for many projects in their states and districts. Over a long period of time the states of H.P.W.C. members will have disproportionately large numbers of authorized projects eligible for funding; if the H.A.C. Public Works Subcommittee samples from this list according to some independent criteria (for example, two possible criteria are the benefit-cost ratio and the length of time the project has been authorized), then, after a time lag of several years, appropriations decisions will come to be biased toward states represented on the H.P.W.C. Second, members of the H.A.C. Public Works Subcommittee have projects in their own districts and states that require authorization, and so the subcommittee may favor members of the H.P.W.C. to gain reciprocity. It is possible that only one of these mechanisms is operative. If this is so then each can be considered as an explanatory model of favoritism for states represented on the H.P.W.C. Under the first model, membership on the H.P.W.C. will not have an immediate effect. After several years of membership, however, a congressman's state will begin to receive more projects. Under the second model, current membership will have an immediate effect on receiving projects. In this chapter both of these models will be explored empirically.

When a congressman joins the committee he normally works very hard to get projects in his district authorized. A senior committee member remarked, "When I first got here I worked hard and got most of the authorizations that I needed. Now it's just a problem of getting them funded and keeping the money coming."[4] This remark illustrates that both long-run and short-run effects of committee membership should be significant. Many congressmen get on the committee, get a few projects authorized, and leave it—whether to go to another committee or for some other reason (death, electoral defeat, election to another office, and so on). Of the 138 members of the H.P.W.C. from 1947 to 1970, 40 transferred to other committees and 65 left Congress. If these people added authorizations from their states before they left the committee, there might be a long-run membership effect observed, but not necessarily an immediate effect.

It goes almost without saying that those who leave the committee for another committee leave it relatively early in their congressional careers. Of 37 members who came to Congress and the H.P.W.C. after 1947 and who left the committee, 28 left with less than four years of committee seniority. Of the other nine, eight went to the prestige committees (Ways and Means, Rules, and Appropriations). No one who had more than eight years of seniority left the House Public Works Committee. This phenomenon might be expected to lead to one of two peculiar distributions of seniority on the committee: (1) the whole committee might be a "low-seniority committee," with few members with much seniority; (2) the committee might be top-heavy because of high turnover in the bottom ranks and very little turnover in the top ranks.

The Democratic and Republican sides of the committee fall cleanly into these two categories. On the Democratic side in 1970, nine of the 18 members had more than 12 years of seniority. Seven of these nine Democrats had seen more than 16 years of committee service. On the other hand, 14 of 15 Republicans had less than ten years of committee experience. The Democrats seem to have a solid core of committee careerists, unlike the Republicans.

Those who stay on the committee learn to work closely with the Corps of Engineers and with the appropriations subcommittee to get projects funded for their states. Committee members have a great deal of respect for the Corps of Engineers and for their colleagues on the House Appropriations Committee Public Works Subcommittee. They realize that Corps and H.A.C. subcommittee support is vital to getting a pet project funded. Committee members sometimes cultivate associations and friendships with Corps officers and H.A.C. subcommittee members. Former Mississippi Congressman Frank Smith remarked in his autobiography that one of the fruits of being on the H.P.W.C. was his new friendship with General Lewis Pick, then Chief of Engineers. A senior H.P.W.C. member said, "I work with the [H.A.C. Public Works] subcommittee chairman most of the time and with the guys on the subcommittee." The same member went on to say that while he was very successful in getting the Budget Bureau to fund his projects, "I also got some money put in by the Appropriations Committee." Frank Smith, who was a member of the committee for 12 years, described his role in lobbying his colleagues on the H.A.C. Public Works Subcommittee: "Beyond the authorizations ... I had to press for funds for anywhere from five to a dozen flood control projects each year."[5]

Committee members are aware that if a project is in the budget request it will seldom be cut out of the budget by either the H.A.C.

or the S.A.C. A Democratic member remarked, "Well, if a project's in the budget it'll get funded; for this sort of thing you may as well go fishing as testify." The kinds of things that can be affected by working with the appropriations subcommittee are new starts initiated by the House.

Most of the work in this and the following chapters will employ new starts rather than dollar amounts as the dependent variable. The argument for this choice is that every project is a new start at one time or another. About half of all new starts are initiated by Congress rather than by the Budget Bureau. This means that if new starts initiated by the House and Senate as well as by the Budget Bureau can be "explained," then the project initiation decisions will have been accounted for. The project initiation decision is particularly important since once a project is started, it is almost always continued on to completion. Once the initial start is made, a fairly rigid construction timetable tends to dictate most of the year-to-year allocations in dollars going to the project. Furthermore, only about 5 percent of the total cost of the project is spent in the first year of construction. Only about .5 to 1 percent is spent in the first year of planning. The total amount of current dollars spent on House construction new starts had ranged from $1.4 million to $37.2 million in the fiscal years 1959–70. The current dollar totals for House planning new starts for the same period have ranged from zero to $4.5 million. These amounts are small compared to total House changes in the construction bill. A materials shortage on one large project can change current dollars in the budget by five to ten million dollars. A few technical miscalculations, contract difficulties, or unusual weather can therefore produce variation in the budget that will swamp the budget variation resulting from House new starts.

The obligation on the Treasury created by House new starts is substantial. In a typical year the total federal contribution required to complete the House planning starts will usually run well over $400 million. The primary budgeting effect of a House new start is therefore felt not in the current year but in the future. The major budgetary impact of planning new starts is delayed much longer than is the impact of construction new starts.*

These considerations make it clear that new starts are the most important and sensitive part of the construction budget, since they index actual decisions at approximately the time they are made. The aver-

* The reader may refer to Chapters 1, 4, and 5 for additional background on these points.

age value to a state of a new start, measured by the amount of federal money to be expended for the project, was about $28 million for fiscal year 1967. There were 63 House-initiated new starts in that year. Other budgetary changes generally are of much less consequence.* For these reasons we will utilize new starts by the Budget Bureau, the House, and the Senate as the major dependent variable in the following discussion. Expenditure data will be referred to occasionally, but only time series of expenditures can be relied on because year-to-year variations owing to technical factors are so large.†

The major hypotheses of this chapter concern the effects of committee membership and of various intracommittee institutions (seniority, the subcommittee, the party) in explaining the distribution of House new starts. Some of these hypotheses are inherently cross-sectional rather than longitudinal. That is, one would expect H.P.W.C. members to do better than nonmembers do, but not necessarily better than H.P.W.C. members did last year.

On the other hand, some of the hypotheses could in principle be tested in cross section or in time series. For example, the effects of seniority might be considered in a time-series perspective. The analysis of the earlier chapters, which showed clear evidence of structural change in the process, makes the time series appear to be the more dangerous of the two possible approaches though, because the rules governing distribution might well change over the period. For this reason the major analysis is carried out on a cross section and is supplemented by the over-time data where that seems helpful.

Long- and Short-Term Effects of H.P.W.C. Membership

The first question to examine is whether or not H.P.W.C. members get "more" projects constructed than nonmembers. Two theoretical effects of H.P.W.C. membership on House construction starts were

* Changes in the rate at which a project is constructed merely shift expenditures backward or forward in time. If a project costs 100 million dollars to build, then the fact that one million dollars is spent next year rather than this year is considered to be a less "important" decision than the decision to break ground on the project in the first place, even though the initial year's expenditure may total only a hundred thousand dollars or less.

† If a state is regularly favored by the Budget Bureau or the Public Works Subcommittee and receives a disproportionate share of new starts over a period of time, Corps construction expenditures will tend to exhibit a secular increase. On the other hand, if a state receives a large construction appropriation in a given year, this may result from the fact that several projects in the state have construction schedules that simultaneously require large expenditures, or perhaps from the fact that rainstorms the previous year held up ongoing construction until the current year.

outlined above: a long-term effect and a short-term effect. There is some difficulty in making the long-term effect operationalistic separately from the short-term effect.

The long-term effect of committee membership, it will be recalled, is the tendency of states represented on the H.P.W.C. to accumulate more and more authorized projects. Now, the H.A.C. Public Works Subcommittee picks its new starts out of the set of authorized projects in some as yet unknown manner. Two possible rules it could be using are the following: (1) it could choose new starts in rough proportion to the number of projects a state has authorized; or (2) it could choose new starts on the basis of how long projects have been authorized. Unfortunately, it has not been possible to utilize these variables explicitly, so proxy variables have been employed.

Under the second hypothesis—that project age is what matters in choosing a new start—the membership of the H.P.W.C. in 1956 (ten years prior to the period of study) was coded. The expectation was that the states represented on the committee in the past would have an accumulation of old projects that would be considered eligible for initiation. Under the alternative hypothesis that the number of new starts is approximately proportional to the number of authorized projects, the total number of years each state was represented on the H.P.W.C. from the 84th to the 88th Congress was employed as a proxy variable.

An attempt was made to investigate the question of whether there were separate long-term and short-term effects of H.P.W.C. membership on the distribution of House-initiated new starts. A regression equation was estimated employing the number of House-initiated new starts for fiscal year 1967 as a dependent variable. The independent variables were the number of congressmen each state had on the H.P.W.C. in 1956 and, separately, in 1966. Table 8.1 presents the results. The state with the largest representation on the H.P.W.C. in 1956 was Texas, with three members. California had the largest delegation on the H.P.W.C. in 1966 with four members. Both current and past representation of a state on the H.P.W.C. appear to have a measurable effect on the number of House-initiated new starts a state receives.* This analysis would seem to suggest that there are distinct long- and short-term effects of H.P.W.C. membership.

If the estimated equation is correctly specified, then having a member on the current H.P.W.C. is worth about 80 percent of a House

---

* Both variables had significant effects at the .05 level. Residual analysis did not reveal evidence of interaction effects.

TABLE 8.1

Estimated Number of House New Starts for Fiscal Year 1967 for States
Represented on the H.P.W.C. in 1956 and 1966

Number of H.P.W.C. members in 1956	Number of H.P.W.C. members in 1966				
	0	1	2	3	4
0	.306	1.110	1.914	2.718	3.522
1	.928	1.732	2.536	3.340	4.144
2	1.640	2.354	3.158	3.962	4.766
3	2.262	2.976	3.780	4.584	5.388

NOTE: $\bar{R}^2$ for the equation was .540; $N = 50$.

new start to a state per year. This translates into approximately $22.4 million in a year. If a state had a member on the committee in 1956, that was worth about $17.4 million in the year 1966.

This regression equation did not have any sort of control for "need" or "demand."* In order to properly estimate the importance of having a member on the H.P.W.C., one must develop a model of what the state would have received in the way of House new starts if it had had no members on the committee. Various models were experimented with, and Appendix B explores these considerations in some detail. The variable that is utilized here and in the following chapters as an indication of need is the current amount of budgeted construction in the state.

This measure has the desirable property of reflecting the relatively stable demand for water projects by various states. For example, Oregon "needed" in some sense a very large federal outlay for water projects in 1950, 1960, and 1970. In large part this was the result of the potential for many hydroelectric projects that could be developed on Oregon waters. Consequently, the Corps' construction budget for Oregon was large compared with that of other states in all of these

* The idea of a state having a certain need for federal expenditures under a given program has, inevitably, a good deal of ambiguity. What is meant here is the notion that in the absence of any political advantage in Congress (or elsewhere in the government) each state would be expected to receive some appropriations under the program. In the present case, states with a lot of potential water projects (rivers with certain characteristics, harbors needing dredging, and so on) are expected to receive large expenditures from the federal government for water projects. The reasons for this expectation are multiple and complicated. The Corps of Engineers desires an expanding bureaucratic mission and will desire to build all projects that meet its technical standards. States with free-running rivers tend to have floods that are sometimes disastrous; as several authors have argued, Congress responds with particular enthusiasm to major flood disasters. See Wallace's "The Politics of River Basin Appropriations."

TABLE 8.2

Estimated Number of House New Starts for Fiscal Year 1967 for States
Represented on the H.P.W.C. in 1956 and 1966, Controlling for Need

Number of H.P.W.C. members in 1956	Number of H.P.W.C. members in 1966				
	0	1	2	3	4
0	.032	.819	1.606	2.393	3.180
1	.536	1.323	2.110	2.897	3.684
2	1.040	1.827	2.614	3.401	4.188
3	1.544	2.431	3.118	3.905	4.692

NOTE: Figures were obtained from the following equation ($N = 50$):

$$\text{House new starts for fiscal year 1967} = \underset{(.163)}{.032} + \underset{(4.20)}{.787} \text{ number of members on the H.P.W.C. in 1966}$$
$$+ \underset{(2.25)}{.504} \text{ number of members on the H.P.W.C. in 1956}$$
$$+ \underset{(3.26)}{.017} \text{ size of current construction budget for fiscal year 1967}$$
$$\bar{R}^2 = .618$$

years, regardless of Oregon's representation on the relevant committees. Representation on the H.P.W.C. may (and, under the hypotheses here, should) cause some year-to-year variation, but Oregon always receives a large share of federal expenditures relative to the shares of the other states.

One difficulty with this measure is that representation on the committees of Congress is extremely stable. Consequently, some political effects are going to be mixed in with "need" effects; therefore, variation properly resulting from political factors will be attributed to "need." This argument (presented more rigorously in Appendix B) indicates that the estimates obtained by the methods of this chapter will be conservative measures of the political effects.[6]

The regression equation used in Table 8.1 was reestimated with the control for "need" incorporated. The resulting estimates, smaller than those of the original equation, are presented in Table 8.2. According to these estimates, the dollar impact of a member currently on the H.P.W.C. is $22.1 million. The value of having had a member on it in 1956 is about $14 million. The argument presented in Appendix B for using budget size as a control would lead us to expect that the estimate of the value of past membership would be affected more than that of current membership. Consequently, the estimate of the value of a member in 1956 ought to be regarded as a lower bound on the true value.

The second conceptualization of past membership was tried with slightly less success. In order to examine the effects of past representation on House new starts, another equation was estimated utilizing the same dependent variable but substituting the total number of man-years each state was represented on the H.P.W.C. for the variable that counted the number of members on the H.P.W.C. in 1956. This equation is presented here (values greater than 2.01 are significant at the .05 level; $N = 50$):*

House new starts for fiscal year 1967	=	.365 (1.91)	+	.632 (2.32)	number of members on the H.P.W.C. in the 89th Congress
			+	.099 (2.31)	number of years served on the H.P.W.C. from the 85th to the 88th Congress

$$\bar{R}^2 = .529$$

Both variables in this regression have significant impact on House new starts. Having an additional member on the current H.P.W.C. is worth about 63 percent of a House new start. An additional year served on the H.P.W.C. in the previous four Congresses is worth about 10 percent of a new start to a state independently of the short-term (or current membership) effect. There might be some spurious relationship in the regression owing to the fact that congressmen from states that receive large public works allocations tend to join the H.P.W.C. In other words, the causation might run from a large public works budget to committee membership, and separately to House new starts. Consequently, another regression was run that controlled for current budget requests for the state. The resulting equation follows ($N = 50$):

House new starts for fiscal year 1967	=	.083 (.420)	+	.666 (2.67)	number of members on the H.P.W.C. in the 89th Congress
			+	.077 (1.92)	number of years served on the H.P.W.C. from the 85th to the 88th Congress
			+	.017 (3.23)	size of the 1966 construction budget request in the state, in millions of dollars

$$\bar{R}^2 = .608$$

* It is not feasible to present these data in tabular form, since the variable (number of years served on the H.P.W.C. from the 84th to the 88th Congress) takes values from 0 to 25. Evidently most of the cells of a table constructed from this equation would be empty.

We can see that budget size has a significant effect, since an extra million dollars in the budget request results in 1.7 percent of a new start. This means that if a state already has a $60 million budget, it will tend to have a House new start added. The term for past membership on the committee becomes (just barely) insignificant at the .05 level when the budget variable is added.

This analysis suggests that current committee membership is an important variable in considering House new starts and that it is distinct from past membership only because of *cooperation* or *logrolling* between the authorizing and appropriating committees. The fact that current members of the H.P.W.C. obtain more new starts than nonmembers when controlling for past membership and "need" implies that current membership is useful in obtaining favorable treatment from the H.A.C. Public Works Subcommittee. Current members of the H.P.W.C. have the authority to authorize projects and to pass committee resolutions instructing the Corps to restudy projects previously found to be unfeasible. Authorizations and restudy resolutions are scarce and desirable commodities to states that have potential water projects in the pipeline. Therefore, if the members of the H.A.C. Public Works Subcommittee come from such states, they have a real incentive to give favorable consideration to projects in states currently represented on the H.P.W.C.

The Significance of Political Party

The committee is formally divided up into a number of different groupings: into Democrats and Republicans; into subcommittee chairmen, ranking minority members, and other members; and into members of one subcommittee rather than another. These formal distinctions may have some measurable effect on the ability of a congressman to get new starts for his district. To begin with, does political party make any difference within the committee in explaining the distribution of House new starts? In 1966 there were 11 Republicans and 23 Democrats on the H.P.W.C. If the committee were run on a partisan basis, one might expect Republicans to be less successful in getting projects for their states than Democrats.

Murphy found that the committee is partisan on much of the legislation it considers, but not on "Rivers and Harbors" items.[7] He reports that junior members of both parties are able to get projects authorized and that at this stage partisan differences do not appear to be particularly important. However, his research does not include a study of cooperation between members of the authorizing and appropriations committees, or between the House and the Senate, for that matter. Thus, on the basis of Murphy's study there is no particular reason to expect to find significant party effects through either long-term or short-term effects of committee membership. The regression results were as follows ($N = 50$):

House new starts $= .181 + 1.21$ number of Republican
for fiscal year 1967 $(.90)$ (3.95) members on the H.P.W.C.

$+ .93$ number of Democratic
(3.69) members on the H.P.W.C.

$+ .019$ size of budget request for
(3.20) fiscal year 1967

$\bar{R}^2 = .579$

This equation would seem to indicate that committee Republicans "do better" than committee Democrats—though not much better. This result must be considered paradoxical in light of the earlier discussion of the membership of the H.P.W.C. The Democratic side of the committee is characterized by a group of between seven and nine "careerists" who have a great deal of seniority and who have the reputation of being in the "rivers and harbors club." Frank Smith claimed in his autobiography that the H.P.W.C. is run by a collegial group of high-ranking Democrats. It would seem, too, that the Democratic members should receive better treatment than the Republicans from the Democratic-controlled H.A.C. Public Works Subcommittee.

The fact that the 50 states represent the entire statistical universe, rather than a mere sample from a larger population, makes it necessary for the differences between the coefficients in the equation to be taken at face value. For this reason, the results cannot be explained away by pointing out that the coefficients are not significantly different from each other. The fact is that the coefficients are different—and in a way we would not expect. Further analysis must be carried out to determine whether 1966 was merely an exceptional year or whether this finding is replicated in other analyses.

The Significance of Seniority

Committees in Congress are internally organized according to party, seniority, and subcommittees. Party effects considered by themselves are not pronounced. Both Republicans and Democrats profit from committee membership, and in about the same amounts. The next important variable to consider is seniority.

Seniority operates in varying ways within different committees, within the two parties in the same committees, and even within the same committee at different times. The seniority system in Congress is a method of choosing committee chairmen from among majority party members. Sometimes seniority means little more than that. On some committees the chairman rules absolutely, and the fact that one member has more seniority than another signifies nothing more than that he is closer to acceding to the chairmanship. On some committees, however, seniority may be a useful index of power and influence; this is especially true where senior members run the committee jointly. On still other committees, seniority is simply an index to subcommittee chairmanships, and that is where power is influence. We can easily give examples of committees that have operated in each of these ways. First, we have Public Works before 1950: chairman Will Whittington (Democrat–Mississippi) ran the committee; subcommittees seldom met and never made decisions because members would never oppose the chairman.[8] Second, we can take Public Works under Charles Buckley (Democrat–New York) and George Fallon (Democrat–Maryland). The senior members were the subcommittee chairmen and ran the committee collegially.[9] Frank Smith describes this period succinctly: "Under [Buckley's] chairmanship, committee policy was set by a team of ranking Democrats working together, rather than by dictation from the chairman."[10] Third, we find Appropriations under George Mahon (Democrat–Texas), which works like a set of independent committees with little intervention from the chairman.[11] There are, of course, many other ways that committee seniority can relate to the attainment of influence.

As a proxy for the effect of seniority on attaining new starts, the committee was split into those members with high seniority and those with low seniority within each party. An equation was run for 1966, and it was expected that there would be important seniority effects ($N = 50$):

$$
\begin{aligned}
\text{House new starts} &= .208 + .91 \quad \text{number of members} \\
\text{for fiscal year 1967} &\quad (1.05) \quad (3.99) \quad \text{on the H.P.W.C.} \\[1ex]
&\quad + .025 \quad \text{number of high-seniority} \\
&\quad\;\;\; (.05) \quad \text{Democrats} \\[1ex]
&\quad + .982 \quad \text{number of high-seniority} \\
&\quad\;\;\; (1.62) \quad \text{Republicans} \\[1ex]
&\quad + .017 \quad \text{budgeted construction for} \\
&\quad\;\;\; (3.15) \quad \text{fiscal year 1967} \\[1ex]
\bar{R}^2 &= .591
\end{aligned}
$$

High-seniority Democrats are the top nine in rank (out of 23). High-seniority Republicans are the top four (out of 11).* Using this formulation, high-seniority Democrats are found to do very little better than low-seniority committee members (.025 new starts). On the other hand, high-seniority Republicans did much better than low-seniority members (the total effect for high-seniority Republicans was 1.892 new starts a year).

Separating Democrats and Republicans at the low-seniority level gives results very similar to those above ($N = 50$):

House new starts $=$ .207 $+$ .904 number of Republicans
for fiscal year 1967 (1.03) (2.26) on the H.P.W.C.

$+$ .914 number of Democrats
(3.11) on the H.P.W.C.

$+$ .025 number of high-seniority
(.05) Democrats on the H.P.W.C.

$+$ .987 number of high-seniority
(1.48) Republicans on the
H.P.W.C.

$+$ .017 budgeted construction
(3.11) for fiscal year 1967

$\bar{R}^2 = $ .582

This equation demonstrates that at the low-seniority level there is no difference at all between Republicans and Democrats. The incentive for first joining the committee seems to be the same for Democrats and Republicans—it gains the member's state just under one House new start a year.

The procedure here underestimates the effects of high-seniority members the longer their tenure and the more successful they have been at attaining new starts while on the committee. As was indicated earlier, the H.P.W.C. Democrats are divided distinctly into a high-seniority group and a low-seniority group. The Republicans have very few high-seniority members. Only W. Cramer (Republican–Florida) would place among the top group of Democrats. If the high-seniority Democrats have been successful in adding new starts during

* These cutoff points were chosen because there appeared to be a significant gap in seniority at them. In addition, some of the people interviewed, as well as the author, could recognize those people in the high-seniority group as being part of the "club." Their names came up repeatedly in this connection.

their tenure on the committee, the current construction budget will partially reflect this success; consequently, a portion of their influence may be attributed in the calculations to budget size.

The Significance of the Subcommittee

The third formal element that is operating within the committee is the subcommittee structure. There were six subcommittees of the H.P.W.C. in 1966, and most members were on three of them. Three subcommittees had jurisdiction over water projects: Rivers and Harbors, Flood Control, and Watershed Development. The Rivers and Harbors and Flood Control subcommittees meet jointly to hold hearings on the Omnibus Rivers and Harbors and Flood Control Bill. The Watershed Development Subcommittee had jurisdiction over some small projects undertaken by the Department of Agriculture. It is omitted from the following analysis since only Corps of Engineers projects are being considered.

The first relationship examined was the regression of new starts on the H.P.W.C., the Rivers and Harbors Subcommittee, and the Flood Control Subcommittee, with a control for the size of the current construction budget. The equation follows ($N = 50$):

$$
\begin{aligned}
\text{House new starts} \ = \ & .164 \ + \ .282 \quad \text{number of members on} \\
\text{for fiscal year 1967} \ & (.91) \quad (.839) \quad \text{the H.P.W.C.} \\[6pt]
& \qquad\quad + \ .302 \quad \text{number of members on} \\
& \qquad\quad\ \ (.887) \quad \text{the Flood Control} \\
& \qquad\qquad\qquad\quad\ \text{Subcommittee} \\[6pt]
& \qquad\quad + \ 1.08 \quad \text{number of members on the} \\
& \qquad\quad\ \ (3.24) \quad \text{Rivers and Harbors} \\
& \qquad\qquad\qquad\quad\ \text{Subcommittee} \\[6pt]
& \qquad\quad + \ .020 \quad \text{budgeted construction} \\
& \qquad\quad\ \ (3.96) \quad \text{for fiscal year 1967} \\[6pt]
\bar{R}^2 \ = \ & .649
\end{aligned}
$$

This equation indicates that members of the Rivers and Harbors Subcommittee do much better than both members of the Flood Control Subcommittee and members of the H.P.W.C. who belong to neither of the two subcommittees.

The reason for this difference is difficult to pin down, but it may stem from some basic policy disagreements between Congress and the

Budget Bureau. The Budget Bureau has long believed that the Corps of Engineers, with the backing of Congress, seriously overestimates the economic benefits of navigation projects.* Owing to this overestimation of benefits, many navigation projects which appear to be economically feasible on the basis of their benefit-cost ratios are actually not. For this reason, when the Budget Bureau recommends new starts it evaluates proposed navigation projects according to its own tough criteria. As a result, very few navigation projects appear as budgeted new starts (that is, approved for initial construction or planning by the Budget Bureau), since few of the authorized navigation projects meet the standard of economic feasibility when benefits are evaluated by the Budget Bureau. Since the members of the committees with jurisdiction over the Corps of Engineers are aware of the Budget Bureau's bias against navigation projects, they realize that the only way most navigation projects will ever get started is by House or Senate initiative. On the basis of this argument it may be expected that congressional new starts will show a bias toward navigation projects in order to compensate for the opposite bias on the part of the Budget Bureau.

In order to gather some evidence on this phenomenon, the Omnibus Rivers and Harbors and Flood Control Bill of 1968 was examined. Seventy-two projects were authorized in that bill; of those, 16 derived their benefits principally from navigation features. The procedure followed was to examine which of these newly authorized projects received funding from the Budget Bureau and which received it from Congress. Table 8.3 summarizes the results of the inquiry. The small number of projects considered here prevents the drawing of strong conclusions, but the table does suggest a congressional bias toward initiating projects whose principal features are navigational. Since jurisdiction over such projects at the authorization stage is held by

* The Corps of Engineers estimates navigation benefits in the following way. If there is a proposed canal between two cities whose principal current mode of shipping is by rail, then the Corps uses the actual ton-mile rates charged to shippers as their estimate of the current ton-mile cost of shipping. In order to estimate costs if the project is built, the Corps utilizes an estimate of the variable costs of shipping to barge owners (and no toll is charged into these costs). If the railroad is the sole shipper of certain commodities (as it is likely to be for things like coal, iron ore, and so on), then it may be charging monopoly rates to shippers so that the differential between current ton-mile costs and project ton-mile costs—if the project is built—will be artificially large. Part of what the Corps considers to be benefits under this method is nothing other than wealth transfer from the railroads to the shippers.

TABLE 8.3

Budgeted and Congressional New Starts by Project-type in 1969

Number	Navigation projects	Other projects
Authorized in the 1968 Omnibus Bill	16	56
Initiated by the Budget Bureau	2	6
Initiated by Congress	6	8

SOURCE: House and Senate reports accompanying the Omnibus Rivers and Harbors and Flood Control Bill of 1968.

the Rivers and Harbors Subcommittee, one might expect its members (who join the subcommittee in order to aid their constituents) to be among the major beneficiaries of this policy.

The equation estimated above contained a variable accounting for those who were members of the H.P.W.C. but were not on either the Flood Control or the Rivers and Harbors subcommittees. The coefficient of this variable was an insignificant .282, so the equation was reestimated without the variable. Substantially the same results were obtained. Membership on the Flood Control Subcommittee was worth .52 new starts per year ($t = 5.62$). For this equation, $\bar{R}^2 = .651$.

One assumption made in these equations is that the effects of subcommittee membership are *additive*: if a member is on both the Flood Control and the Rivers and Harbors subcommittees his state will receive $.52 + 1.28 = 1.80$ new starts per year. If the state merely had a member on one of the subcommittees it would receive the number of House new starts indicated by one of the estimated coefficients. However, because there is substantial overlap between the two subcommittees, it is quite possible that members of both will do better than the sum of the two coefficients. When this possibility was explored, it was found that membership on both subcommittees estimated without the additive restriction was worth 1.91 new starts, which is *not* a significant improvement over the additive model.

The next thing to examine is the effect of party membership within the subcommittee. The remarks already made about navigation projects would seem to indicate that water policy in the navigation area is primarily made in Congress. More specifically, it is made by the Rivers and Harbors Subcommittee working with the H.A.C. Public Works Subcommittee. Flood-control policy is made chiefly in the Budget Bureau, with some modification (incremental if one likes) in Congress. If Democratic dominance in 1966 made a difference, we would expect to find it in the area of navigation projects rather than in that of flood control. The following equation bears out our expectations ($N = 50$):

House new starts for fiscal year 1967	$=$	.227 (1.30)	$+$	.02 (4.08)	Budgeted construction for fiscal year 1967
			$+$	.115 (.405)	number of Democrats on the Flood Control Subcommittee
			$+$	1.39 (3.03)	number of Republicans on the Flood Control Subcommittee
			$+$	1.34 (4.16)	number of Democrats on the Rivers and Harbors Subcommittee
			$+$	.678 (1.42)	number of Republicans on the Rivers and Harbors Subcommittee

$$\bar{R}^2 = .672$$

This equation confirms the existence of party effects in the direction that we expected. Democrats on the Rivers and Harbors Subcommittee do twice as well in getting new starts as Republicans on the subcommittee. However, an additional unanticipated result shows that Republicans do far better than Democrats on the Flood Control Subcommittee. No explanation for this fact is offered here.

The H.P.W.C. and Budgeted New Starts

Each year the Budget Bureau recommends starts on a number of projects. Theoretically, it chooses the "best" projects available to receive funding.* The Budget Bureau defines "best" in a fairly complicated way, and its evaluation agrees only coincidentally with the Corps' evaluation of a project. The Bureau will frequently recompute the benefit-cost ratio according to its own methods and then evaluate the ratio in the light of its priority ranking of projects by type. It generally prefers urban flood-control projects and power

---

* A careerist in the Budget Bureau was asked, "What is a 'good' project as far as the Budget Bureau is concerned?" He replied: "First it has to have a good benefit-cost ratio. But that is not all. We had a priority system. We gave preference to urban flood protection. If you only looked at the benefit-cost ratio you would come up with all recreational boat harbors—they're all around five or six. We try to keep them out if we can."

projects (if it is "good power" according to a high-ranking official) to rural flood-control projects and navigation and recreation projects. Thus a project with a benefit-cost ratio not much greater than one in a preferred category will be chosen over a project with a high benefit-cost ratio in a nonpreferred category.

Every year the Budget Bureau receives a proposed budget from the Corps of Engineers. It attempts to prune the requests drastically, both removing requested new starts and cutting back on funded amounts. Projects will be added only if they appear to be better ways of accomplishing some agreed-upon objectives. Generally, the Budget Bureau does not see itself as either the initiator of water projects or the designer of a water program; it simply reacts to the very strong and coordinated stream of inputs put forward by the agency and by individual congressmen. The power of the Budget Bureau is the power to withhold, and congressmen realize that if the Bureau can be persuaded to put in a new start everyone else in the process will go along.

Since congressmen and other groups interested in water projects view the Budget Bureau as a major bottleneck, it is the focus of a great deal of lobbying—from congressmen, from the White House, and from local groups desiring projects. Some of this lobbying is highly institutionalized. Each year many states send organized delegations led by congressmen and senators to the Budget Bureau to see the deputy director in charge of the Corps' budget. States give informal presentations, the requests of delegation members usually having been worked out or coordinated in advance. Among the states with cohesive delegations that make strong presentations are Florida, Texas, California, Missouri-Arkansas-Oklahoma (together), Ohio, Kentucky, the Columbia River states, the Tennessee-Tombigbee River states (Alabama and Tennessee), and the member states of the Mississippi Valley Association. This list was given by a former high-ranking Budget Bureau official off the top of his head. It was checked with other people, and there was general agreement that these states and state groups do in fact stand out.

Another type of formal or institutionalized political influence is exerted at the budget-making stage by the White House. The former Budget Bureau official said that "each year someone else and myself would go over there [the White House] with a list of projects and who was affected. . . . They would look it over and make changes. Occasionally they would formally intervene to get a project for someone." When asked whom he would see in the White House, he replied. "Harlow usually [under Nixon]. He would usually ask for projects for Republicans, of course, but there would be a few for Democrats. . . . Under Johnson we'd see Wilson and Manatos . . . and they would usually ask for projects for strategically placed Republicans: John Rhodes, Allott, etc. . . . Occasionally they would cut out a project." The practice of White House clearance apparently goes on at the staff level in the process of budget formulation. When the budget is having its final review the President may personally take some interest in the budgeted new starts. Johnson apparently reviewed the proposed budgeted new starts each year and rejected with some profanity those that aided congressmen who had not "kept the faith."

These formal processes that allow political considerations to affect the choice of budgeted new starts do not exhaust the political influences on the budget. The prestige and the influence of the Budget Bureau rest heavily on its ability to have Congress accept its proposals. If the final agency budgets as signed by the President bear little resemblance to the Budget Bureau's proposals, then we might consider the Bureau to have little influence in the budget process. Political analysts have found, though, that the Budget Bureau's initial request for an agency bears a very strong relationship to what the agency finally gets.

There are two chief reasons why Budget Bureau requests are very influential with Congress. First, the Bureau is the President's agency, and its requests are regarded to some extent as his requests. Second, the Bureau works hard to propose budgets that will pass Congress more or less intact. It tries to anticipate congressional reaction and if possible to incorporate changes it thinks Congress will make in the budget request. This practice helps it retain its power and prestige by protecting the proposed agency budgets from congressional changes.

The practice of anticipating congressional changes and demands is likely to be most fully developed for those agencies that Congress regards as constituency-serving. The Corps of Engineers has long considered itself, as Congress has considered it, to be an agency of Congress.[12] Appendix A, in fact, indicates that the congressional bodies taken together have a larger total influence on the Corps' final budget than the Budget Bureau has. The Budget Bureau has developed an extremely open method of treating the Corps' budget—a method that allows congressional requests and White House requests to be routinely incorporated.

The political officials in the Budget Bureau are very aware of who the powerful members of Congress are in the area of water project appropriations.[18] Each Budget Bureau official interviewed seemed to have a list of names of members who have to be satisfied if the budget is to be acceptable to the Congress. Among those most often mentioned were the late Michael Kirwan, John Rhodes (Republican–Arizona), Jennings Randolph (Democrat–West Virginia), the late Allen Ellender (Democrat–Louisiana), James Wright (Democrat–Texas), and former Senator John Sherman Cooper (Republican–Kentucky). Many other names came up as well. Budget Bureau officials acknowledged that projects that affected these people tended to be incorporated at the budgeting stage, but they usually went on to add that the projects had to be "good" ones nonetheless. As one former official said, "Everyone wanted to help Kirwan out on the Ditch . . . but not too much. . . . People wrote letters, held meetings and so on. . . . There was a lot of movement but somehow it never got built." In response to another question he stated, "Well, we would look for good Ohio and Louisiana projects and stick those in but it had to be a good project . . . , that was the main thing."

The impression gained from these interviews is that the Budget Bureau is not willing to stray too far from its own standards in anticipating congressional changes. The officials seem to recognize that they must maintain a balance to retain power. By doing so they can make the budget achieve desirable ends (as they define them) and not have to add many inefficient and unjustifiable projects (which they see as undesirable). Since the Budget Bureau refuses to go "too far" in the direction of adding new starts for the purpose of maintaining the integrity of the budget, the Corps of Engineers' budget does appear to undergo significant changes in Congress. In Chapters 4 through 7 we examined part of this phenomenon. This chapter and the following ones will attempt to examine the degree to which the Corps anticipates congressional reactions.

The size and the relative formality of the House make it likely that the allocation of influence in a particular issue area will conform fairly well to the formal distribution of authority. In other words, we may expect the same formal institutions that exhibited pronounced effects on House new starts to exhibit noticeable effects on budgeted new starts. Since we have already outlined the reasons for the effects examined here, the results can be presented briefly.

Committee Membership and Budgeted New Starts

The members of what Budget Bureau officials call the "public works club" dominate the H.P.W.C. Budget Bureau personnel feel that these representatives are influential in the appropriations process even though they have no formal part in it. Consequently, we should expect to find in the budget some reflection—however veiled —of this potential to shape the outcome of the budgeting process. A regression equation was run to determine the effect of current H.P.W.C. membership on budgeted new starts ($N = 50$):

Budgeted new   =   .397   +   .50   number of members on
starts for fiscal   (1.90)   (3.09)   the H.P.W.C.
year 1967

          +   .014   budgeted construction for
           (2.40)   fiscal year 1967

     $\bar{R}^2 = $ .250

The $\bar{R}^2$ is much lower than that found for the equation determining House new starts, but the coefficient for committee membership is highly significant and is of the expected (positive) sign. The coefficient for committee membership when House new starts was the dependent variable was 1.05. Apparently, therefore, the short-run value of H.P.W.C. membership to a state amounts to one-half of one budgeted new start and to one House new start per single session of Congress. The average total federal expenditure to complete a project involved in a budgeted new start in fiscal year 1967 was $12.7 million.

The next equation run was an attempt to separate the long-term and short-term effects of membership on the H.P.W.C. The motivation for this approach was given earlier. The equation follows ($N = 50$):

Budgeted new   =   .307   +   .307   number of members on
starts for fiscal   (1.42)   (1.50)   the H.P.W.C. in 1966
year 1967

          +   .361   number of members on
           (1.47)   the H.P.W.C. in 1956

          +   .012   budgeted construction for
           (2.16)   fiscal year 1967

     $\bar{R}^2 = $ .268

The long- and short-term effects appear to be roughly of the same magnitude. When House new starts was the dependent variable, short-term effects were more pronounced than long-term ones. This indicates that part of the Budget Bureau's response to political factors may actually be an artifact resulting from the biasing of the pile of authorized projects toward the states represented on the committee over a long period of time. This is consistent with the general impression gained from interviews that anticipated reaction by the Budget Bureau certainly exists but is not substantial. According to this equation, if a state had just placed a representative on the H.P.W.C. it could expect about one-third of a budgeted new start. This would involve a federal commitment of about $4 million, a very small expenditure.

Political Party and Budgeted New Starts

Since the Democrats controlled the executive branch in 1966, we might expect budgeted new starts to go in disproportionate numbers to Democratic H.P.W.C. members. We should expect the Budget Bureau to add new starts for Democrats based on the belief that otherwise the Democrats would add them in committee, thus effecting large changes in the budget. Additionally, H.P.W.C. Democrats are by and large avid partisans, and we might expect a Democratic administration to reward these tendencies if possible.

In reality, the Johnson Administration was active in passing legislation that required the occasional assent of Republicans. Consequently, we might also expect the White House and Budget Bureau to leave the Democratic members to take care of themselves, since they controlled the committee, and to focus their attention on Republicans. The interview results appear to convey this impression. According to one Budget Bureau official, Johnson's aides Mike Manatos and Henry Hall Wilson looked out for the interests of Representative Rhodes (Republican–Arizona), who was a member of the H.A.C. Public Works Subcommittee, Senator Allott (Republican–Colorado), and other prominent Republicans.*

There appears to be no compelling reason to believe in the prominence of the first process outlined above over the second—or vice versa. The Budget Bureau might be thought to favor the first process, since it would seem to preserve the integrity of the budget. On

* Rhodes and Allott are both prominent in the public works club, if such club can be said to exist. Both men come from states in which agencies of the Department of Interior are more important than is the Corps of Engineers. Rhodes is the ranking Republican on the H.A.C. Public Works Subcommittee and Allott is a member of the Senate Interior Committee and the S.A.C. Public Works Subcommittee. Budget Bureau officials thought that both of these Republicans had to be reckoned with if the budget proposals were not to become objects of partisan conflict.

the other hand, since the results of the analysis of House new starts indicate that committee Republicans do slightly better than committee Democrats, the Bureau might favor adding new starts for Republicans in order to maintain the budget's integrity. If this is the case, both the Budget Bureau and a Democratic White House would be in favor of aiding Republicans over Democrats. The equation that was estimated was as follows ($N = 50$):

$$
\begin{aligned}
\text{Budgeted new} &= .449 + .217 \quad \text{number of members on}\\
\text{starts for fiscal} & \quad\;\; (2.13) \;\; (.82) \quad \text{the H.P.W.C.}\\
\text{year 1967} &\\
& \qquad\qquad + .852 \quad \text{number of Republicans on}\\
& \qquad\qquad\;\; (1.33) \quad \text{the H.P.W.C.}\\
& \qquad\qquad + .013 \quad \text{budgeted construction for}\\
& \qquad\qquad\;\; (2.33) \quad \text{fiscal year 1967}
\end{aligned}
$$

$$\bar{R}^2 = .262$$

H.P.W.C. Republicans do about four times as well as Democrats in getting budgeted new starts for their states. This is a much more pronounced advantage than these same committee Republicans have in getting House new starts. This finding must be regarded, though, as no more than an indication of an interesting direction for further research, for there has as yet been no systematic work done on the use of tangible incentives to form and maintain legislative coalitions, and without such studies it is difficult to interpret the results obtained here.

Seniority and Budgeted New Starts

Budget officials seem to think of the Congress, and the House in particular, as a large group of people dominated by a few very interested, knowledgeable, and above all powerful men in each issue domain. Those officials with responsibilities in the water resources area are accustomed to thinking about and dealing with a small group of congressmen and senators. In the House, this small group coincides with the high-seniority members of the authorizing and appropriating committees. There is a close relationship between seniority and influence over issue areas. The interviews repeatedly produced references to a "club," which implies that senior members share common interests and perceptions and that there is a certain chumminess among them. Budget officials realize that the representatives they have to deal with are an extremely stable group; consequently, if these officials want the Budget Bureau to have maximum leverage on the final budget they must be prepared to accommodate the "club" members—particularly in their policy preferences.

Accommodation between the Budget Bureau's objectives and the perceived desires of the senior committee members is a matter of some difficulty for the Bureau, since it often runs counter to the Bureau's ideology (what Morton Halperin calls its organizational "essence").[14] Some of the senior men are believed to care only about what goes in or near their districts. Others have policy goals for the development of water resources—especially the building of canals. The Budget Bureau finds it relatively easy to accommodate representatives who care only about what goes into their districts. However, there are representatives who have formed an ideology of building dams and canals and who consequently take a personal interest in projects that are not located near them. In the area of navigation, in particular, this interest has led to prolonged and bitter disputes between such representatives and the Bureau.

The Bureau does try to accommodate senior committee members as long as the issue is relatively local in its implications. Officials admit that if they can find a good project in a senior committee member's district they will try to speed it through if possible. The following equation illustrates this phenomenon ($N = 50$):

$$
\begin{aligned}
\text{Budgeted new} && = .452 & + .261 && \text{number of members on} \\
\text{starts for fiscal} && (2.15) & (1.08) && \text{the H.P.W.C.} \\
\text{year 1967} \\
&&& + .339 && \text{number of high-seniority} \\
&&& (.648) && \text{Democrats on the H.P.W.C.} \\
&&& + 1.03 && \text{number of high-seniority} \\
&&& (1.59) && \text{Republicans on the} \\
&&&&& \text{H.P.W.C.} \\
&&& + .012 && \text{budgeted construction for} \\
&&& (2.02) && \text{fiscal year 1967} \\
\end{aligned}
$$

$$\bar{R}^2 = .261$$

The equation indicates that added seniority does make a representative somewhat more effective in obtaining budgeted new starts. The difference is more marked for Republicans than for Democrats; once again, Republicans appear to be more successful than Democrats. We must again note the caveat included when House new starts were examined: for high-seniority members the effects are likely to be confounded with the proxy variable being employed for "need" (budgeted construction), so that the estimates are likely to be too low. The implications of the equation are nonetheless clear. The Budget Bureau does "defer" to high-seniority members of the H.P.W.C. and does attempt to anticipate their demands. However, the earlier analysis showed that high-seniority members also do well in House new starts; consequently, this deferential strategy of the Budget Bureau is not pronounced enough to protect the budget effectively from severe congressional changes.

The Effect of Subcommittee Membership on the Budget

The H.P.W.C. handles rivers and harbors and flood control legislation in two separate subcommittees, as we have seen: Rivers and Harbors, and Flood Control. There is some overlapping of membership between the two. There are 11 Democrats on Rivers and Harbors and 13 Democrats on Flood Control. Six Democrats are on both subcommittees. There are five Republicans on each of the subcommittees; two Republicans are on both subcommittees. Hearings are held jointly by the two subcommittees on the Omnibus Rivers and Harbors and Flood Control Bill, and the bill is reported out in two pieces corresponding to the jurisdictions of the two subcommittees. Before a project can be authorized (i.e. included in the Omnibus Bill) it must receive "clearance" from the Budget Bureau. Each project report, therefore, contains a paragraph outlining the Budget Bureau's evaluation of the project. Members who want particular projects approved show concern over Budget Bureau objections, since if the Bureau does not like a project at this stage, it will probably oppose funding later on.

Nevertheless, we must not overemphasize the importance of Budget Bureau clearance at the authorization stage. In the 1970 Omnibus Bill 43 projects were finally authorized, only 21 of which had received final clearance from the President (or the O.M.B.). As mentioned in Chapter 1, Congress sometimes authorizes projects contingent upon the approval of the President, and several of the projects authorized without the approval of the O.M.B. were in this category.

Ranking members of the subcommittee are in contact with the Budget Bureau, the Corps, and concerned congressmen in order to try to remove Budget Bureau objections to the project before those objections become part of the public record. At this stage the Bureau has at least some ability to change the plans of proposed projects; the Bureau preserves its power to alter projects by being neither too demanding nor too unyielding on criteria and by obtaining the cooperation of subcommittee members. To the extent that subcommittee members seek to satisfy Budget Bureau objections before authorization of a project, they act as allies of the Bureau. We can show that subcommittee members profit from this arrangement as well. The following equation illustrates this phenomenon ($N = 50$):

$$
\begin{aligned}
\text{Budgeted new} &= .429 + .562 \quad \text{number of members on} \\
\text{starts for fiscal} & \quad\;\;(2.07)\;\;(2.11) \quad \text{the Rivers and Harbors} \\
\text{year 1967} & \qquad\qquad\qquad\qquad \text{Subcommittee} \\
& \quad\;\; + .230 \quad \text{number of members on the} \\
& \qquad (.869) \quad \text{Flood Control Subcom-} \\
& \qquad\qquad\qquad\quad \text{mittee} \\
& \quad\;\; + .014 \quad \text{budgeted construction for} \\
& \qquad (2.48) \quad \text{fiscal year 1967} \\
\bar{R}^2 &= .237
\end{aligned}
$$

Members of the Rivers and Harbors Subcommittee generally do better than members of the Flood Control Subcommittee. To explain this assertion we may venture the reason used to explain why Rivers and Harbors members did better on House new starts. The Rivers and Harbors Subcommittee has jurisdiction over navigation projects, whose funding the Budget Bureau generally opposes. The Bureau is aware that Congress will start some navigation projects anyway, so if it wishes to have any influence over the shape of these projects, it must be reasonable in its evaluations at the authorization stage. Unfortunately there is no interview material available to support this conjecture, but it does seem consistent with the spirit of the interviews.

When subcommittees were broken down by party, it was found that the Democrats on Flood Control did less well than the Republicans. The Democrats on Rivers and Harbors, on the other hand, did somewhat better than the Republicans. The set of institutions studied consisted of those internal to the House Public Works Committee. All the hypotheses examined rest on the assumption that policy-making in the area is highly routinized and is characterized by a fairly elaborated structure of quid pro quo.

The results indicate that although the H.P.W.C. has no formal or legal authority to initiate or ratify public works new starts, it seems to exercise considerable informal influence over the choice of new starts. This informal influence can only be exercised within the stable or patterned arrangements that characterize policy-making in this area, for it is only in this context that reciprocating behavior is well defined. To take an example which has actually occurred, if the Appropriations Committee stopped giving preference to new starts for members of the H.P.W.C., the informal expectations that exist in the minds of H.P.W.C. members would be violated. After a period of time, those members who felt "wronged" would attempt to restore the status quo ante either by "rolling" the Appropriations Committee on the floor or by penalizing the individual members of that committee. In the next chapter we will examine such a situation in greater detail.

Within the H.P.W.C., the formal division of authority and labor that exists tends to have some demonstrable impact on policy outcomes also. Generally speaking, specialization and formal influence within the committee lead to increased ability to "get more" of the distributed benefits of committee membership. There are some rather intuitive reasons for these findings. If a member is on the Rivers and Harbors Subcommittee, he has a vote in marking up the navigation projects section of the Rivers and Harbors Bill. He has—formally at least—the prerogative of bringing up an objection to a project at executive session; if the project is not defended by another member, one objection may knock it out of the bill. How much influence he has over the final result of committee deliberation and how much influence he has within the informal structure relating the appropriations and authorizations committees depend on strategic and personal factors as well as on formal ones, at least for younger members. But when the top of the seniority ladder is approached in the H.P.W.C., the "clubby" manner in which the committee does its business and the operating consensus among the top eight or nine Democrats give these members a pivotal position on water-project legislation. This makes for a stable operating system in this area, since when the operating consensus is violated the "club" can mobilize a strong coalition on the House floor (and has done so) to restore the old balance.

This stable system has existed for only about 15 years (1956–71), a period during which there has not been a great deal of turnover at the top of the H.P.W.C. It is therefore impossible to evaluate just how important personal factors are in the system's operation. One gets the feeling that if one member were not interested in maintaining the system as it is, others would easily take up the slack. The recruitment process, the opportunities to go to other committees, and the processes of socialization make this problem a rare one and, for that reason, one that is difficult to research. All that can be done with the data of this chapter is to indicate that rewards appear to be distributed in rough conformity to formal authority over the legislative arena under observation. The fact that the formal structure appears to define the observed reward structure fairly well would appear to limit or constrain the role that personality can play in the distribution of projects.[15] Chapter 10—on the Senate—will throw more light on this subject.

9

Committee Effects on Project Choice:
The House Appropriations Committee

The authority to initiate congressional consideration of appropriations measures has rested with the House Appropriations Committee since the early 1920's. Prior to that time, some legislative committees, including the Rivers and Harbors Committee, had the right to report appropriations bills to the House. Formally, therefore, the budget of an agency must be ratified by the House Appropriations Committee in order for that agency to spend any funds from the general revenues of the government. This delegation of effective power over appropriations decisions from the House to its Appropriations Committee is reflected in real influence only insofar as the House respects the committee's decisions. On the whole, the Appropriations Committee is considered to be among the most powerful in the House. The preliminary investigation carried out in Chapter 5 indicates that this general attribution of influence to the committee has to be tempered by taking into account the agency under consideration. For some agencies the committee's decisions are effectively final for both the House and the Senate. For other agencies the House goes along with committee recommendations but the Senate makes large changes. In the case of still other agencies, the House makes substantial changes through floor amendments after the Appropriations Committee has submitted its recommendations.

The House Appropriations Committee has traditionally divided itself into subcommittees with separate jurisdictions in order to consider appropriations measures. Unlike the House Public Works Committee, the Appropriations Committee predated the Legislative Reorganization Act of 1947; as a result, although some of the subcommittees of the H.P.W.C. existed as legislative committees before 1946

(Flood Control and Rivers and Harbors), the subcommittees of the H.A.C. were formed and given jurisdictions by the chairman with no natural precedent to follow. Subsequently, some of the subcommittees of the H.A.C. have been relatively stable in membership and jurisdiction, though others have changed from year to year. Some agencies have had to face the same chairman and much the same membership each time they have appeared to ask for their annual budget requests; over the same period, other agencies have been shuttled from one subcommittee to another.

Those agencies that face the same subcommittee each year tend to develop ongoing ties with that subcommittee. These ties are reflected in continuing consultation between the subcommittee chairman and the agency during the year, and in staff contacts with agency personnel. The permanent relationship between agency and subcommittee tends to foster stable relations throughout the congressional appropriations process for that agency. For example, an agency such as the F.B.I., which enjoys the support of its appropriations subcommittee, will not try to subvert that subcommittee's decisions by appealing to its friends in the House (usually on the relevant legislative committee) or in the Senate. Conversely, an agency that has its budget cut deeply each year in the House (for example, the Agency for International Development) may try to develop support elsewhere in the process.

Utilizing Fenno's data on agency success in the House and the Senate, we can develop some idea of the prevalence of these patterns. Table 9.1 indicates that agencies that are successful with the House committee do not get their budgets revised substantially in the Senate. Those that do suffer major cuts in the House receive succor in the Senate. Unfortunately, Fenno does not present similar data relating the House floor decisions by bureau to the House committee decisions. Even more regrettable is the fact that he did not construct comparable tables for conference outcomes. An example of where such data would be useful is in the area of appropriations for the Interior Department. Interior Department agencies suffer very large cuts at the hands of the H.A.C., according to Fenno.[1] However, these same agencies receive very generous restorations from the S.A.C. Senator Carl Hayden's (Democrat–Arizona) position as chairman of the S.A.C., as chairman of its subcommittee on the Interior and related agencies, and as head of the panel of the S.A.C. Public Works Subcommittee that handles appropriations for assorted agencies in the Interior Department (in particular the Bureau of Reclamation) enabled him to

TABLE 9.1

Relation Between House Success and Senate
Success for 24 Bureaus

Category	12 most successful bureaus in the House	12 least successful bureaus in the House
Above median in restorations by Senate	4	11
Below median in restorations by Senate	8	1

SOURCE: Fenno, *The Power of the Purse*, pp. 368 and 586.

restore to the Interior agencies' budget most of the funds cut by the H.A.C. The fact that Hayden, who came from a Western state that receives many projects from the Interior Department, was well situated to reconstruct the Interior Department's budget requests seems to have given H.A.C. members license to cut freely and deeply into the Interior Department's budget. The final effects of this arrangement on the budgets cannot be examined without data on conference outcomes.

If the agency is successful in developing support outside the House Appropriations Subcommittee, and if the decisions of the subcommittee are substantially revised on a regular basis, then the subcommittee will in effect have lost a major part of its influence over the agency. Members of the House Appropriations Committee, and in particular its chairman, are likely to view such a state of affairs as unsatisfactory. If the pattern cannot be changed through the use of the institutionalized advantages of the H.A.C. on the floor or in conference, then either the subcommittee will have to learn not to cut the agency's budget so deeply or, failing this, the agency will sometimes have to be switched by the chairman of the H.A.C. to another jurisdiction. The point is that if the power of the H.A.C. to affect agency budgets is to be preserved, the responsible subcommittee must adjust its behavior to the realities of the extent of that agency's support in Congress.

These remarks, when combined with the analysis offered in Chapter 5, suggest a modification of Fenno's view of the goals and expectations of the members of the House Appropriations Committee as expressed in *The Power of the Purse*. Fenno argues in that book that there is a "remarkably solid consensus" on committee goals among the members. To recapitulate, the goals that everyone appears to agree on are (1) protecting the power of the purse, (2) guarding the federal treasury, (3) reducing the budget estimates of agencies, and (4) serving member constituency interests. In day-to-day application these shared goals appear to reduce to a primary emphasis on economy and on "cutting" agency budgets. There are bound to be deficiencies in any approach that attempts, like Fenno's, to explain the behavior of committee members in dealing with thousands of different budgeted items each year by reference to a short list of goals or desires shared by the members. The difficulty with the particular list of goals that Fenno employs is that those goals are not always consonant with the individual member's desires and expectations in joining the committee.

In both *The Power of the Purse* and his paper "Congressional Committees: A Comparative View," Fenno argues that the major reason members wish to join the H.A.C. is because "that is where the power is." By "power" the congressmen quoted by Fenno appear to mean that through membership in the committee they are able to effectively set limits (in most cases upper limits) on what activities a sizable number of government agencies can undertake in a given year. This ability means that both agencies and other members of Congress must come to them to ask for things they want agencies to do (or not to do, as the case may be). Members of the H.A.C. are acutely aware that the root of their power depends on the fact that their decisions stand more or less intact or that they are not frequently changed on the floor of the House or in conference with the Senate.

The decisions of the H.A.C. are not automatically invulnerable to change. The reason the committee's recommendations are seldom changed is precisely because it does not attempt to impose a single standard on every agency. Committee goals and expectations are tailored to each agency individually and depend on the amount of House and Senate support for the particular agency in question. Fenno presents some evidence (in his Chapter 8) that would support this revised view, but he does not attempt to modify his theory to incorporate an explanation of these phenomena. Instead, he is content to present a table which contrasts agency support in the H.A.C. with the agency's "external support."

The argument presented here would indicate that one of the cells of his table is "unstable" and should generate some unusual behavior over time. If an agency has weak support on the committee but strong external support, then that agency's budget should receive a lot of successful floor amendments, and major changes should occur in the Senate. In his Table 9.8 Fenno presents evidence of this instability.[2] Eight of the 12 least successful agencies before the House Appropriations Committee are in the Interior Department; the Interior Department Appropriations Bill receives more successful amendments on the House floor than does the appropriations bill for any other department.[3] We should note that the Bureau of Reclamation and the Bonneville Power Administration are included in the public works budget, which also undergoes substantial revision on the floor. In Fenno's own framework this indicates that the House Appropriations Committee has been repeatedly sanctioned by the House on the floor. Over a period of time committee members may find this loss of influence intolerable, and consequently the committee's behavior may exhibit a change toward increased agency support. The Corps of Engineers' budget is an excellent example of this phenomenon, and it is likely that much of the changing relationship between the H.A.C. and the House can be explained by a simple "equilibrating" mechanism based on the individual member's desire to preserve his influence (and therefore his committee's influence) in the House. There is some indirect evidence in support of this equilibrating tendency presented in Figure 5.5, which shows that the number of amendments to appropriations measures has been regularly declining. Figure 5.1 shows that the House Appropriations Committee has been growing generally more lenient over time. The theory being advanced here would suggest a causal relationship between these two phenomena.

The magnitude of this theory is too great to be adequately supported within the confines of this work; however, the theory provides an adequate explanation for the ways the Corps' budget has been treated by the H.A.C. since the Legislative Reorganization Act of 1947. A brief historical account will indicate how the Corps of Engineers' budget was shifted from one jurisdiction to another from 1947 to 1955 in relation to the subcommittee's treatment of the budget and the resulting floor reaction. In the Republican 80th Congress, the Corps' budget was examined by the Deficiencies Subcommittee, chaired by Congressman Taber (Republican–New York) with Cannon (Democrat–Missouri) as the ranking minority member. In both sessions, the Corps' budgets were revised upward in the Senate, and substantial fractions of the upward changes survived the conference. In 1947, the Senate more than doubled the House subcommittee's recommendation, and the conference figure remained more than double the House subcommittee's figure. Though the House subcommittee was much more openhanded in 1948, the Senate still added on more than $100 million, only $35 million of which was retained in conference.

In the 81st Congress, the Corps' budget was handled in the House by the Deficiencies and Army Civil Functions Subcommittee, chaired by John Kerr (Democrat–North Carolina). This was substantially the same subcommittee that had had authority over the Corps' budget in the 80th Congress. There were only five members, and the top two members on each side were the same as in the 80th Congress. In 1949, the House subcommittee cut $180 million from the President's budget for the Corps, and subsequently 22 floor amendments were offered, four of which were successful (adding $11 million). The Senate then restored about $155 million, and after a bitter four-month-long conference about $69 million was retained. In the second session of the 81st Congress, the House and Senate were again far apart on the Corps' budget ($130 million), and the final figure was $53.4 million above the House figure.

The 81st Congress appears to have marked a period when the leadership of the H.A.C. thought that it could control agency expenditures by controlling which congressmen went onto the subcommittee considering each agency's budget. In particular, Cannon and Taber attempted to screen off the subcommittee members who had substantial constituency interest in the agencies within their subcommittee's jurisdiction. It is instructive to compare the amount of Corps construction funds going into states represented on the subcommittee with the amount going into states not so represented.

The Corps' construction budget request for fiscal year 1950 contained $42.6 million for the states of members of the subcommittee and $495.7 million for all other states. If these figures are adjusted for size of the state delegation, then congressional districts in states with a delegation member on the subcommittee averaged $440,000 in Corps expenditures; the comparable statistic for districts in other states was about $1.3 million. The figures are of about the same order of magnitude (one to three) when the final House recommendations are considered. They remained roughly the same in the second session. It is worth noting, as an aside, that most of the expenditures within the subcommittee went to the states of the chairman (John Kerr) and ranking minority member (Taber).*

If anything, the attempt to institute the economy norm through controlling subcommittee membership was carried further in the 82d Congress. The average per district expenditure (A.D.E.) recom-

---

* Of $42.57 million budgeted for states represented on the Civil Functions Subcommittee of the H.A.C., Taber's and Kerr's states received $30.53 million. The average per district expenditure amounted to $1.37 million for North Carolina and $310,000 for New York.

mended in the budget for states represented on the subcommittee was $455,000. The A.D.E. (in the budget request) for states not represented was $1.4 million. In the first session the Subcommittee on Deficiencies and Army Civil Functions slashed $126 million out of the President's budget. There were 18 amendments offered on the floor, of which two passed, adding $25 million to the House recommendation. The Senate added to the House figure about $100 million, of which $60 million was retained in conference.

The second session of the 82d Congress was similar to the first. The subcommittee cut nearly $200 million from a budget request for the Corps of $575 million. Nineteen amendments were offered on the floor and none was successful. The Senate figure was $178 million more than the House recommendation, and $92 million of the Senate increases were retained in conference. During each of the three Congresses mentioned (80th to 82d), the Corps of Engineers had substantial "external support"; consequently, the subcommittee's attempts to hold down spending failed, for the final budget figures were far from the House's figures.

The following Congress received from a Republican President budget requests that were much smaller than those that had been regularly proposed by the Truman Administration. Cutting by the subcommittee that handled the budget of the Corps of Engineers (the subcommittee was called Civil Functions and Military Construction) was consequently much less severe than it had been in previous years. The Republican Senate added to the House request, but the differences between the House and the Senate figures were not more than $60 million. The Cannon-Taber practice of keeping agency supporters off the subcommittee was still operative. The A.D.E. recommended in the budget for states represented on the subcommittee was only $43,000; at the same time, the A.D.E. for those states not represented on the subcommittee was over $1.1 million (New York and Missouri received *all* the expenditures going to states represented on the subcommittee).

This exposition indicates that when Congress is controlled by Republicans the Corps does not have nearly as much "external support" (support outside the House Appropriations Committee) as it does when Congress is Democratic. In the Democratic 81st and 82d Congresses, there were repeated and partially successful attempts made by House members to sanction the House subcommittee responsible for the Corps' budget through substantial amendments offered to its appropriations bill, but Cannon and Taber continued to pursue the economy goal by stacking the subcommittee. The first session of the 84th Congress (1955) was the first time that House sanctions were completely successful. The floor revolt of 1955 marked the effective end of the Cannon-Taber practice of keeping congressmen who were "interested" in Corps expenditures off the subcommittee.

With the 84th Congress under Democratic control, those Democrats who had a constituency interest in the expenditures of the Corps of Engineers expected a substantial change in the orientation of the House Appropriations Committee away from what they saw as the meager budget recommendations given to the Congress under Eisenhower's "no new starts" policy. Their expectations were fueled by the fact that Cannon had formed a new Public Works Subcommittee that was more than twice as large as the Civil Functions Subcommittee of the previous Congress. In addition, the A.D.E. (in the Corps' budget) for members of the Public Works Subcommittee was $507,000 in contrast to the $43,000 per member of the former Civil Functions Subcommittee of the 83d Congress. This indicated that members of the new subcommittee had substantially more constituency interest in the Corps of Engineers' budget than members of the old Civil Functions Subcommittee had had.

The jurisdiction of the Public Works Subcommittee encompassed that of the Civil Functions Subcommittee (the civil functions budget of the Corps of Engineers) and included control over the Bureau of Reclamation (previously under the Interior Subcommittee) and several agencies previously under the jurisdiction of the Independent Offices Subcommittee. Cannon and Davis (Republican–Wisconsin) were chairman and ranking minority member, respectively. The Public Works Subcommittee handled appropriations measures for agencies within the legislative domain of the Public Works Committee and the Interior Committee.

The subcommittee recommended a 10.5 percent cut in the President's budget for the Corps (compared with an 8.1 percent cut by the Civil Functions Subcommittee in the second session of the 83d Congress) as well as a substantial cut in funds for the Bureau of Reclamation. Congressmen interested in the budgets of these agencies were infuriated, particularly members of the legislative committees on Public Works and the Interior. Members of these two committees dominated the floor debate over the budgets for the Corps and for the Bureau of Reclamation, and with the assistance of other interested members they were able to add $55.2 million to the Corps' budget (the subcommittee had cut $54 million). The Public Works Subcom-

TABLE 9.2
Some Effects of the 1955 Floor Revolt

Effect	1949–55	1956–64
Ratio of A.D.E.'s for those off the subcommittee over those on the subcommittee	9.89	2.14
Average cut by the subcommittee in the President's budget	18.80%	2.04%
Average number of floor amendments	15.50	4.40
Average number of successful floor amendments	3.00	.40

mittee never again attempted to cut deeply into budget requests. Table 9.2 brings out some long-term effects of the 1955 floor revolt. This table adds support to the theory that the conflict between the House Appropriations Committee and the Corps' supporters outside the H.A.C. was institutionalized in the Cannon-Taber method of keeping agency advocates off the subcommittee responsible for a particular agency. Once the House forced the leadership of the H.A.C. to stop cutting the Corps' budget deeply, the Cannon-Taber recruitment method was no longer applied. Since 1955 there has been an observable downward trend in the ratio of A.D.E.'s for those off the subcommittee over those on the subcommittee.

The defeat of the "economy norm" with respect to the Corps' budget has associated with it a dual phenomenon that is the emergence of a public works or water projects "subgovernment" (to employ Douglas Cater's terminology).[4] Beginning in 1955, we can note the clear establishment of cooperative relations between the H.P.W.C. and the H.A.C. Public Works Subcommittee.* Cuts in the Corps' construction budget by the H.A.C. Public Works Subcommittee were examined to see which congressmen they affected, and the results are shown in Table 9.3. It is evident that members of the H.P.W.C. have enjoyed a privileged or protected position with respect to budget cuts by the H.A.C. Public Works Subcommittee since 1956. The previous

---

* If there is a club in the public works issue area, then by all odds 1955 marks its inception. The organization of the 1955 floor revolt took place in a "rump caucus" presided over by Representative Overton Brooks (Democrat–Louisiana), who was at that time the president of the National Rivers and Harbors Congress. Frank Smith of Mississippi was, by his own testimony, one of the principal organizers who arranged the floor strategy. The men who spoke on the floor and who offered the amendments came principally from the Interior Committee, the H.P.W.C., and the H.A.C., which failed to hold together. The floor revolt was organized and carried mainly by members of these committees.

TABLE 9.3

*Membership on the H.P.W.C. and Cuts by the H.A.C. Public
Works Subcommittee*

Membership	1949–55	1956–68
Number of times cuts in states with members on the H.P.W.C. exceeded those in "other" states	5	0
Number of times cuts in "other" states exceeded those in states with members on the H.P.W.C.	2	13

chapter presented evidence of this cooperative relationship for one year—1966. New starts initiated by the subcommittee were concentrated in the states represented on the H.P.W.C.

The relationship of cooperation with the H.P.W.C. has been accompanied by an increased program-advocacy orientation on the part of H.A.C. Public Works Subcommittee members. Membership on this H.A.C. subcommittee has come to confer a definite constituency advantage to congressmen since 1956. Table 9.4 indicates in one respect the degree to which subcommittee membership aids members' states. This table indicates that projects in the states represented on the subcommittee have become largely invulnerable to cuts since 1956.

The changes in the figures presented in Table 9.4 correspond to changes in the membership of the subcommittee after 1955. Among the members after that date are men who have been recognized as forming part of the water resources "club" that was repeatedly referred to in interviews. The late Mike Kirwan (Democrat–Ohio) was known as "one of the great developers in the Congress" (according to a Democratic member of the H.P.W.C.). Jamie Whitten (Democrat–Mississippi), a representative from the Mississippi Delta region, became a water projects advocate because of the nature of his constituency. Joe Evins (Democrat–Tennessee), James Murray (Democrat–Illinois), John Phillips (Republican–California), T. Millett Hand (Republican–New Jersey), and Ben F. Jensen (Republican–Iowa) all had substantial constituency interests in water projects and in the growth of the budget of the Corps of Engineers and became members of the Public Works Subcommittee after 1955.

We can make an even stronger generalization: from 1956 on, members of the H.A.C. Public Works Subcommittee not only came from states with strong interests in Corps expenditures, they also were not averse to using their power as subcommittee members to protect and

TABLE 9.4
Constituency Benefits of Membership on the H.A.C.
Public Works Subcommittee

Membership	1949–55	1956–68
Number of times H.A.C. recommendations for projects in subcommittee members' states were *smaller* than budget requests	7 (7)	3 (10)
Number of times H.A.C. figures for subcommittee members were *greater* than budget requests	0 (0)	10 (3)

NOTE: The number in parentheses is the corresponding number for the *total* construction budget.

extend Corps expenditures in their states. The H.A.C. subcommittee, in other words, developed a pork barrel orientation to the Corps' construction budget. If each state's portion of the Corps' construction budget is considered to be a "state line," then the H.A.C. Public Works Subcommittee had a total of 44 state lines from 1949 to 1955 and 115 state lines from 1956 to 1965. Table 9.5 indicates state-by-state outcomes of the H.A.C. review of the Corps' budget for those states represented on the subcommittee. Cuts in the state lines of states represented on the H.A.C. subcommittee have become relatively infrequent while budget increases have become common.

The results obtained in this chapter are to be understood within the context of an H.A.C. Public Works Subcommittee that is an active participant along with the H.P.W.C. in the pork barrel. The equations to be presented will parallel, insofar as possible, those of the previous chapter in the hope of aiding the reader in making comparisons between the two committees. Once again, the data used here are construction new starts (House-initiated and budget-initiated) for fiscal year 1967. During 1966 the Public Works Subcommittee had only nine members: six Democrats and three Republicans. Kirwan was in his second year as subcommittee chairman, and John Rhodes had been the ranking minority member since the beginning of the 89th Congress. The top four Democrats on the subcommittee in 1966 (Kirwan, John Fogarty [Democrat–Rhode Island], Evins, and Edward Boland [Democrat–Massachusetts]) had all joined it in 1955; Whitten had joined the subcommittee in 1962. Of these five Democrats, all but Boland were H.A.C. subcommittee chairmen. Their ranks in the H.A.C. as a whole were 2d (Kirwan), 3d (Whitten), 6th (Fogarty), 9th (Evins), and 10th (Boland). The sixth Democrat, Robert Casey (Democrat–Texas), was the last-ranked Democrat on the H.A.C. and did

TABLE 9.5
Pork Barrel Orientation of H.A.C. Public Works
Subcommittee Members

Members	1949–55	1956–65
Number of cuts in state lines	17	14
Number of "no change" outcomes in state lines	22	52
Number of raises in state lines	5	49

not retain his seat on the subcommittee in the 90th Congress. The three Republicans were Rhodes (6th ranking on the H.A.C.), Glenn Davis (Republican–Wisconsin), and Howard Robison (Republican–New York). The latter two were 12th and 13th among 16 Republicans on the H.A.C. (Glenn Davis had returned to Congress after an eight-year absence. He had been the chairman of the H.A.C. Subcommittee on Army Civil Functions during the 83d Congress, and had returned to his law practice for several years before being reelected to the House.) The H.A.C. Public Works Subcommittee thus not only had a two-to-one Democratic majority, but also included some of the most powerful Democrats from the full committee.*

The Effects of Membership
in the House Appropriations Committee

Though the budget for the Corps of Engineers is examined by the Public Works Subcommittee, the relatively fluid nature of the subcommittee when viewed over a long period of time emphasizes the fact that it is the tool of the full committee. The facts that the subcommittee operates autonomously in any given year and that the full H.A.C. virtually always accepts its recommendations should not obscure the equally evident fact that the H.A.C. chairman, acting on behalf of the full committee, has juggled the jurisdictions and membership of the subcommittee on some occasions.†

* No conclusive reasons for this subcommittee structure can be given. We might conjecture that after 1956 the increased floor success of the subcommittee convinced Cannon not to juggle its membership or its jurisdiction in an attempt to change its behavior. He may have come to terms with the constituency interests many congressmen had in Corps expenditures. The Democratic members may have found, in the absence of intervention from Cannon, that subcommittee membership was valuable to them and thus did not try to transfer off the subcommittee. The low-seniority composition of the Republican side of the subcommittee is not accounted for by this argument and remains an enigma.

† The fact that these are rare and exceptional events within the H.A.C. should

One of the reasons that the full committee accepts subcommittee recommendations is that the individual members of the full committee are happy with these recommendations. H.A.C. members expect to receive and apparently believe that they do receive preferred treatment at the hands of their peers on the H.A.C. subcommittees. Fenno remarks on "the unanimously held member belief that committee membership will enhance one's ability to get projects for his constituents." He quotes a member: "Naturally you want to do as much to help the people of your district as you can.... When you are interested in something, any appropriations subcommittee will listen to you a lot more if you're a member of the committee than if you aren't."[5] This expectation seems to work across party lines as well. "One Republican newcomer noted that the Democratic chairman of his subcommittee wrote into the committee report that construction should begin immediately on the newcomer's pet project."[6] But the amount of reciprocity across subcommittees appears to depend to some extent on agreements between members. A member commented that influence "depends on the friends you make on other subcommittees. There's the fellow who asked me about a hospital he's got coming up. Then when I want something done, I will go and see him. They'll pay more attention to me when I'm a member of the commit-

---

not lead one to overlook the fact that similar events would be of historical importance if they occurred among the Standing Committees. The nature of the tasks of the H.A.C. has required that its subcommittees approach the workings of the Standing Committees more nearly than is the case with any other committee's subcommittees. In particular, a fairly stable set of jurisdictions and a seniority norm for advancement have long been at work within the H.A.C. Stable rules for advancement and stable jurisdictions would appear to provide strong incentives for specialization in subcommittee work. If the chairman of the H.A.C. were to transfer people regularly from subcommittee to subcommittee or to make major changes in jurisdictions with any frequency, members would cease to find it beneficial to invest their time and effort in becoming experts in the subject matter of their subcommittees.

For these reasons, Cannon's advancement of Otto Passman over Vaughn Gary to the chairmanship of the Foreign Operations Subcommittee, his abolition of the Civil Functions Subcommittee and creation of the Public Works Subcommittee, and many other changes in jurisdictions and subcommittee memberships he made assume a particular importance when we consider that they took place in the H.A.C. Each extraordinary change has the effect of reducing the effectiveness of the H.A.C. to do its job (as its members see it). This argument would suggest that the chairman would institute an extraordinary change only in extreme cases. One such case might be the application of strong sanctions by the House to the committee. Another instance (perhaps the likely one in the choice of Passman for a subcommittee chairmanship) might be the strong desire of the chairman for a certain sort of policy to be followed (or not followed) by an agency or set of agencies.

tee. You trade back and forth across subcommittees that way.... It's a matter of scratching each other's backs, I suppose. But that's the only way you get any specific project accomplished around here."[7] This expectation on the part of committee members is focused—not surprisingly—on certain issue areas. Fenno remarks that "A chairman may be placed under greater pressure to bargain, for example, in the public works bill than he is in the Justice Department bill."[8] One would expect, therefore, that committee members' expectations for special treatment would be highest on public works bills.

The first equation adduced here, with House new starts as the dependent variable, gives some indication of the reality behind these expectations ($N = 50$):

$$\begin{array}{l}\text{House new} \\ \text{starts for fiscal} \\ \text{year 1967}\end{array} = \begin{array}{c}-.056 \\ (-.260)\end{array} + \begin{array}{c}1.32 \\ (8.13)\end{array} \begin{array}{l}\text{number of members on} \\ \text{the H.A.C. in 1966}\end{array}$$

$$\bar{R}^2 = .570$$

Having a member on the H.A.C. was worth about 1.32 House-initiated new starts to a state. This equation indicates that members of the committee do in fact fare better at the hands of their peers than do those not on the committee. The coefficient for membership on the H.A.C. survives when the regression is controlled for the size of the current construction budget.

The second component of the belief that membership on the H.A.C. will enable a member to "get more" for his district is the belief that the agencies will be more willing to help a congressman who is on the H.A.C. Once again Fenno provides interview material that helps to add some flesh to this idea. One member said, "It's the committee that gives you the most power with the government agencies; and you're in touch with them all the time for your constituents." Another member said, "The committee is a good grab-bag place. Bureaucrats kowtow to you a lot more when they sit across the table asking you for money than they do in a legislative committee."[9]

The H.A.C. is in a position to affect in a critical way the aspirations and goals of the agencies that must ask for money each year. There is therefore a natural tendency for agencies to be responsive to H.A.C. members in terms of aiding their constituents. Each year the Corps of Engineers submits its proposed construction budget to the Budget Bureau with a list of proposed construction starts that it will have the "capability" to undertake in the upcoming year. The Budget Bureau, in consultation with the White House staff and sometimes with the President himself, generally approves some of these starts and rejects the rest. The previous chapter discussed this process in somewhat greater detail, but we can note here that the motivation of the Budget Bureau tends in this case to parallel that of the agencies in part. The Corps would like to put new starts in or near the districts of congressmen on the H.A.C. in order to maintain rapport with Congress. The Budget Bureau will tend to "go along" with this general pattern of distribution because its power depends in large part on its relations with the H.A.C.

As we have already seen, the Budget Bureau and the Corps disagree substantially on goals and operate under different constraints. The Corps wants to expand its program and its mission (into sewage treatment, design of complete ecological systems, recycling, and so forth); the Budget Bureau, on the other hand, is trying to hold down expenditures and to coordinate, as far as possible, a rational fiscal policy. Nevertheless, for both institutions success depends largely on good relations with the H.A.C. Consequently, we might expect a pronounced preference for H.A.C. members in the budgeted new starts as a result of the compounding of agency and Budget Bureau desires to please H.A.C. members. This expectation is amply borne out in the following equation ($N = 50$):

$$\text{Budgeted new starts in fiscal year 1967} = \underset{(.274)}{.061} + \underset{(4.35)}{.693} \text{ number of members on the H.A.C.}$$
$$+ \underset{(2.33)}{.012} \text{ budgeted construction for fiscal year 1967}$$
$$\bar{R}^2 = .357$$

It appears that a state will get about seven-tenths of a budgeted new start for each member it has on the H.A.C.

This brief examination of the effects of H.A.C. membership appears to confirm the statements in the interview material found in Fenno's study. The relationships reported were further examined to see if they were a spurious result of the effects reported in the previous chapter; i.e., if membership on the H.A.C. and H.P.W.C. are highly correlated, then the fact that H.P.W.C. members "get more" would logically imply that H.A.C. members would appear to "get more" as well. There was in fact a substantial correlation between memberships on the H.A.C. and the H.P.W.C. ($\bar{R} = .64$), but the regressions run with both variables still displayed significant and independent relationships.

*The Effects of Membership on the H.A.C. Public
Works Subcommittee*

The line-by-line appropriations decisions made by the House Appropriations Committee are made in its subcommittees. The subcommittees operate more or less autonomously in any given year, and nearly all of their decisions are accepted by the full committee—generally without any but the most cursory review. There are several mechanisms documented by Fenno by which the full committee ensures that subcommittee decisions are consistent with the goals of the committee. These mechanisms include, first, the fact that the committee chairman and the ranking minority member select the membership of the subcommittees. Second, the chairman, and frequently the ranking minority member (R.M.M.), sits *ex officio* on all of the subcommittees. Third, the chairman and the R.M.M. are formally in control of the subcommittee staffs. Fourth, the chairman allocates the jurisdictions of the subcommittees and can create or abolish subcommittees. In addition, it sometimes occurs that a subcommittee decision will be appealed—rarely successfully—to the full committee. These mechanisms taken together define some of the constraints within which each subcommittee operates.

It has already been argued that committee goals are to some extent tailored to agencies. That is, the full committee might expect a subcommittee to cut one agency's budget requests deeply, and it might reinforce this expectation by utilizing one or more of its autonomy-limiting constraints listed above. The best-known example of this occurred when Cannon made Otto Passman, who was very critical of foreign aid, chairman of the Foreign Operations Subcommittee[10] over a more senior subcommittee member. The application of the Cannon-Taber recruitment norm is an example of the use of a control mechanism to ensure budget-cutting in certain of the subcommittees.

Fenno documents the use of control mechanisms to reinforce the economy norm operative in the H.A.C. As we argued earlier, however, certain agencies with widespread support in the House are more or less invulnerable to severe cuts by the H.A.C., and some of the same mechanisms that reinforce budget-cutting in some subcommittees can be used to limit it in other subcommittees. The argument is familiar. The chairman will "stack" certain subcommittees with congressmen who support the agency's programs so that the subcommittee's recommendations will stand a better chance of being accepted by the House. Some major examples of this phenomenon are the subcommittees on

Defense,[11] Military Construction,[12] Agriculture, Labor and H.E.W., and Public Works (after 1955). The placement of the Public Works Subcommittee in this group is justified on the basis of the data presented earlier in this chapter. The by-products of having congressmen with constituency interests in an agency's program on the appropriations subcommittee for that agency are twofold: first, the agency's programs will be supported and expanded; second, agency growth will most likely occur in a way that particularly benefits the states of the congressmen on the agency's appropriations subcommittee. In the case of the Corps of Engineers, the congressmen on the subcommittee will make sure that their states receive a large share of new construction starts.

The Public Works Subcommittee has the authority to change the budget requests submitted to it by the Budget Bureau. Each year it holds extensive hearings, taking testimony about particular projects from officials of the Corps of Engineers, from local groups, and from interested congressmen. The hearings are divided into two parts: official testimony, and testimony of outside witnesses (congressmen and interest groups). The testimony of outside witnesses informs the subcommittee of the Corps' "capabilities" for the upcoming fiscal year on each project as opposed to what the Budget Bureau has recommended for each project. This is made possible by the established Corps practice of indicating to local interests the amount of construction the Corps is capable of undertaking on a given project in the upcoming year.* Thus the subcommittee has before it in markup sessions (on its official markup notes) not only the budget request for a project but also the Corps' capability on that project, which is almost always a higher figure. Local groups and congressmen usually support the Corps' expenditure figures rather than the Budget Bureau's requests.

A frequent practice, and one that is considered to be successful with the subcommittee, is for both a state's entire delegation to the Congress (representatives and senators) and the major interest groups supporting projects in the state to agree on recommendations for projects in the state. Then at the hearings the witnesses from that state present a united front for the subcommittee with each witness supporting the others' recommendations. Generally, the total state delegation requests are not just the sum of the Corps' recommendations, though this varies by state (see Chapter 3). Rather, there is an

---

* This is usually accomplished by a letter from the district or division engineer to the local congressman.

attempt to ask for the largest increase over the budget request that stands some chance of being adopted. If there are severe disagreements between groups within a state, they are worked out to as great a degree as is possible; the conflict is not revealed in the hearings.*

The Subcommittee on Public Works recognizes the fact that some state delegations are highly cohesive and organized, and that they have made an attempt to iron out internal conflicts and disagreements and have also tried to come up with a feasible request. It also recognizes the fact that some states will get most of what they want from the Senate, so that the House does not have to accede to their requests. Finally, it realizes that in some states congressmen must appear to be extreme advocates of local water projects and will recommend high figures that they realize will not be fully accepted by the committee. It is with these factors in mind that the subcommittee responds to state delegation requests. The correlation between total state delegation requests (obtained from a reading of the *Hearings*) and changes in the budget by the House subcommittee during 1966 was .33.

One example of the strategic limitations on the size of this correlation is revealed in studying the budget requests for Corps construction in Arkansas in 1966 (fiscal year 1967). The budget estimate for construction was $143.81 million (the highest of any state), and the state delegation supported a requested increase of $6.295 million. The House subcommittee granted only a $1.1 million increase. The Senate subcommittee added another $4 million, and virtually the entire Senate increase was retained in conference. In this case, the House subcommittee was aware that since Senator John McClellan (Democrat–Arkansas) was a high-ranking member of the Senate Subcommittee on Public Works Appropriations, the Arkansas budget requests would receive careful and favorable consideration from the S.A.C. Public Works Subcommittee.

While the H.A.C. Public Works Subcommittee evidently does respond to state delegation requests (which in most cases bear a strong relationship to the Corps of Engineers' requests to the Budget Bureau), it does not merely accept a fixed proportion of the increases proposed by the state delegations. Some states get most of what they ask for, and other states get very little. There are several reasons for state delegation success before the subcommittee. One reason that we have dealt with already is the cohesion of the delegation (see Chapter 3). Another—the focus of the present chapter—is rooted in state rep-

* As was noted in Chapter 3, there is considerable variation among states in their attempts to coordinate requests to the H.A.C. Public Works Subcommittee.

resentation on the H.A.C., and especially on its Public Works Subcommittee. We have examined the effects of representation on the
H.A.C. in a previous part of the present chapter. In this section we
are investigating the effects of membership on the H.A.C. Subcommittee on Public Works. The following equation indicates that Public
Works Subcommittee members get more House-initiated new starts
than do other members of the H.A.C.; they also do much better than
those House members not represented on the H.A.C. ($N = 50$):

$$
\begin{aligned}
\text{Number of house} \\
\text{new starts for} \\
\text{fiscal year 1967}
\end{aligned}
=
\begin{aligned}
-.345 \\
(-1.64)
\end{aligned}
+
\begin{aligned}
1.38 \\
(4.32)
\end{aligned}
\quad
\begin{aligned}
&\text{number of members on} \\
&\text{the H.A.C. Public Works} \\
&\text{Subcommittee}
\end{aligned}
$$

$$
+
\begin{aligned}
1.18 \\
(7.19)
\end{aligned}
\quad
\begin{aligned}
&\text{number of members on the} \\
&\text{H.A.C. but not on the Pub-} \\
&\text{lic Works Subcommittee}
\end{aligned}
$$

$$
+
\begin{aligned}
.018 \\
(3.61)
\end{aligned}
\quad
\begin{aligned}
&\text{budgeted construction for} \\
&\text{fiscal year 1967}
\end{aligned}
$$

$$
\bar{R}^2 = .651
$$

This relation indicates that to some extent the subcommittee's decisions favor those states with a large representation on the H.A.C.
over other states (even when budget size is controlled) and favor even
more those states with representation on the Public Works Subcommittee. In order to shed more light on this phenomenon, time-series
data were examined. Figure 9.1 gives the percentage cuts by the
H.A.C. subcommittee in construction budget requests for those states
with representatives on the Public Works Subcommittee compared
with the percentage cuts for all other states for the years 1949–64. (In
reading this figure a negative cut is to be interpreted as an addition.)
In 14 of the 16 years the percentage cuts for states represented on the
subcommittee were smaller than the percentage cuts for other states.
In the ten years from 1955 to 1964, states represented on the subcommittee had their construction requests cut only three times; during
the same period, the other states had their aggregate construction requests reduced by the subcommittee eight times. These data make it
apparent not only that the H.A.C. Public Works Subcommittee has
become a program-advocate committee, but that its members regularly reap constituency rewards for being on the subcommittee. The
rewards described here have taken the form of increased numbers of
House new starts and generally favorable treatment of the budget
requests for members' states.

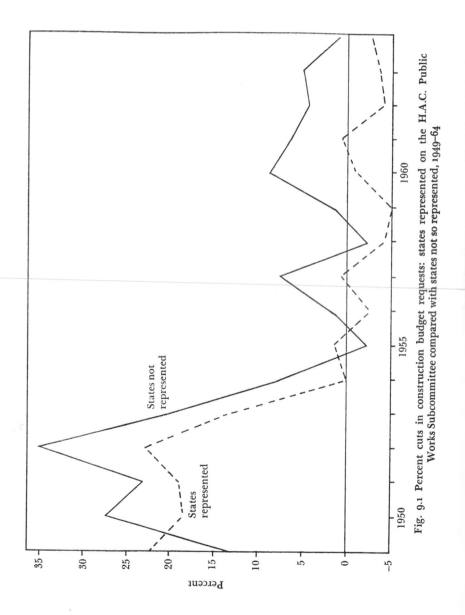

Fig. 9.1 Percent cuts in construction budget requests: states represented on the H.A.C. Public Works Subcommittee compared with states not so represented, 1949–64

The next question to be examined is the extent to which the Budget Bureau and the Corps of Engineers show preference to Public Works Subcommittee members in their decisions. Previous sections of this chapter indicated that members of the H.A.C. receive more budgeted new starts than nonmembers. In a previous chapter it was argued that the ability of the Budget Bureau to achieve its desired goals was critically dependent on the relationship between the Budget Bureau and the H.A.C.—in particular the H.A.C. subcommittees. In day-to-day operations, the Budget Bureau is divided into small working units that operate with some degree of autonomy during the budget cycle. In recent years, the Corps of Engineers' programs, along with those of other agencies working in the area of water resources, have been grouped under the natural resource division. Decision-makers in this area realize that their superiors in the Budget Bureau are sensitive to the desires of congressmen on the appropriations committees and that decisions will sometimes be changed to help out such congressmen. As a result, there is a tendency for Budget Bureau decision-makers to "look out for" the interests of congressmen who can affect the degree to which they can achieve their goals. It would appear that this should lead to an observed preference in the decisions of the Budget Bureau for members of the H.A.C. Subcommittee on Public Works. The following regression equation examines this relationship $(N = 50)$:

Budgeted new starts for fiscal year 1967	$=$	.081 (.361)	$+$	.775 (4.42)	number of members on the H.A.C.
			$-$	.416 (−1.11)	number of members on the H.A.C. Public Works Subcommittee
			$+$	.012 (2.16)	budgeted construction for fiscal year 1967

$$\bar{R}^2 = .360$$

This equation indicates that, contrary to expectation, members of the H.A.C. subcommittee do not do as well in terms of budgeted new starts as other members of the H.A.C. They still do better than those not on the H.A.C. At this point no explanation can be given for this finding, but a few conjectures may be in order.

Interview material presented in the previous chapter indicated that Budget Bureau decision-making personnel considered members of the

H.A.C. Public Works Subcommittee to be among the most powerful and important congressmen. One formerly high-ranking official, when asked for a list of congressmen whose desires had to be taken into account when putting together the Public Works Appropriations Bill, mentioned several members of the subcommittee. Among those named (and also named by other Budget Bureau officials) were Rhodes, Kirwan, Whitten, Boland, and Evins. However, Budget Bureau personnel insisted that while they would make an effort to put in an extra project to appeal to these people, it had to be a "good" project (see Chapter 8 on this point). It is conceivable, given the stability of the membership of the subcommittee, that there were not a great enough number of "good" projects in the states of the members of the H.A.C. subcommittee to produce a positive effect. Unfortunately, there is no really convincing way to examine this hypothesis, since it depends on the idea of a "good" project from the point of view of the Budget Bureau.

Although only a rough indication can be gained from such an exercise, active authorized projects* that had not yet been started as of 1968 were grouped according to whether or not they were primarily navigation projects. The Budget Bureau generally considers navigation projects to be bad projects, since according to their method of computing benefits and costs few of them have benefit-cost ratios even approaching 1.0. In 1968 there were 290 active, authorized projects that could have received initial planning or construction funds. The hypothesis is that members of the H.A.C. Public Works Subcommittee will have relatively more "bad" projects in their states than "good" ones, according to this rough indicator of Budget Bureau evaluation. The data are consistent with this hypothesis. Of the navigation projects eligible to be new starts in 1968, 23.4 percent were in the states of H.A.C. Public Works Subcommittee members; only 15.3 percent of other types of projects were in their states. Now of course, not every nonnavigation project is considered acceptable by the Budget Bureau, so the 15.3 percent may be an overestimate. In any case, there appears to be a limitation on the data reported in the previous regression equation which would prevent the Budget Bureau from initiating many new starts in the states of H.A.C. Public Works Subcommittee members—the "good" projects may simply not have been available for choice.

* A project is considered to be active if it is either receiving planning or construction funds or is eligible to do so. Inactive projects include those currently being studied and hence without a "plan" for construction.

Just as we did with respect to the House Public Works Committee, we can break the H.A.C. Public Works Subcommittee down into component groups in order to examine further the processes at work within it. The H.A.C. Public Works Subcommittee had only nine members in 1966, so only the crudest of breakdowns can be attempted in the cross-sectional (1966) data. The H.P.W.C. was broken down by subcommittees, seniority, and party in our analysis. In the case of the H.A.C. Public Works Subcommittee, however, there are no subcommittees (there were regional subpanels in 1955, but that practice was subsequently discontinued), and a seniority breakdown would be nearly identical with the party division (as was pointed out earlier, four of the six Democrats were subcommittee chairmen at the time). For this reason only the party division can be looked at within the subcommittee.

The first equation presented here examines the effect of party on the new-starts decisions made by the H.A.C. Public Works Subcommittee. A demonstrable tendency for the Democrats to get more House new starts than the Republicans was expected, since there was a six-to-three Democratic majority, since the Democrats were very senior to the Republicans on the H.A.C. as a whole, and since the H.A.C. Public Works Subcommittee Democrats were considered strong members of the rivers and harbors club. The equation below confirms this expectation ($N = 50$):

House new starts for fiscal year 1967	=	$-.339$ (-1.63)	+	1.23 (7.31)	number of members on the H.A.C. but not on the H.A.C. Public Works Subcommittee
			+	1.51 (4.52)	number of Democrats on the H.A.C. Public Works Subcommittee
			+	$.791$ (1.38)	number of Republicans on the H.A.C. Public Works Subcommittee
			+	$.017$ (3.30)	budgeted construction for fiscal year 1967

$$\bar{R}^2 = .654$$

This equation indicates that Democratic members of the H.A.C. Public Works Subcommittee got nearly twice as many House new starts for their states as Republican members did. It is also evident that the

Democratic members of the H.A.C. Public Works Subcommittee did somewhat better than the other members of the H.A.C. Owing to the high correlation between seniority and party on the subcommittee, it is not possible to argue conclusively that party membership was the real causative factor at work here. Only one of the subcommittee Republicans, John Rhodes, was considered by observers to come from a state having really substantial interests in water resource projects. The other two Republicans came from states that might not be expected (for different reasons) to have many water projects.

Glenn Davis (Republican–Wisconsin), chairman of the Army Civil Functions Subcommittee in the 83d Congress, was vociferously economy-minded and tended to regard much of the Corps' budget as a pork barrel. Wisconsin has received very little in construction funds since 1947. Howard Robison (Republican–New York) was the only member of the H.A.C. Public Works Subcommittee to have been on the H.P.W.C. The New York delegation as a whole is among the least cohesive in the House of Representatives, according to Barbara Deckard* (see Chapter 3); over the years, New York's Republican representation on the H.A.C. Public Works Subcommittee has included the economy-minded John Taber and John Pillion. Until Pillion joined the subcommittee (in 1959), Taber held Corps expenditures in New York to a low level, apparently since the issue of the size of the Corps' budget was a partisan one during the Eisenhower years. The Democrats generally were in favor of expanded spending on public works. Eisenhower's vetoes of the Rivers and Harbors Bill of 1956 and of the Public Works Appropriations Bill of 1959, as well as his policy of opposing budgeted new starts, helped to crystallize the partisan division over public works spending. Since Taber was the ranking Republican on Appropriations and was a major congressional opponent of large public works budgets, he consequently could not try to expand New York's budget share too voraciously. Robison had the additional handicap of being a junior member of the subcommittee.

The relationship between budgeted new starts and party member-

* The New York Republican delegation, though it exhibits more cooperation on constituency matters than does the state's Democratic contingent, still ranks lower in this respect than most of the state delegations examined by Deckard in her dissertation. Deckard observes that New York Republicans do not cooperate with each other on district matters (see Chapter 4 of her "State Party Delegations" thesis). Since as she says in her article of the same title "both [New York] delegations are split" (p. 208), it seems likely that there is little cooperation among New York congressmen on constituency matters.

ship was examined, and the results indicated that Republican members of the H.A.C. were substantially favored over Democrats by the Budget Bureau. No convincing explanation for this phenomenon has been uncovered as yet.

To summarize, party membership appears to have different consequences for the decisions made by the subcommittee as opposed to those made by the Budget Bureau. The argument advanced here is that the reasons for this disparity are rooted first in the professional and political criteria for project evaluation utilized by the Budget Bureau, and second in the fact that the Democrats are highly senior program-advocates for the Corps of Engineers. The analysis indicates that fairly substantial effects on new-starts decisions (and hence on future spending) can be attributed to party, and that House Appropriations Committee members uniformly do much better than nonmembers even though in the regressions the relative effectiveness of Democratic and Republican members switches.

Seniority and the Subcommittee Chairmanship

The H.A.C., like many other committees in the House, does nearly all of its work in subcommittees. Within these smaller units the subcommittee chairman has an impressive amount of influence—influence comparable to that of committee chairmen in the legislative committees. The decentralized and largely autonomous workings of the subcommittees, and the norms regarding participation in subcommittee work (apprenticeship, hard work, and specialization), create a wide area of discretion for chairmen. The chairmen of subcommittees are appointed largely according to subcommittee seniority, although there have been some exceptions. Fenno regards the practice of appointing chairmen according to subcommittee seniority as a constraint on the full committee chairman's power and therefore as an independent source of influence for the subcommittee chairmen.

The practice of using seniority to advance members within subcommittees and to appoint subcommittee chairmen when raised to the level of a norm or expectation constitutes, within a committee, an institutional distribution of a power resource (or set of resources). A principal hypothesis of this study—that the distribution of divisible policy outputs will conform largely to the distribution of power —suggests that subcommittee chairmen would be expected to benefit disproportionately from the policy decisions made within the H.A.C. This argument rests on some additional theoretical linkages that have been only partially established by the data presented in the preceding sections. First, the reciprocity between subcommittees of the H.A.C. is strong enough for members of the H.A.C. not on the subcommittee considering an appropriations act to benefit more than nonmembers of the H.A.C. Second, subcommittee chairmen are much more influential within their subcommittee than are nonchairmen; their influence rests largely on their independent resources rather than on an operating consensus within the subcommittee. If subcommittees regularly opposed their chairman whenever he departed from their policy desires to any degree, then the chairman would in reality have little influence over the subcommittee other than his own vote in markup sessions. Third, members of the H.A.C. Public Works Subcommittee have policy desires and goals within the discretion of some of the other subcommittees which nonmembers of the H.A.C. Public Works Subcommittee can affect. If all three of these conditions hold, then we would expect subcommittee chairmen and ranking minority members to get more House-initiated new starts than others would get.

The data presented in earlier sections of this chapter give some support to the first proposition. Members of the H.A.C. do get more new starts than nonmembers get. Fenno's work in *The Power of the Purse* documents the fact that members of the H.A.C. expect preferential treatment by the subcommittees. Fenno also gives some reason to believe that the second proposition is true, although he does not confront it squarely. His study suggests that most chairmen are very influential within their subcommittees (though there is some variation), and that subcommittee members are deferential toward them and willingly grant them wide discretion. This is not enough to establish the truth of the proposition, for it may be that chairmen do not venture outside what they know their subcommittees will accept. Indeed, Fenno argues, they cannot stay long outside this area without strong external support by the full committee chairman and a large portion of the membership of the full committee. It is precisely this question that is at the center of some major studies of influence on Capitol Hill* and that must be answered for subcommittee

* John Manley's study of Wilbur Mills, the chairman of the House Committee on Ways and Means, broaches the dilemma of whether a particularly influential committee chairman is more of a leader than a follower. Manley terms this phenomenon a paradox, saying "The paradox of leadership is that it always involves followsmanship" (*The Politics of Finance*, p. 100). Manley attributes Mills's record of seldom losing on votes within committee or on the floor to the facts that

chairmen in order to affirm or deny the truth of the second proposition.

The third proposition, like the first, is amenable to direct empirical study. The members of the H.A.C. Public Works Subcommittee may care little about policies in areas other than in water resources. They may confine their interests in congressional action to making policy in the natural resource arena and to getting water projects for their districts and states. If this is so, the H.A.C. Public Works Subcommittee members will have little reason to engage in trade with other subcommittees. There is no pretense here of providing a complete description of the degree to which subcommittee members are concerned with the decisions of other subcommittees, but it should be noted, first, that reciprocity has been observed (H.A.C. members do get more new starts than nonmembers get) and, second, that many subcommittee members have expressed concerns and observable constituency interests in other areas.

These three propositions must be true to establish the theoretical expectation that subcommittee chairmen and ranking minority members will do better than other H.A.C. members. Of the three, only the second seems speculative; however, if one accepts Fenno's impressions in this area, it must be regarded as largely true. The following equation examined the resulting hypothesis ($N = 50$):

$$
\begin{aligned}
\text{House new starts for fiscal year 1967} = &-.359 &+ &1.26 &&\text{number of members on the H.A.C.} \\
&(-1.70) &&(7.16) \\
& &+ &.289 &&\text{number of subcommittee} \\
& && (.942) &&\text{chairmen on the H.A.C.} \\
& &- &.265 &&\text{number of ranking minor-} \\
& && (-.840) &&\text{ity members on the H.A.C.} \\
& &+ &.016 &&\text{budgeted construction for} \\
& && (3.23) &&\text{fiscal year 1967} \\
\bar{R}^2 = &.654
\end{aligned}
$$

This equation indicates that subcommittee chairmen get more House new starts than other H.A.C. members do, but that the ranking minority members get fewer. It should be remembered that five of the subcommittee chairmen are also on the H.A.C. Public Works Sub-

---

he is responsive to the desires of the committee and that the committee, for many reasons, is fairly representative of the House as a whole.

committee. Is this finding the result of the "importance" of subcommittee chairmen to their colleagues on the H.A.C. Public Works Subcommittee or is it the result of the preference that the subcommittee shows to its own members? An equation was run to examine this question; it is reproduced below ($N = 50$):

$$
\begin{aligned}
\text{House new starts} \ = \ & .171 \ + \ 1.05 \quad \text{number of members on} \\
\text{for fiscal year} \ & (.634) \quad (2.26) \quad \text{the H.A.C. Public Works} \\
1967 \ & \qquad\qquad\qquad\qquad \text{Subcommittee} \\
\\
& \qquad + \ .446 \quad \text{number of H.A.C. subcom-} \\
& \qquad\quad (1.02) \quad \text{mittee chairmen} \\
\\
& \qquad + \ .859 \quad \text{number of H.A.C. ranking} \\
& \qquad\quad (2.29) \quad \text{minority members} \\
\\
& \qquad + \ .026 \quad \text{budgeted construction for} \\
& \qquad\quad (3.86) \quad \text{fiscal year 1967}
\end{aligned}
$$

$$\bar{R}^2 \ = \ .335$$

This equation indicates that if a subcommittee chairman also happens to be on the H.A.C. Public Works Subcommittee he gets an average of about 1.5 House new starts in a year. If he is not on the subcommittee, his state receives only about .45 new starts, or just half of what a ranking minority member receives. This demonstrates that subcommittee chairmen and ranking minority members do *not* do as well as the members of the H.A.C. Public Works Subcommittee in terms of receiving House new starts. The conclusion drawn here is that power or influence in the full committee is not particularly important in accounting for the distributional characteristics of the H.A.C. Public Works Subcommittee's decisions. Therefore, it is necessary to look inside the subcommittee to see if the most influential members appear to do better than the less influential ones. As we pointed out earlier, this requires time-series data which are not strictly comparable to those presented so far.

The chairmen of the subcommittee dealing with the budget of the Corps of Engineers from the 81st to the 91st Congresses are as follows:

> John Kerr (Democrat–North Carolina), 81st and 82d Congresses
> Glenn Davis (Republican–Wisconsin), 83d Congress
> Clarence Cannon (Democrat–Missouri), 84th to 88th Congresses
> Michael Kirwan (Democrat–Ohio), 89th to 91st Congresses

Wigglesworth (Republican–Massachusetts) was the ranking minority member for the 81st and 82d Congresses, Davis was the ranking minority member in the 84th Congress, Ben Jensen (Republican–Iowa) was the ranking minority member in the 85th to 88th Congresses, and John Rhodes (Republican–Arizona) has been the ranking minority member through the 91st Congress.

The subcommittee chairmen have come from states with different interests in Corps spending. In the 81st and 82d Congresses, North Carolina (the state of John Kerr, the chairman) received more Corps construction money than any of the other states represented on the subcommittee in three out of four years. Similarly, while Kirwan was chairman of the subcommittee, Ohio received more construction money than any other state on the subcommittee. On the other hand, while Glenn Davis was chairman of the subcommittee Wisconsin received no construction funds. During Cannon's ten years as subcommittee chairman, Missouri got more construction money than most states on the subcommittee, generally ranking in the top five or six (out of the ten to fourteen states represented).

The graph in Figure 9.2 plots the average budget request per district for the subcommittee chairmen and for other members of the subcommittee from 1949 to 1968. It is worth pointing out that only during the Republican 83d Congress with Glenn Davis as subcommittee chairman did nonchairmen get more in budgeted construction than did the chairman. This figure supports the hypothesis that the subcommittee chairman will benefit disproportionately from programs of agencies over which his subcommittee has jurisdiction.

Figure 9.2 plots budgeted-construction district averages over time, and therefore represents agency–Budget-Bureau decisions for the 20-year period. It shows that the Corps of Engineers and the Budget Bureau appear to weight their distributive decisions in favor of the subcommittee chairman. A similar graph can be constructed indicating the decisions of the subcommittee over the same period, and Figure 9.3 presents the average change per district in the budget by the subcommittee. Evidently the chairman does not regularly do better than other subcommittee members in terms of changes in the budget request. On ten occasions in the last 20 years congressional districts in the chairman's state did less well (got cut more or raised less) than districts in the states of the other members. The reasons for this are not fully known, but one plausible conjecture is that the Corps and the Budget Bureau might try to anticipate the demands

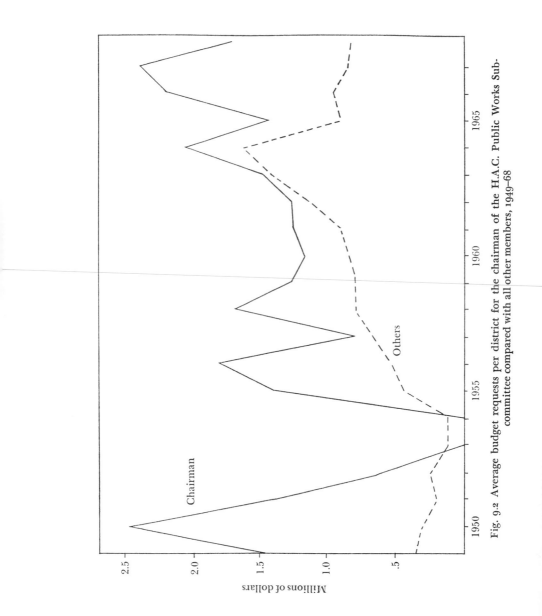

Fig. 9.2 Average budget requests per district for the chairman of the H.A.C. Public Works Sub-committee compared with all other members, 1949–68

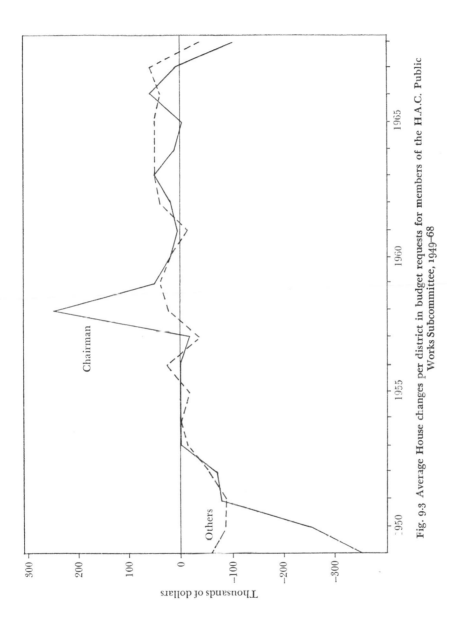

Fig. 9.3 Average House changes per district in budget requests for members of the H.A.C. Public Works Subcommittee, 1949–68

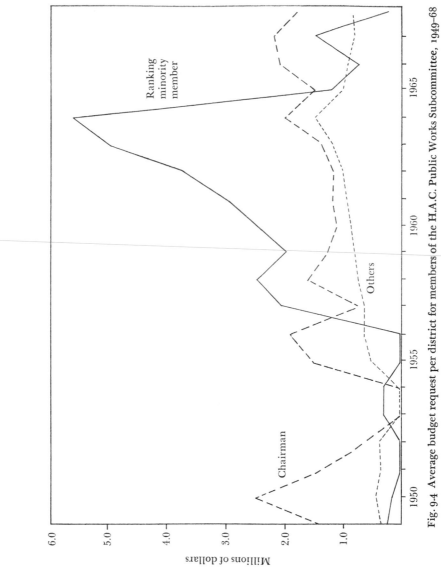

Fig. 9.4 Average budget request per district for members of the H.A.C. Public Works Subcommittee, 1949–68

of the chairman and incorporate them into the budget, which they would not do for others, especially for junior subcommittee members. In other words, the subcommittee chairman may get all he wants in the original budget request. Several Budget Bureau officials (cited earlier in several places) who actually made such decisions candidly admitted that this practice was quite usual.

On combining the information in these two figures, it becomes apparent that the following description of the process would generate similar data to those already observed. The agency's budget contains most of what the chairman wants for his state and substantial portions of what other subcommittee members desire. The Budget Bureau trims the requests for the lower-ranking subcommittee members and for those who are not on the subcommittee, leaving the chairman's share more or less untouched. The subcommittee acts partially as an appeals board for Budget Bureau cuts and particularly restores funds for its own members other than the chairman, since most of what he wanted was already in the budget. The chairman may willingly allow cuts in his state's budget share in order to increase subcommittee support for the final bill, since these cuts will not, in any case, be a large part of his state's total Corps construction budget. This theory is consistent both with the budget data presented in this and previous chapters and with the interviews.

One would expect a similar mechanism to work for the ranking minority member of the subcommittee. Figure 9.4 presents the average district budget request in the states of the ranking minority member, the chairman, and the other members of the subcommittee. This figure should be broken into two parts for proper comprehension: 1949 to 1954, and 1955 to 1968. In the pre-1955 period the ranking minority member averaged more than others on the subcommittee only twice out of six times; both of those times occurred when the Democrats were in the minority. In the post-1955 period the ranking minority member (R.M.M.) averaged more than the other members (excluding the chairman) ten out of 14 times. The R.M.M. averaged more than the chairman on eight of 14 occasions. This figure indicates several things: first, the orientation of subcommittee Republican leaders toward getting public works for their states increased after 1957 (when Ben Jensen became the R.M.M.); second, taken together, the most institutionally powerful members of the H.A.C. Public Works Subcommittee—the chairman and the R.M.M.—benefit more than the other members; third, of passing interest is the fact that while Cannon was chairman and Jensen was R.M.M., Iowa always received more Corps construction than Missouri.

The material presented in this section should leave little doubt that to some extent institutional power within the H.A.C., and especially within the H.A.C. Public Works Subcommittee, is rewarded with public works expenditures. It is important to add that the rewards which accrue to the subcommittee chairman and the ranking minority member appear to be the product of agency and Budget Bureau decisions rather than of subcommittee decisions. Other subcommittee chairmen and ranking minority members not on the H.A.C. Public Works Subcommittee, as well as the more junior H.A.C. Public Works Subcommittee members, appear to benefit from subcommittee actions (House new starts, for example) rather than from agency and Budget Bureau decisions. Obviously much more work needs to be done in this area before anything approaching a complete description can be ventured. It appears on the basis of this evidence that the anticipation of subcommittee reactions by the agency and by the Budget Bureau may account for much of the observed advantages of chairmen and ranking minority members. Their power attracts the deference of those whose futures they can affect.

Conclusion

This chapter and the previous one have explored the general hypothesis that the distribution of divisible policy rewards is related to the distribution of power in the House. The assumption underlying the approach of this chapter was that the size and the relative formality of the House of Representatives make it likely that the power distribution will be closely related to the distribution of institutional resources such as committee memberships and chairmanships. The formal rules for allocating institutional power within the House are largely embodied in the seniority system, the committee assignment system, and the prerogatives of the chairmen of the standing committees. The committee assignment system does not function as automatically as does the seniority system, but there are nonetheless many formalized aspects of the process, one example being norms concerning geographic representation.

The results reported in this chapter appear to support the hypothesis that committee membership, subcommittee chairmanship, and subcommittee membership are strongly related to the distribution of rewards in the appropriations process. This relationship is reflected in decisions made both by the House Appropriations Committee and by the agency and the Budget Bureau.

In addition, these chapters have reported some differing relationships within and between the two congressional parties represented on the committees. These results were not altogether anticipated, and only conjecture or guesswork has been advanced to try to account for them. Among these results were the findings that the H.A.C. Public Works Subcommittee Democrats got more House new starts than the Republicans, but that the Republicans averaged more of the budgeted new starts. The analysis of the previous chapter indicated that Republicans on the H.P.W.C. received more House- and budget-initiated new starts than did committee Democrats. These findings beg for additional research examining varying party orientations to divisible policies within the different committees.

The relationship between institutional resources and the distribution of divisible policies appears to have two separable components. Institutional power resources are generally issue-specific to some degree. That is, a congressman who is assigned to the Armed Services Committee acquires some potential for direct influence over some decisions made in that committee; generally, these decisions will concern the armed services most directly. His influence (if he is able to translate his having a seat on the committee into real influence) in the committee may or may not help him to get more of what he wants in other policy areas. On the other hand, the member of the House Appropriations Committee attains a more widespread grant of potential influence since H.A.C. members accord preferential treatment to their colleagues on the H.A.C. For this reason, when studying the Corps of Engineers' civil construction projects one must examine both the issue-specific power distribution (power in the H.P.W.C. and the H.A.C. Public Works Subcommittee) and the overriding power structure of the House (membership on the H.A.C., committee chairmanships and so forth). In this chapter we found that members of the H.A.C. who were not on the Public Works Subcommittee did do better than nonmembers of the H.A.C. This would give some support to the idea that non-issue-specific institutional resources are related to the distribution of policy outputs.

In order to shed more light on this question, the effects of committee chairmanship were examined and were compared with the effects of some more highly issue-specific resources ($N = 50$):

House new   =   −.305   +   .707   number of members on
starts for fiscal   (−1.62)   (3.69)   the H.A.C.
year 1967
                                +   .657   number of members on
                                   (3.66)   the H.P.W.C.

                                +   .464   number of members on
                                   (1.43)   the H.A.C. Public Works
                                            Subcommittee

                                −   .129   number of chairmen of
                                  (−.785)   committees

                                +   .018   budgeted construction for
                                   (3.97)   fiscal year 1967

          $\bar{R}^2 =$ .724

This relationship suggests that states with committee chairmen and
no other resources are not able to convert that one resource into divisible outputs in the form of Corps water projects. This outcome
tends to affirm the hypothesis that issue-specific resources are more
valuable to a state desiring House new construction starts than generalized influence within the House is. This topic will not be explored in detail, for it would too greatly expand this study, but the
evidence presented here suggests the hypothesis that most of the influence exercised over divisible policy is issue-specific. This hypothesis is in line with Cater's description of certain policy areas (sugar
policy, defense spending) as "subgovernments" that are more or less
closed from outside influence.[13] It also corroborates the view of some
Budget Bureau officials that there is a "rivers and harbors club" which
operates more or less autonomously.

    If these findings are substantiated in other research now being car-
ried out, there will have to be a new formulation made of the contemporary images of the effects of the distribution of power on policy
in Congress. The results reported here indicate that to a considerable
extent the geographic distribution of policy outputs depends on who
in Congress has the power to make decisions over that policy. This
means that the necessity of congressional consideration of policy
shapes the sort of policy made in a predictable and regular manner
irrespective of the distribution of need or demand for the public
projects to be produced.*

    * These remarks would seem to be most relevant to policies that may be charac-
terized as divisible—that is, policies on which it is possible to vary the money

Contemporary advocacy journalists and public interest lobbyists have lately been given to criticizing the fact that old distributive policies never seem to die. The direct tie between the congressman and his constituency makes it extremely difficult for an administration to close military bases which are not needed (at least for military ends). A recent Nader report[14] and some eminent economists have pointed out the senselessness of a continued policy of bringing new lands under irrigation for agricultural use while other lands are being taken out of agricultural use as a result of other federal policies. Environmental groups have recently been frustrated by the very strong congressional support of the Highway Trust Fund set up in 1956 to build and maintain the interstate highway system. Many of the same groups have found it difficult to get congressional support in opposing Corps projects.

There are many other examples of distributive policies pursued by the government with congressional support which appear to have perverse effects on the national welfare (however it is measured). The argument here is that the reasons for strong congressional support for these sorts of policies can be found in the following factors. First, the congressman who desires a career in the House (or Senate) has the incentive and, to a varying extent, the ability to utilize certain policies to achieve his personal career goals. Second, the policies that can be used most easily for this purpose are the distributive ones. Third, the "subgovernment" structure that surrounds decision-making on distributive policies gives a large number of congressmen the ability to extend their influence on projects important to them and to their constituencies. Fourth, the distribution of power within the subgovernments is related to seniority and to committee and subcommittee membership, and as a member stays in Congress he increases his ability to influence decisions in distributive areas. Fifth, some stable system of power distribution in the House is made necessary by its size and work load, and distributive policies generate rewards which can be used to maintain support for the power distribution. In nondistributive areas additional institutional power may not increase one's ability to affect decisions of a majority (even of the less powerful members) all on the other side of the issue. Distributive

---

spent, the services provided, or the projects constructed in one geographical area without affecting the quantity delivered to any other area. This notion of a divisibility issue seems closely related to Theodore Lowi's concept of a distributive issue. For elucidation of this notion, see Lowi's review article "American Business and Public Policy, Case Studies and Political Theory."

policies can be used to provide rewards for career advancement within the House. Sixth, as a member becomes increasingly senior, attains his desired committee, and begins to enlarge his influence over distributive outputs important to his district his opportunities for reelection should increase (he attains more security); consequently, he becomes more influential and has more projects adopted.

This complicated mechanism, if it is a moderately accurate description of a part of congressional behavior, indicates a causal relation between the structure of Congress and the policies that come out of it. It helps explain why the federal government is so adept at "pouring cement" and not at redistributing wealth or opportunity even where that is a desired policy goal on the part of many policymakers.

Many historical questions are posed by this formulation as well. The increase of career orientation on the part of congressmen since the turn of the century has been documented in part by H. Douglas Price,[15] and its role as a causal factor in the increasing "institutionalization" of the House[16] has had the additional consequence—when combined with its effects (the seniority system, etc.)—of determining a part of the policy mix that emerges from the congressional process. Some policy studies of pre-institutionalized Congresses must be made before we can even guess at the magnitude of these effects.

10

The Senate Committees and
the Corps of Engineers' Expenditures

*Power is not where the rules say or appearances suggest it
should be, but where it is found.* —*Ralph Huitt*

The two previous chapters have been based on the hypothesis that
power in the House of Representatives is associated with formal or
institutional resources. Although it has been recognized that two
successive chairmen of the same committee may exert greatly differing amounts of influence within their jurisdictions, as a rule the
chairman will be among the most powerful congressional participants in the issue arena. A position of formal influence in the House
carries with it the automatic deference of junior House members,
bureaucrats, White House program advocates, and senior House colleagues on other committees (who naturally expect reciprocal deference). A House member's small staff, the incentives for legislative
specialization in the House, and the formal and informal prescriptions barring direct interference in the jurisdictions of other committees all enlarge the grant of real influence accompanying chairmanship or membership on a committee whose business is seen as
"important." There have been, to be sure, maverick chairmen in the
House—men who have had less internal influence in the House than
they might have attained had they behaved differently (Wright Patman, Democrat–Texas; Adam Clayton Powell, Democrat–New York).
These men were exceptional, though. They had to be willing to
"go against" the norms and expectations of their colleagues, which
requires a rare perversity. There have also been lazy chairmen and
chairmen who have been unintelligent or uninterested in committee
business; when this has occurred, the ranking minority member (or
sometimes a high-ranking majority member or a group of members)

has sometimes exercised the prerogatives of the chairman. When a chairman (or, more generally, someone vested with formal authority) in the House does not use his potential influence, some other person or group *from within the jurisdictional hierarchy will.* It may be someone on the committee, someone in the agency, someone from the corresponding committee in the Senate, or someone on the House Appropriations Committee.

In the Senate, despite the fact that there are similar grants of formal influence organized by the seniority system and the committee assignment process, the deference that accompanies a chairmanship in the House is not generally forthcoming. Many senators have staff members who work on subjects not within the jurisdictions of those senators' committees and who keep them relatively well informed on the topics before the Senate and its committees. Senators expect to have and to voice opinions on subjects outside their committee jurisdictions. They frequently try to get information about a piece of legislation from sources other than the committee and the (usually allied) agencies. When a senator is made a committee or subcommittee chairman, he must establish his real influence by using the formal resources given to him by seniority. The resulting distribution of influence is much less in accordance with the original distribution of resources than is the influence distribution in the House.

The validity of these remarks varies greatly by committee, since the formal prerogatives of the chairmen vary substantially. The chairmen of the House and Senate Armed Services Committees both have access to classified information not automatically available to other members. In some Senate committees the chairman, the ranking minority member, and ranking majority members are ex officio members of the Appropriations Committee's subcommittee dealing with legislation in the area of their jurisdiction. Some committees in both chambers have established subcommittee structures that the chairman is not completely free to alter to any great extent (Public Works, Appropriations, and others); other committees have no subcommittees (Senate Finance) or a flexible subcommittee system (both Armed Services and Judiciary in the House). Nevertheless, the relative small size and the informality of the Senate restrict the ability of Senate chairmen to act arbitrarily as their House counterparts sometimes do. The resulting distribution of influence is thus more even in the Senate than in the House; it is also more dependent on the personal attributes and initiatives of senators and on chance and circumstance than is the case with the House. The Washington mystique about the

Senate is revealed in talk of "uncrowned kings," "inner clubs," or "one of the ten most powerful men." Journalists and bureaucrats spend substantial amounts of time trying to figure out where influence lies in the Senate, although they all seem to know where it is in the House (they just look at the committee and subcommittee lists). Congressional scholars have repeatedly confirmed the essential informality of power in the Senate that has been attested to by journalists. Huitt says, "Formal powers are less important than the brains and self-confidence to assume a larger role, tempered by the sensitivity to internal controls necessary not to overplay it."[1]

In previous chapters we have suggested that influence in the House is relatively issue-specific. In a sense, there is no single distribution of power in the House but rather many separate ones. The ability of a House member to intervene in setting parity prices on cotton may or may not help him to keep a military base open in his district. The size and the formality of the House make it unlikely that substantial exchanges take place across issues. A more probable arrangement is that a House member decides what sorts of policies he most wants to influence and makes his career choices to maximize influence in those areas. If he wants to exert some influence in other issue areas he must work through his state delegation (if it is large enough to have a wide committee "spread"), his informal group memberships (the Wednesday Club, the Democratic Study Group, Members of Congress for Peace Through Law, and others), his friends on the relevant committees, or the party leadership. Of course trades do take place. Though every congressman, journalist, and bureaucrat has several stories to tell of how this dam was exchanged for a vote on this or that issue, the structures of influence over issues make trades difficult to strike and even more difficult to consummate.*

This chapter will present results roughly comparable to those presented in the two previous chapters. The analysis will focus on two committees: the Senate Public Works Committee (S.P.W.C.) and the Senate Appropriations Committee's Subcommittee on Public Works. The greater procedural informality in the Senate, the more even distribution of influence, and the overlapping characteristics of Senate committees must be expected to modify the results obtained. For this

---

* Exactly who is believed to execute trades seems to depend on the storyteller. Many liberals in and out of Congress claim that the conservative coalition utilizes its strong hold on many policy centers in the Congress to make deals to inhibit the passage of liberal legislation. On the other hand, conservatives have complained about the President's use of certain policies to enhance the chances of passage for parts of his program.

reason, and because of a desire to avoid redundancy, the examination of these two committees will be united in one chapter.

It was noted earlier that members of the H.P.W.C. fell (more or less neatly) into two groups: first, those who were put on the committee, stayed for only one or two Congresses, and then transferred off; second, those who made a career on the committee. Among Democrats, committee "careerists" appeared to include a rather large group of seven to nine members. Once a member had stayed on the committee for more than four terms he stayed on "for good," so to speak. There seemed to be a committee rank, perhaps ninth or tenth among the Democrats, above which continued membership on the H.P.W.C. was more to be desired than a junior spot on a "prestige" committee. If there is a similar rank among Democrats on the S.P.W.C. it would be between second and fifth. Between 1947 and 1970, 72 different senators served on the S.P.W.C. Of these, 20 left the committee because they left the Senate, 37 transferred to another committee, and 15 remained on the committee. Six of the transfers from the S.P.W.C. were to the Appropriations Committee. The average rank on the S.P.W.C. of those who went to the S.A.C. was 3.2 (2.5 for Democrats, 3.5 for Republicans). There were seven transfers to Finance (five Republicans and two Democrats, with average ranks of 9.5 for the Democrats and 4.8 for the Republicans). Three went to Foreign Relations (all three were Democrats), with an average rank of 5. There were five transfers to Armed Services (four Republicans with an average rank on the S.P.W.C. of 3.8, and one Democrat whose rank was 9).

Little can be concluded from these data except perhaps that Democrats showed a preference for Appropriations and Foreign Relations over Finance and Armed Services as measured by the rank they gave up on the S.P.W.C. to obtain the transfer. Republicans appeared to prefer Appropriations and Armed Services to Finance and Foreign Relations. The phenomenon of interest here is that members of both parties gave up the highest ranks for transfers to the S.A.C.

A major reason for this observed willingness to forgo a strong position on the S.P.W.C. appears to have been the expectation of receiving a subcommittee assignment on the Public Works Subcommittee of the S.A.C. Both Democrats who transferred from the S.P.W.C. to the S.A.C., as well as three of the four Republicans, soon went onto the Public Works Subcommittee. The jurisdiction of the two committees is quite similar, so that transferees were not really surrendering any substantial power in the transfer. Rather, they were gaining additional subcommittee assignments over a wider range of agencies and were also obtaining a share of the appropriations power over the Corps of Engineers in return for a share of the power to authorize expenditures. It has been argued that the appropriation decision is much more crucial than the authorization one for most projects.

The Senate Public Works Committee appears to be the lowest ranking major committee in the Senate (eleventh), based on Goodwin's data on committee transfers.[2] It is also ranked low (twelfth) when committees are compared on the basis of the average number of years in the Senate that newcomers to the committee have served before joining the committee.[3] Only a few senators have based their senatorial careers on their membership on the S.P.W.C. The best known of these are John Sherman Cooper (Republican–Kentucky), Robert Kerr (Democrat–Oklahoma), who was also high-ranking on Finance and Aerospace, Edmund Muskie (Democrat–Maine), and perhaps Jennings Randolph (Democrat–West Virginia). Other senators have been on the committee for long periods of time, but few of them have focused as much of their efforts on it as on their other committee assignments.

By way of contrast, the Public Works Subcommittee of the S.A.C. is one of the two or three most prestigious subcommittees of the Senate Appropriations Committee (itself among the most prestigious and influential of Senate committees). Recruitment to subcommittees in the S.A.C. is based on full committee seniority rather than on the discretion of the chairman. For this reason, the measures used by Goodwin and others for evaluating the relative prestige of committees can be usefully applied to the S.A.C. subcommittees. Stephen Horn found that the Defense Subcommittee and the Public Works Subcommittee were the most attractive S.A.C. subcommittees among Democrats on the basis of three different attractiveness measures (proportion of freshman appointees, average seniority, and transfer patterns). For Republicans these two subcommittees were near the top on two of the three measures.[4] The Public Works Subcommittee is characterized by stability and by the fact that its members are among the most influential men in the Senate. Of 13 Democrats on the subcommittee in 1965, ten were full committee chairmen. If one counts the chairman of the Public Works Committee, who sits with the subcommittee ex officio during deliberations on the Corps of Engineers' budget, a subcommittee meeting would include 11 of the 16 committee chairmen in the Senate. The year 1965 was not unusual in this respect.

The Senate Appropriations Committee's
Subcommittee on Public Works

The apparent attractiveness of the Public Works Subcommittee to senators on the Appropriations Committee indicates that senators expect the rewards of subcommittee membership to exceed the costs (in terms of the forfeited membership on another subcommittee and its attendant rewards). There are three policy areas over which the subcommittee has jurisdiction: the Corps of Engineers, the Bureau of Reclamation and certain other agencies within the Interior Department, and the Tennessee Valley Authority. Each of these areas produces policies that have considerable economic impact on particular states and regions. We might therefore expect the potential for distributive benefits implicit in the subject area of the subcommittee to provide a strong attraction to members of the S.A.C.

Membership on the subcommittee would be considered attractive only if it provided members with a greater opportunity to influence budgeting decisions in the three areas than would be available to nonmembers. It is of interest, therefore, to sketch the ways in which decision-making takes place within the subcommittee. The best description of this process can be found in Stephen Horn's *Unused Power.*

First, it is worth noting that on rivers and harbors items the subcommittee is joined by three ex officio members from the Public Works Committee. The influence of the ex officio members over budgetary decisions in this area is formally the same as that of the other subcommittee members—they have a vote in the markup sessions. However, in practice they are not usually as influential as the regular subcommittee members. Fenno quotes a subcommittee chairman: "I don't want to discredit any of those people, but their opinions don't change the result very much. We're a lot more apt to listen to the regular members of the committee and take their advice."[5] Of course, one would expect the relative influence of ex officio members to vary according to the issue area and the personal characteristics of each ex officio member and of the members of the subcommittee. For many years Robert Kerr (Democrat–Oklahoma) was an ex officio member from the Public Works Committee, and no one would dispute his influence in the rivers and harbors policy arena. In fact, Horn writes: "When Robert S. Kerr of Oklahoma was an ex officio member, . . . his aggressiveness and his power within the Senate establishment enabled him to transcend the restriction to rivers and harbors items only and to engage in battle in a markup session on matters of reclamation policy as well."[6]

A second important fact to realize is that though the subcommittee holds markup sessions (just as its House counterpart does) that all subcommittee members can attend, to a great extent most of the actual decisions are made (at least they were during the period under study) by three powerful subcommittee members prior to the markup session. Carl Hayden handled the Interior agencies, sitting through all the hearings and producing a marked up bill pretty much by himself. Senators Hill (Democrat–Alabama) and Ellender (Democrat–Louisiana) had the same sort of authority over the T.V.A. budget and the Army Civil Functions budget. Horn describes Ellender's unquestioned preeminence with respect to Corps spending. "With respect to the army civil functions aspects of the Public Works Subcommittee, Senator Ellender provided a solo performance. After sitting through months of hearings—usually alone—he met with his professional staff members and submitted his recommendations to the subcommittee clearly labeled 'Senator Ellender's recommendations.' "[7] Horn points out in a different part of his book that Ellender's recommendations "were seldom revised because of the respect his colleagues had for his diligence and judgment."[8] Horn also presents a table comparing the percentage of questions asked by subcommittee members for each subcommittee. Ellender asked 88.8 percent of the questions in the Public Works Hearings (1965). This subcommittee had the lowest level of member participation at hearings of any subcommittee.[9]

There are, of course, pre-markup sessions held by the subcommittee chairman and the ranking minority member of the House subcommittees, but subcommittee members expect to participate in markup sessions, especially if they have specialized in an area within the subcommittee's jurisdiction. One gets the impression that if senators on the Public Works Subcommittee want to get a project in a bill, their best strategy would be to pay a visit to Ellender or Hayden or Hill—depending on whose jurisdiction the project was in—rather than to raise the request in the markup session. It appears from Fenno's and Horn's work that even though the Senate as a body is characterized by a more even distribution of resources, the major part of subcommittee decision-making is done by one, two, or three high-ranking members.

Assuming that the preceding remarks are true, and therefore that most of the actual decisions in the public works area are made by two or three men, why would so many powerful senators want to join the subcommittee? It is difficult to answer this question persuasively, although several conjectures may be advanced. The first is that it serves as an economizing device—members of the subcommittee are not expected to attend hearings and rarely do so. Therefore, members are not called upon to expend much effort on this subcommittee (each senator will have five or six subcommittee memberships). The second possibility is that Ellender, Hill, or Hayden may be more likely to take the preferences of their subcommittee colleagues into account before those of other members of the S.A.C. Third, the mere fact of subcommittee membership may be helpful to senators in their home states. There may be other motivations as well. Only the second possibility, that subcommittee members may receive favorable treatment from the Senate subcommittee, will be examined here.

Two personal staff members of a senator who had just joined the subcommittee were asked whether the senator had been having increased success in getting new starts since having gained a subcommittee spot.

We didn't expect to get one-half as much as we did. I was surprised at how much the door was opened once we got on the subcommittee. . . . Before he got on the subcommittee the boss would send a letter to the chairman asking for an addition. When we got one, I'll tell you, it was a strange day. This year we did just the same thing. We wrote a letter to the chairman asking for some new starts. But when the returns came in we had fared a lot better. It was just because we had become a member of the subcommittee. I'll bet we had three new starts out of 16 for the whole country.

The impression gained from this and other interviews can be compared with some statistical information.

Using cross-section data for fiscal year 1967, we can estimate an equation regressing Senate-initiated new starts on membership on the S.A.C. and on the S.A.C. Public Works Subcommittee. The results are presented below ($N = 50$):

$$
\begin{aligned}
\text{Senate new starts} \ = \ &.459 \ + \ .662 \quad &&\text{number of members on the} \\
&(2.09) \quad (1.55) \quad &&\text{S.A.C. Public Works} \\
& &&\text{Subcommittee} \\[6pt]
&\quad\quad\ - \ .381 \quad &&\text{number of members on} \\
&\quad\quad\ \ \ (.904) \quad &&\text{the S.A.C.} \\[6pt]
&\quad\quad\ + \ .007 \quad &&\text{budgeted construction for} \\
&\quad\quad\ \ \ (1.39) \quad &&\text{fiscal year 1967} \\[6pt]
\bar{R}^2 \ = \ &.044
\end{aligned}
$$

The explanatory power of this regression is quite low compared to the results we found in the chapters on the House. Nevertheless, it is worth pointing out that members of the Public Works Subcommittee did do better than those full committee members not on the subcommittee. Subcommittee members averaged about two-thirds of a Senate new start more than full committee people not on the subcommittee. However, this is not a particularly big difference in dollars. It should also be evident that as a result of the attractiveness of the Public Works Subcommittee the membership is generally more senior than the membership of the S.A.C. as a whole. Consequently, part of the small difference could be a result of seniority rather than of subcommittee membership.

The regression equation indicates that Public Works Subcommittee members got more Senate new starts than nonmembers in the calendar year 1966. To add an extra dimension to our analysis of the subcommittee's behavior, we can look at the data on its actions on the House recommendations for states represented on the subcommittee. The first thing to notice is that the S.A.C. Public Works Subcommittee increased the House recommendations for the states represented on it in each of the 20 years from 1949 to 1968. The increase ranged from a high of more than 36 percent in 1949 to lows of just over 2 percent in 1961 and 1966.

These figures can be usefully contrasted with the subcommittee's treatment of states not represented on it. Figure 10.1 compares the subcommittee's recommendations for represented states with its recommendations for nonrepresented states. In 16 of the 20 years the states not represented on the subcommittee received *greater* percentage increases than the states represented on the subcommittee. These data taken by themselves might seem to indicate that members of the S.A.C. Public Works Subcommittee treat their own states worse than they treat other states. What would explain this behavior?

Senate increases above House recommendations come from two sources: Senate-initiated new starts, and restorations of House cuts in the recommendations for projects. The regression equation for fiscal year 1967 indicated that the states represented on the S.A.C. Public Works Subcommittee did a little better than other states with respect to obtaining Senate new starts. It is appropriate, therefore, to examine the hypothesis that since states represented on the subcommittee receive fewer cuts in their budgets than other states to begin with, they are in need of fewer restorations. The small Senate increases over the House recommendations may be explained by the more lenient treat-

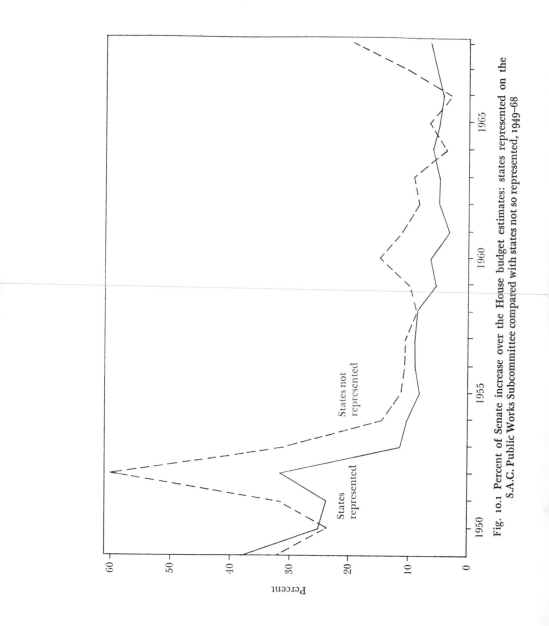

Fig. 10.1 Percent of Senate increase over the House budget estimates: states represented on the S.A.C. Public Works Subcommittee compared with states not so represented, 1949–68

ment of the Corps' budget requests by the House Appropriations Committee for the states represented on the Senate subcommittee.

This theory is plausible from the point of view of the H.A.C. Public Works Subcommittee. After all, it was argued earlier that one way for the H.A.C. Public Works Subcommittee to preserve its influence is for it to make recommendations that will not be overturned in the appropriations process. The subgovernment notion advanced in this study would seem to lead to the House subcommittee's favorable treatment of projects located in the states of senators who have institutional leverage over the Corps of Engineers' budget. In the temporal context of the appropriations process this phenomenon might be considered institutionalized anticipated reaction. Table 10.1 examines this hypothesis. Note that states represented on the S.A.C. Public Works Subcommittee tend to receive smaller cuts than other states, and that they receive (for that reason) smaller Senate increases.

This analysis provides further evidence about the nature of the shift in behavior in 1955. House cuts were frequently very large prior to that year, and the Senate consequently responded by restoring large amounts to the Corps' budget. Interestingly enough, in comparing those states represented on the subcommittee with others for the years 1949–54, the Senate recommendation constituted a higher percentage of the original budget request for those states on the subcommittee than for the others for five of the six years. The comparable figures for the 1955 to 1968 period showed that the states represented on the subcommittee did better than the other states eight out of 14 times. Between 1949 and 1954 the Senate recommendation for states represented on the subcommittee was lower than the budget request in four of the six years. For states not represented on the subcommittee the Senate figure was lower than the budget figure in five of the six years. After 1955 the Senate figure was lower than the budget request

TABLE 10.1

House Cuts and Senate Additions for States Represented
on the S.A.C. Public Works Subcommittee

		SENATE ADDITIONS	
		States on subcommittee get larger additions than other states	States on subcommittee get smaller additions than other states
HOUSE CUTS	State on subcommittee get larger cuts than other states	2	1
	States on subcommittee get smaller cuts than other states	2	15

only once for the states not represented on the subcommittee, and it was never below the budget estimate for the states represented on the subcommittee.

These results must be compared with those obtained in Chapter 9 for the H.A.C. Public Works Subcommittee. The Senate data reveal only a limited amount of favored treatment by the S.A.C. Public Works Subcommittee for its own members. What is revealed, though, is the tendency of the H.A.C. Public Works Subcommittee not to cut funds for the states of senators on the S.A.C. Public Works Subcommittee. A senator will find it desirable to join the S.A.C. Public Works Subcommittee, then, for two separate reasons. The first is that membership will accord him status in the public works "subgovernment" and therefore favored treatment by its constituents outside the Senate (the House subcommittee, the O.M.B., and the Corps of Engineers). The second, and apparently lesser reason, is that his state's construction requests will receive somewhat better treatment from the S.A.C. Public Works Subcommittee itself. There appears to be a tendency for the states of senators on the subcommittee to end up with higher proportions of the budget estimates than other states receive, but much of the difference since 1955 has been the direct result of the behavior of the House subcommittee rather than the Senate subcommittee. These data do not tell conclusively how the S.A.C. Public Works Subcommittee would have acted if the House cut the budget relatively more deeply in the states represented on the subcommittee than in the remaining states. Thus it remains possible that the reason for the observed House preference for states on the S.A.C. Public Works Subcommittee rests on the expectation on the part of the House subcommittee that were they to cut deeply their actions would merely be reversed.

These findings provide a limited answer to the question asked at the beginning of this section: Why is the Public Works Subcommittee so attractive to S.A.C. members? There is only a weak relationship between committee membership and Senate new starts. It is possible that the relatively even distribution of resources in the Senate makes these small differences all that can be expected. This possibility is certainly consistent with the egalitarian and informal image of the Senate presented in Huitt's articles. The distribution of House-initiated new starts turned out to be dominated largely by institutional factors; Senate new starts may be determined more by strategic factors beyond the scope of this work than by the institutional factors being studied here.* Some senators may find that their electoral fate depends less on their ability to get a few projects for their state than on their ability to produce some larger policy. They may then find it useful to employ whatever leverage they have over public works policy to help win support for some other policy. Bolling's conjecture that public works spending is a hidden buttress of the conservative coalition may be much more appropriate in reference to the Senate than in reference to the House.[10] For what it is worth, the composition of the S.A.C. Public Works Subcommittee is heavily weighted with key members of the conservative coalition. However, this possibility must be explored in another piece of research. It is advanced here only as a plausible explanation for some of the results observed in this section. Nonetheless, these remarks should not downgrade the more or less unexpected finding that subcommittee membership results in favored treatment by the House Appropriations Committee. This finding adds another support to the subgovernment image that we have been constructing.

The Senate Public Works Committee

The Senate Public Works Committee (S.P.W.C.), relative to the S.A.C. Public Works Subcommittee, is a low-prestige, low-seniority committee. It has, of course, no authority over budgetary decisions (other than the fact that it can send three ex officio members† to the S.A.C. Public Works Subcommittee), so that the reasons why we might expect its members to receive favored treatment at the hands of the S.A.C. Public Works Subcommittee, the H.A.C. Public Works Subcommittee, or the Budget Bureau are indirect. The S.P.W.C. has jurisdiction over the Omnibus Rivers and Harbors and Flood Control Bill and can pass committee resolutions to study projects that have received unfavorable reports from the Corps of Engineers (see Chapter 1). In Chapter 8 we found that members of the H.P.W.C. received special consideration from the H.A.C. Public Works Subcommittee

---

* This theory must remain a conjecture since no data in this study demonstrate that Senate new starts are initiated according to the strategic purposes of any group of senators. However, the cross-section regressions I have presented do indicate that institutional factors are incapable of explaining the distribution of new starts.

† The ex officio members from the S.P.W.C. are frequently, though not always, the top two members of the majority party and the ranking minority member. There have been many exceptions to this pattern—especially on the majority side —and one cannot meaningfully speak of a rule or norm governing the choice of ex officio members.

(for example, they received greater numbers of House-initiated new starts than other House members received). A similar set of hypotheses to the ones put forth in that chapter are advanced here with reference to the S.P.W.C.

Since the S.P.W.C., like most Senate committees, does much of its work in subcommittee, for the following analyses attention will be focused on the S.P.W.C. Rivers and Harbors and Flood Control (R.H.F.C.) Subcommittee. Jennings Randolph (Democrat–West Virginia), the second-ranking Democrat on the full committee, was the chairman of the R.H.F.C. Subcommittee. The chairman of the full committee, Pat McNamara (Democrat–Michigan), was known to take little interest in the Corps' construction program. John Sherman Cooper (Republican–Kentucky) was the ranking minority member on both the full committee and the subcommittee.

In order to examine the relationship between committee membership and constituency benefits, the Senate new-starts variable will be employed. "Senate new starts" was regressed on "number of seats held on the S.P.W.C.R.H.F.C. Subcommittee" controlling for budget size, and it was found that the subcommittee members averaged only a little over one-fifth of a Senate new start more than nonmembers. The $\bar{R}^2$ for the equation was .025. The relationship is in the expected direction, although there is considerable unexplained variation, as above. In other words, the institutional factor of subcommittee membership appears to have a barely noticeable, though positive, effect on how many Senate new starts a senator's state receives; however, there are apparently many other variables operating at the same time. Possible explanations for the generally low explanatory power of the "institutional effects" model were ventured in the previous section and need not be reiterated.

It was argued in the previous section that two types of benefits accrue to a senator as a result of membership on the S.A.C. Public Works Subcommittee. One type is his increased ability to get things he wants from the subcommittee. The other type is the preferred treatment he receives from other decision-makers in the water projects decision area. In particular, we found that the H.A.C. Public Works Subcommittee tended to make fewer cuts in the budget requests of states represented on the S.A.C. Public Works Subcommittee than it did in the requests of other states. Do these two categories of benefits extend as well to membership on the S.P.W.C.R.H.F.C. Subcommittee?

"House cuts in the budget request" for states represented on the

S.P.W.C.R.H.F.C. Subcommittee were compared with cuts for other states from 1949 to 1968. In 13 of the 20 years, all those states not represented on the subcommittee had their budget requests cut more deeply than those represented on the subcommittee. The House actually increased the budget request for states represented on the subcommittee in seven of the 20 years, whereas states not represented on the subcommittee received an increase in only four years. Evidently, membership on this subcommittee does produce *both* kinds of benefits for senators.

The House tends to cut the Corps' construction budgets for states not represented on the S.P.W.C.R.H.F.C. Subcommittee more deeply than it does for those states that are so represented. At the same time, we might expect that the S.A.C. Public Works Subcommittee, acting as an "appeals court," would tend to restore more funds to those states that had their budgets cut most deeply in the House. Indeed, in 15 of the 20 years, the states not represented on the S.P.W.C.R.H.F.C. Subcommittee received larger percentage increases than those represented on the subcommittee received. Table 10.2 compares House cuts for states on and not on the subcommittee with Senate additions. Senate additions were consistent with the "appeals court" hypothesis on 16 of 20 occasions.

How do the benefits obtained from membership on the S.A.C. Public Works Subcommittee compare with those gained from membership on the S.P.W.C.R.H.F.C. Subcommittee? Comparing the two reported regression equations indicates that the S.A.C. Public Works Subcommittee members average about one-third of a new start more than nonmembers, whereas S.P.W.C.R.H.F.C. Subcommittee members average approximately one-fifth of a new start more than nonmembers. Running a "combined model" equation utilizing membership on both subcommittees as independent variables yields Table

TABLE 10.2
House Cuts and Senate Additions for States Represented on the S.P.W.C.R.H.F.C. Subcommittee

		SENATE ADDITIONS	
		States on S.P.W.C.R.H.F.C. get larger additions than others	States off S.P.W.C.R.H.F.C. get larger additions than those on subcommittee
HOUSE CUTS	States on S.P.W.C.R.H.F.C. get larger cuts than others	3	4
	States off S.P.W.C.R.H.F.C. get larger cuts than those on subcommittee	0	13

TABLE 10.3

The Effects of Subcommittee Membership

	On Senate R.H.F.C.	Off Senate R.H.F.C.
On S.A.C. Public Works	.963	.675
Off S.A.C. Public Works	.558	.260

NOTE: Entries are the estimated number of Senate new starts for fiscal year 1967 after controlling for budget size.

10.3 (with $\bar{R}^2 = .053$). This table indicates that membership on the S.A.C. Public Works Subcommittee is slightly more valuable in terms of Senate new starts than membership on the S.P.W.C.R.H.F.C. Subcommittee. Four states (California, Maine, Oklahoma, and West Virginia) had senators on both committees; as can be seen from the table, these four states averaged nearly one Senate new start for fiscal year 1967 (under the linear combined effects model).

It is instructive now to turn to the second category of benefits: preferred treatment at the hands of the H.A.C. Public Works Subcommittee. The House cut budget requests of the S.P.W.C.R.H.F.C. Subcommittee more deeply than the S.A.C. Public Works Subcommittee on 14 out of 20 occasions. Moreover, the S.A.C. Public Works Subcommittee members reecived net budget increases from the House for their states on eight occasions, whereas S.P.W.C.R.H.F.C. Subcommittee members received such increases only seven times. It can be tentatively concluded from this longitudinal data that the H.A.C. Public Works Subcommittee shows a preference for the states represented on the S.A.C. Public Works Subcommittee over the states represented on the S.P.W.C.R.H.F.C. Subcommittee, and that membership on either subcommittee results in more favorable House treatment than is received by states without any such representation.

One final comparison between the two subcommittees is possible. When examining data on Senate additions to House recommendations over time, it was apparent that House cuts in effect "caused" a substantial portion of the Senate additions under what is termed the "appeals court" hypothesis (see Chapter 6). Two tables have been presented (Tables 10.1 and 10.2) that examined the degree to which the appeals court idea explained the Senate increase in the budget. An observation was considered to be consistent with the appeals court notion if the group of states receiving the deepest House cuts sub-

TABLE 10.4
Deviant Cases from the Appeals Court Hypothesis

	S.A.C. Public Works Subcommittee	S.P.W.C.R.H.F.C. Subcommittee
Subcommittee states are cut deeper than other states but get smaller Senate additions	1	4
Other states are cut deeper but subcommittee states get larger Senate additions	2	0

sequently received the largest Senate additions. It was found that the data comparing states represented on the S.A.C. Public Works Subcommittee with those not so represented (Table 10.1) were consistent with the appeals court theory on 17 of 20 occasions. The data comparing states represented on the S.P.W.C.R.H.F.C. Subcommittee with others (Table 10.2) were in line with the appeals court idea 16 of 20 times. It is instructive to examine the cases that did not fit in with the appeals court idea and to compare them for the two subcommittees. Table 10.4 presents this comparison. Obviously there are not many cases examined here, but the thing to notice is that the data show a clear advantage for the S.A.C. Public Works Subcommittee members over the S.P.W.C.R.H.F.C. Subcommittee members in gaining benefits for their states.

The comparisons ventured in this section appear to fit neatly into a single fabric. Two categories of benefits resulting from representation on a water-resources-related committee have been isolated and identified. As we found when we examined the House, in the Senate the Appropriations Subcommittee accords itself clear preference over the Authorization Committee in its allocation of new starts. But membership on the Authorization Committee does seem to bring some rewards to the state of the senator. The interesting phenomenon of favorable treatment by the H.A.C. Public Works Subcommittee for what may be called "subgovernment members" in the Senate has been shown to extend beyond the two appropriations subcommittees to the members of the Authorization Committee in the Senate as well as in the House (see Chapter 8).

The Effects of Political Party Within the Committees

The S.A.C. Public Works and the S.P.W.C.R.H.F.C. subcommittees are internally organized according to political party and seniority in the full committee. The facts that recruitment to the subcommittees is conducted within each party separately, that the subcommittee staff is allocated separately to the majority and the minority, and that succession to the chairmanships is organized within the party provide ample reason to suspect that the benefits accruing to the members of the two subcommittees may vary according to political party. In the chapter on the H.P.W.C. it was reported that the committee Republicans averaged more new starts than the Democrats (this difference was accounted for by the fact that the high-seniority Republicans received more new starts than the high-seniority Democrats did, whereas the low-seniority groups in both parties received about the same number of new starts). On the H.A.C. Public Works Subcommittee, however, the Democratic members were more successful than the Republicans in getting new starts for their states. On the Senate side, the collegial nature of the chamber and the importance of the reciprocity norm might lead us to expect only small differences in benefits between the parties. On the other hand, since the Democrats have controlled Congress since 1955, it is possible that we might find a reflection of this party dominance in the distribution of benefits to committee members.

In the previous section, two sorts of benefits that accrue to the members of each of the two Senate subcommittees were identified. One benefit was that a senator's state would receive more favorable treatment at the hands of the Senate and its committees with respect to water projects if that senator was a member of a committee with jurisdiction over the Corps of Engineers. The second benefit was the preferred treatment a senator's projects would receive at the hands of the House and its committees. It will be easier to examine the second type of benefit first, since otherwise the "appeals court" role of the Senate can obscure its actions as a *de novo* initiator of benefits to senators.

Democratic and Republican members of the S.A.C. Public Works Subcommittee over the period 1949–68 were compared. On 14 of 20 occasions the House cut (in percentage) funds for the states of Republican senators more than it cut funds for the states of Democratic senators. The Republicans suffered greater cuts than the Democrats did even during the Republican 83d Congress. The states of Democratic members of the S.A.C. Public Works Subcommittee received *increases* from the House in nine of the 20 years, whereas the states represented on the subcommittee by Republicans received increases in eight of the 20 years. These data indicate that the House tends to treat the Democratic Senate subcommittee members slightly better than it treats the Republicans. The differences are not particularly

TABLE 10.5
*House Cuts and Senate Additions for States Represented
on the S.A.C. Public Works Subcommittee, by Party*

| | | SENATE ADDITIONS | |
		Democrats get larger additions than Republicans	Republicans get larger additions than Democrats
HOUSE CUTS	Democrats get larger cuts than Republicans	6	0
	Republicans get larger cuts than Democrats	2	12

large, but they offer some support for the idea that the dominant party members receive more benefits than the minority party members.

Does the Senate (or in particular, the S.A.C. Public Works Subcommittee) show any preference for Democratic subcommittee members? In 12 of the years 1949–68, Republicans received larger increases from the Senate than Democrats did. This observation may be accounted for in the two ways mentioned in the previous section: first, by the appeals court hypothesis; second, by the preferred treatment of one or the other party. Table 10.5 compares the Senate response to House recommendations for Democrats and for Republicans. Eighteen of the 20 cases between 1949 and 1968 conform to the appeals court hypothesis. The two cases that do not conform to that hypothesis show preferred treatment for Democrats.

One hesitates to draw a conclusion from just two cases. We can draw further information from these data, however, through another sort of analysis. By regressing Senate increases on House cuts (in millions of dollars), the following equations were obtained for the states of the Democratic and Republican members of the S.A.C. Public Works Subcommittee ($N = 20$):

Democrats, Senate increases $= \$12.67 + .412$ House cuts
$$\bar{R}^2 = .51$$
Republicans, Senate increases $= \$3.73 + .718$ House cuts
$$\bar{R}^2 = .94$$

These two equations may be taken as estimates of the "decision rule" used by the S.A.C. Public Works Subcommittee in the states of its Democratic and Republican members. The estimated decision rule for the Republicans appears to be a particularly close approximation of the actual behavior of the subcommittee. As an example of the use of these equations, suppose the House were to cut a total of ten million dollars from the construction budgets for the states of both

Democrats and Republicans on the Senate subcommittee. The Senate, according to these "decision rules," would be expected to add $16.79 million to the construction figure for the Democrats and $10.91 million to the construction figure for the Republicans. In this particular case the Democrats receive more in Senate additions than the Republicans receive. Notice that for states represented by either Democrats or Republicans the S.A.C. Public Works Subcommittee acts as an "appeals court," since it simply restores funds according to a different decision rule for each set of states.

Utilizing these two equations we can determine that whenever the House cuts less than $28.8 million from the construction requests for a group of states, the decision rule for the Democrats will produce larger Senate additions than the decision rule for the Republicans will produce. Over the 20-year period from 1949 to 1968, by grouping the states of the S.A.C. Public Works Subcommittee members into those represented by Democrats and those represented by Republicans, we obtain 40 House recommendations. Only nine of these 40 House recommendations entailed cuts greater than $28.8 million. The average House cut was $13.12 million for Republicans and $4.65 million for Democrats. Therefore, we may conclude that for the "normal" range of House decisions (those near the mean) the appeals court decision rule used by the Senate subcommittee for states represented on it by Democrats was more lenient than the decision rule used for states represented by Republicans.

These results indicate that, though it is true that Senate additions are largely explained by the appeals court hypothesis, the Republican and Democratic subcommittee members can expect substantially different treatment before this "court." There appears to be a definite advantage to being a member of the party in the majority on this "jury." This analysis has some implications for the whole "Senate-as-appeals-court" idea. There are many ways for the Senate to act as an appeals court and still exercise considerable distributive discretion in deciding what funds go where. The projects the Senate chooses to initiate, and the ones it decides to "speed up" or to restore funds cut in the House to, are matters of choice to the S.A.C. Public Works Subcommittee, despite the fact that nearly all of this behavior can be accounted for by a crude appeals court model. Such accounting would be deceptive, since much interesting behavior can occur within the confines of the appeals court hypothesis. In other words, the statement that the Senate's behavior is chiefly a response to House action does not exhaust the possibilities of analysis of the Senate's role in

TABLE 10.6

Net Change in Budget Figures for States Represented
on the S.A.C. Public Works Subcommittee, by Party

	Democrats	Republicans
Number of times the conference figure was smaller than the budget request	6	10
Number of times the conference figure was larger than the budget request	13	9

NOTE: Conference data were not available for 1950.

policy-making in the public works area. Rather, it introduces the twin questions considered here. How does the Senate respond to the House action (which items or projects get restored, added, or changed)? What happens in cases in which Senate behavior cannot be classed as a response to House action (are there regularities observed in the deviant cases)?

It is of some interest to compare the final appropriations figure with the Budget Bureau's initial recommendation in order to attempt to assess the net effect of the congressional appropriations process on the allocations by party for members of the S.A.C. Public Works Subcommittee. Table 10.6 makes this comparison. The states of Democratic members of the S.A.C. Public Works Subcommittee fare much better in the appropriations process as a whole than the states represented by Republicans do. Just as was the case with the H.A.C. Public Works Subcommittee, the Democratic members seem to receive more benefits from membership than the Republicans receive. To complete the investigation into the advantages of majority party members in attaining benefits from subcommittee membership, we must examine the data for the S.P.W.C.R.H.F.C. Subcommittee. Democratic dominance during all but two of the years for which data were available prohibited testing with the time-series data the questions of whether the majority party does better or whether the Democrats do better no matter which party is in the majority. Some comparative cross-section studies must be made with project-by-project data in order to separate these two hypotheses conclusively.

Comparing the states of the Democratic and Republican members of the S.P.W.C.R.H.F.C. Subcommittee, it was found that the House cut larger amounts of funds slated for the states represented by Republicans than it cut for states represented by Democrats on 12 of 20 occasions. The House recommended increases over the budget requests for states represented by Republicans in seven of the 20 years, and by Democrats in nine of the 20 years. These data indicate, as did those for the S.A.C. Public Works Subcommittee, that the Democratic members of the S.P.W.C.R.H.F.C. Subcommittee usually receive better treatment than the Republicans at the hands of the House. In terms of the two types of benefits enumerated earlier, the Democratic subcommittee members seem to receive more benefits from membership in the public works "subgovernment" (the second type of benefit) than Republicans do.

The other type of benefit under investigation is that received from Senate action itself. Three tests were made to determine whether Democratic subcommittee members benefited more than Republicans from Senate action (generally, this concerns action by the S.A.C. Public Works Subcommittee on the Corps' construction budget). These three tests were identical to those made for the S.A.C. Public Works Subcommittee. First, we determined the number of times the Democratic subcommittee members received larger percentage increases than the Republicans over the House figures. Second, the "deviant" cases under the crude appeals court model (for example, the group that received the largest House cut received the largest compensatory Senate increase) were examined to see what, if any, bias they displayed. Third, the appeals court decision rule itself was analyzed to see if it entailed a more favorable payoff to members of one party than to members of the other.

It has repeatedly been demonstrated that the Senate increases the budget over the House recommendations. The percentage increases made by the Senate for each year from 1949 to 1968 were computed separately for the states represented on the S.P.W.C.R.H.F.C. Subcommittee by Democrats and for the states represented by Republicans. In only eight of 20 cases did the Republicans receive larger percentage increases than the Democrats. Therefore, we can conclude that Democrats tend to receive larger increases than Republicans do.

Are these data "explained" by the appeals court hypothesis? Do the Republicans receive larger increases than the Democrats only in years when they suffer larger cuts? The answer to this question is yes. Table 10.7 indicates that for each of the eight years that Republicans did better than Democrats before the S.A.C. Public Works Subcommittee the Republicans had suffered greater budget cuts than the Democrats at the hands of the House. Of course, the converse could not be the case since the Democrats had funds cut more severely by the House than the Republicans on only eight occasions, but received the larger Senate increase 12 times. The four deviant cases from the simple

TABLE 10.7

*House Cuts and Senate Additions for States Represented
on the S.P.W.C.R.H.F.C. Subcommittee, by Party*

		SENATE ADDITIONS	
		Democrats get larger additions than Republicans	Republicans get larger additions than Democrats
HOUSE CUTS	Democrats get larger cuts than Republicans	8	0
	Republicans get larger cuts than Democrats	4	8

appeals court model are in the direction of Senate actions favoring the Democratic subcommittee members.

The appeals court decision rules themselves were analyzed. Senate recommendations (in millions of dollars) were regressed on House recommendations (in millions of dollars) for the two sets of states (those represented by Democrats and those represented by Republicans) on the S.P.W.C.R.H.F.C. Subcommittee. The following two equations were estimated ($N = 20$):

Democrats, Senate recommendations $= \$5.01 + .581$ House recommendations

$$\bar{R}^2 = .73$$

Republicans, Senate recommendations $= \$3.15 + .792$ House recommendations

$$\bar{R}^2 = .94$$

Using these estimates, some simple calculations indicate that the Senate will add more dollars to the budgets of states represented by Democrats than it will add to the budgets of states represented by Republicans whenever the House cuts less than $10.87 million. Of 40 appropriations recommendations made by the House over the 20-year period from 1949 to 1968 (20 recommendations for each party), only eight contained cuts greater than $10.87 million. Therefore, we may conclude that over the "normal range" of House cuts the Senate's estimated decision rule for Democratic members of the S.P.W.C.R.H.F.C. Subcommittee is more generous than the corresponding rule for Republican subcommittee members.

The last set of data examined compared the conference figure with the initial budget request for members in each of the two parties within the S.P.W.C.R.H.F.C. Subcommittee. This comparison might

TABLE 10.8

*Net Change in Budget Figures for States Represented
on the S.P.W.C.R.H.F.C. Subcommittee, by Party*

	Democrats	Republicans
Number of times the conference figure was smaller than the budget request	7	9
Number of times the conference figure was larger than the budget request	12	10

NOTE: Conference data were not available for 1950.

be said to evaluate the net effects (in some aggregate sense) of the congressional appropriations process. Table 10.8 presents these results.

It has been demonstrated that, in the Senate, Democratic members of both the relevant subcommittees—authorizations and appropriations—tend to do better than Republican members in both of the categories of benefits employed here. This statement can be made with some confidence since each of the tests of this hypothesis has rendered the same verdict. The clear pattern revealed here is partly to be expected for the following reason: to the extent that the two parties have any ideological focus, the Democrats' philosophy is more consistent with public works undertakings than the Republicans' is. Even those Democrats who are conservative on other issues often favor increased expenditures on water projects and other public works items. The Democrats have controlled Congress for the entire 20-year period we have analyzed—with the single exception of the 83d Congress. The fact that Republican ideology seems to have an anti–public-works bias (or at least had such a bias during the 80th and 83d Congresses) may have inhibited any development of pork barrel politics among Republicans when they had control of Congress. Consequently, what was observed over the whole 20-year period was a preference on the part of decision-makers in the public works area for projects in those states represented in the water-project subgovernment by Democrats. This pattern was broken only in the case of the House Public Works Committee, where high-seniority Republicans were the most advantaged group. This phenomenon needs more investigation before too much is made of it.

The Influence of Seniority

The congressional seniority rule referred to by scholars, pundits, and politicians is a method of choosing the chairman of each standing committee. Nelson Polsby and his coauthors characterize a seniority system as a system in which the choice of chairman is based solely on committee seniority (longest continuous service); therefore, it is an automatic procedure that leaves no discretion in anyone's hands. There is little disagreement among scholars that a seniority system in this sense has prevailed in both houses of Congress for many years —at least since 1925.[11]

There are, of course, other kinds of seniority aside from committee seniority. Barbara Hinckley has demonstrated that there is only an imperfect relationship between chamber seniority and committee seniority, since many congressmen change committees at various stages of their congressional careers.[12] Chamber seniority is employed as the criterion by which office space, Capitol Hill patronage (policemen, pages, elevator operators, and so on), and seating at official gatherings are allocated. In addition, Senate Republicans have traditionally employed chamber seniority as the sole yardstick in allocating committee assignments.[13] In both the House and the Senate, the two parties use chamber seniority as one criterion (or, as with the Senate Republicans, the sole criterion) for determining committee assignments. However, there are many cases in which other criteria are employed.

A third kind of seniority, and one seldom discussed by congressional scholars, is subcommittee seniority. Certain congressional committees apparently utilize this kind of seniority as a criterion for allocating subcommittee chairmanships. The dearth of research in this area, however, precludes anything other than speculation on this point.

Within the party delegations on congressional committees, the principal organizational decisions that are made include the allocation of the committee chairmanship, the establishment of subcommittees and their staffs and jurisdictions, the choice of the membership of the subcommittees, and the choice of the subcommittee chairmen. In many committees "seniority" (usually committee seniority) plays an important part in some of these decisions, although on other committees it plays a lesser part. For example, in some committees recruitment to subcommittees is heavily dependent on the expressed preferences of the committee members, and conflicts are resolved according to committee seniority. This system is employed on the S.A.C., according to Horn.[14] It is difficult to determine from Horn's description if the chairman could intervene in such decisions arbitrarily—as the chairman of the H.A.C. is apparently free to do.[15] If the chairman is not able to intervene, then this method of recruitment would be called a seniority *system* according to Polsby's criteria, and it would constitute a decentralizing force within the committee.[16] On some committees, subcommittee assignments are determined strictly according to members' preferences, and there are always enough seats to go around. The House Foreign Affairs Committee and the House Committee on Education and Labor are two such committees. In such cases we might say that the committees are using a seniority rule for subcommittee recruitment since the chairman exercises no discretion. The abundance of subcommittee seats ensures that conflict over seating rarely occurs.*

Committee seniority is frequently employed to determine subcommittee chairmanships. If there are, say, five subcommittees, then each of the five top-ranking Democrats might be chairman of a subcommittee. This system can work in at least two different ways. On the H.P.W.C. each of the top Democrats must take his allotted subcommittee chairmanship. James Murphy gives the following illustrative anecdote in this regard.[17] A senior committee Democrat became eligible for a subcommittee chairmanship in an area of little interest to him. He proposed forgoing the chairmanship, since accepting it would have forced him to transfer off a subcommittee of more importance to him. The top-ranking committee Democrats objected that his proposal would upset the stable seniority rule, and they insisted that he take the chairmanship for the sake of preserving the rule. In the S.A.C., on the other hand, the top Democrats have "claims" on the subcommittee chairmanships in the sense that they have "the right of first refusal" in order of seniority whenever a chairmanship becomes available. Thomas Wolanon studied the use of committee seniority in allocating subcommittee chairmanships in the House, and he found that although such a rule accounted for most of the subcommittee chairmanships allocated, there were numerous exceptions. The committee exhibiting the most frequent violations of this stable seniority rule was the H.A.C.[18]

According to Polsby's criterion, we should not conclude from Wolanon's analysis that there is a strict or rigid seniority system governing the allocation of subcommittee chairmanships. The frequency of violations of the seniority system indicates that committee seniority

---

* In committees where members' preferences are the major criterion used in recruitment to subcommittees, seniority may or may not be important. The subcommittees may simply change in size from session to session to accommodate the demand for subcommittee seats. Where subcommittees are of fixed size a seniority criterion may be used to routinely resolve conflicts over scarce seats. It would seem to be sensible to speak of a seniority system for allocating subcommittee seats only when seniority was the only criterion in use for adjudicating conflicts.

is only *usually* followed in choosing subcommittee chairmen. The fact that it is not always employed as the sole criterion means that some residual discretion is left to someone—presumably the chairman of the full committee. On the other hand, the apparent violations may be accounted for in another way. Some committees may be employing a different seniority rule—for example, they may be using *subcommittee* seniority to choose subcommittee chairmen. In many cases, and perhaps in most, the two criteria employed would result in the same choices of subcommittee chairmen (depending, of course, on the frequency with which committee members transfer among subcommittees). However, it is possible for both criteria to be used in the same committee when tempered with the discretion of the committee chairman. In such a case there would be no seniority "system" in the sense in which the word has been used.

It would seem that the use of a seniority system (of either sort discussed) within a committee would tend to decentralize authority to subcommittee chairmen and away from the chairman of the full committee. The use of a seniority system (seniority in the full committee in this case) to allocate vacant seats on subcommittees—a frequent practice in Senate committees—would seem to impose limits on the authority of the chairman (and also, of course, on the authority of the ranking minority member). A simple explanation of the possible cases according to the use or nonuse of the available seniority rules for choosing subcommittee members and allocating subcommittee chairmanships yields the results found in Table 10.9. Committees have been only tentatively placed in the table's cells. It may be argued that the H.A.C. ought to be in the upper left-hand cell, or at

TABLE 10.9

Use of Seniority as a Criterion for Making Organizational Decisions Within Committees

RULE FOR CHOOSING SUBCOMMITTEE CHAIRMAN	RULE FOR ALLOCATING VACANT SUBCOMMITTEE SEATS	
	Chairman's discretion	Full committee seniority
Chairman's discretion		House Education and Labor
Full committee seniority	H.P.W.C., S.A.C. Democrats	S.P.W.C., S.A.C. Republicans
Subcommittee seniority	H.A.C.	

least that it used to occupy that cell while Clarence Cannon was chairman. There has not been enough research done on this subject for us to classify committees with any great degree of certainty, but we can make a few remarks about some of the cells in this table.

To begin with, it is obvious that the chairman is most powerful (relative to other committee members) if the committee is in the upper left-hand cell. He would seem least powerful in the two cells on the lower right, for in the committees in these lower right-hand cells decisions are made automatically. Many Senate committees appear to fall into one of these two cells. The practice of utilizing subcommittee seniority rather than seniority in the full committee to choose the subcommittee chairman would tend to reward specialization. We might therefore expect this practice to find greater acceptance in the House than in the Senate.

This analysis indicates that the Senate subcommittee chairmen—and indeed individual subcommittee members—should be if anything more autonomous and therefore individually more consequential than the subcommittee chairmen or individual subcommittee members in the House. This expectation is likely to be partly confounded by the actual workings of the rule for choosing subcommittee chairmen in the Senate. As we indicated above, full committee seniority is employed to distribute the rights of first refusal. In other words, first the highest-ranking majority member is asked what subcommittees he would like to chair, then the second-ranking member is asked about the remaining subcommittees, and so on. This process may lead a senator to chair a subcommittee in which he and his state have little interest. The ubiquity of the reciprocity norm in the Senate, and especially within the Senate committees, seems to guarantee a senator benefits that are relevant to his state. For this reason, the state of the chairman of the Public Works Subcommittee of the S.A.C. may not get more benefits than the states of the other members, since the chairman's state may not have a great interest in public works. It may have happened that Public Works was the only subcommittee left for him to choose after the more senior committee members had chosen their chairmanships.

Therefore, we cannot be certain precisely what to expect from an analysis of the effects of seniority (or, in this case, of the effects of chairmanships and ranking minority memberships) in the Senate subcommittees. There does seem to be some interview evidence on the relation between seniority and benefits in the Senate. Stephen Horn, referring to the S.A.C., reports: "Many senators and staff members believe that there is a direct relationship between seniority and success in getting one's proposals adopted. In 1965–66, a few subcommittee chairmen claimed that in their subcommittees senior members had no advantage when decisions were made. 'The merit of the program or project is what counts,' said one."[19] Horn goes on to indicate his own verdict: "The reality was perhaps best expressed by a long-time staff member when he noted, 'Seniority will not always win, but it will mean you are listened to.' "[20]

A staff aid for a senator on the S.P.W.C.R.H.F.C. Subcommittee was asked: "Speaking generally, does seniority help a senator to get projects he wants authorized?" He replied without hesitation "Yes." More interview data must be gathered to fill out this argument. It seems likely, nonetheless, that senators expect senior members to receive preferential treatment at the hands of the subcommittee. They also expect the chairman and the ranking member of the subcommittee to receive more projects than other subcommittee members get. To determine to what extent these expectations are met by the S.A.C. Public Works Subcommittee's behavior with respect to the Corps of Engineers' budget, we will present some empirical findings.

As in the previous section, two types of benefits are distinguished. The first type includes the benefits gained from favorable treatment at the hands of the House, the Budget Bureau, and other decision-making bodies outside the Senate. The second type includes the benefits accorded by the S.A.C. Public Works Subcommittee in its decisions. Table 10.10 compares the percentage cuts by the House in the budget requests for the states of the chairmen of the two subcommittees (S.A.C. Public Works and S.P.W.C.R.H.F.C.) and the percentage cuts in the requests for the states of the other members, excluding the ranking minority members, for the years 1949 to 1968. On both subcommittees the chairmen suffered smaller percentage cuts than did the other members. However, it is worth pointing out that

TABLE 10.10

House Cuts in Budget Requests for Chairmen Versus Other Members on the S.A.C. Public Works and the S.P.W.C.R.H.F.C. Subcommittees

	Chairman gets larger cut than others	Chairman gets smaller cut than others
S.A.C. Public Works Subcommittee	7	13
S.P.W.C.R.H.F.C. Subcommittee	9	11

TABLE 10.11

House Cuts in Budget Requests for Ranking Minority Members Versus Other Members, Excluding Chairmen, on the S.A.C. Public Works and the S.P.W.C.R.H.F.C. Subcommittees

	Ranking minority member gets larger cut than others	Ranking minority member gets smaller cut than others
S.A.C. Public Works Subcommittee	9	11
S.P.W.C.R.H.F.C. Subcommittee	11	9

the chairman of S.A.C. Public Works did better relative to the other members of his subcommittee than the chairman of S.P.W.C.R.H.F.C. did relative to the remainder of his subcommittee. On direct comparison of House cuts for the states of the two chairmen, the chairman of the S.A.C. Public Works Subcommittee received smaller cuts than the chairman of the S.P.W.C.R.H.F.C. Subcommittee on ten occasions. There were three years when both chairmen received identical treatment, and the chairman of the S.P.W.C.R.H.F.C. Subcommittee did better on several occasions. These data allow three conclusions: first, that the House treats both chairmen better than it treats the other members of their subcommittees; second, that the treatment differential is greater on the S.A.C. Public Works Subcommittee than it is on the S.P.W.C.R.H.F.C. Subcommittee; third, that the chairman of the S.A.C. Public Works Subcommittee generally receives smaller cuts than the chairman of the S.P.W.C.R.H.F.C. Subcommittee.

A similar comparison was made for the ranking minority members of the two subcommittees, and Table 10.11 gives the results. Evidently, the ranking minority member (R.M.M.) of the S.A.C. Public Works Subcommittee receives smaller House cuts than the other subcommittee members more frequently than is the case with the R.M.M. of the S.P.W.C.R.H.F.C. Subcommittee. Comparing the two ranking minority members directly, we find that in eight of the 20 years from 1949 to 1968 the R.M.M. of the S.A.C. Public Works Subcommittee received the smaller cut. There were six ties, and in six years the R.M.M. of the S.P.W.C.R.H.F.C. Subcommittee received the smaller House cut. These patterns are consistent with those obtained for chairmen at every turn.

Table 10.12 compares House cuts for chairmen and for ranking minority members on the two subcommittees. This table indicates

TABLE 10.12

House Cuts in Budget Requests for Chairmen Versus Ranking Minority Members on the S.A.C. Public Works and the S.P.W.C.R.H.F.C. Subcommittees

	Chairman gets larger cut than R.M.M.	Chairman and R.M.M. get same cut	R.M.M. gets larger cut than chairman
S.A.C. Public Works Subcommittee	7	4	9
S.P.W.C.R.H.F.C. Subcommittee	6	4	10

TABLE 10.13

Additions by the Senate over House Recommendations for Chairmen Versus Other Members on the S.A.C. Public Works and the S.P.W.C.R.H.F.C. Subcommittees

	Chairman gets larger % addition than other subcommittee members	Chairman gets smaller % addition than other subcommittee members
S.A.C. Public Works Subcommittee	13	7
S.P.W.C.R.H.F.C. Subcommittee	8	12

that on both subcommittees the chairman receives better treatment from the House than the R.M.M. does. It appears that this preference is a little more pronounced on the S.P.W.C.R.H.F.C. Subcommittee. This table, when combined with 10.10 and 10.11, leads to the conclusion that the chairman and the R.M.M. receive better treatment from the House than do other subcommittee members. The House preference for chairmen over ranking minority members is interpreted as a further effect of party, which we discussed in the previous section.

Do the chairmen and ranking minority members subsequently receive preferential treatment at the hands of the S.A.C. Public Works Subcommittee? Table 10.13 presents data on percentage increases over House recommendations for the chairmen versus other subcommittee members (excluding the R.M.M.) on the two subcommittees. In interpreting this table, it is useful to recall from the introductory discussion in this chapter that the chairman of the S.A.C. Public Works Subcommittee makes most of the Senate decisions being examined here by himself. Therefore, it should come as no surprise

TABLE 10.14

Relation Between Senate Additions and House Cuts for Chairman Versus Other Members on the S.A.C. Public Works Subcommittee

	Chairman gets larger Senate addition than others	Chairman gets smaller Senate addition than others
Chairman gets larger House cut than others	6	1
Chairman gets smaller House cut than others	7	6

TABLE 10.15

Relation Between Senate Additions and House Cuts for Chairman Versus Other Members on the S.P.W.C.R.H.F.C. Subcommittee

	Chairman gets larger House cut than others	Chairman gets smaller House cut than others
Chairman gets larger Senate addition than others	5	3
Chairman gets smaller Senate addition than others	4	8

that the differential between the chairman and the other subcommittee members is so substantial in this table for the S.A.C. Public Works Subcommittee in comparison with the results for the S.P.W.C.-R.H.F.C. Subcommittee. A direct comparison of the two chairmen indicates that on 13 of 20 occasions the chairman of the S.A.C. Public Works Subcommittee received the larger percentage increase.

The advantageous position of the chairman of the S.A.C. Public Works Subcommittee is thrown into still starker relief when Senate additions for the chairman versus other subcommittee members (excluding the R.M.M.) are cross-tabulated with the analogous variable for House cuts. Table 10.14 presents these results. Twelve of the 20 observations are consistent with the crude "appeals court" theory (those states receiving the largest House cut subsequently receive the largest Senate addition). Of the eight cases not in accord with the appeals court prediction, seven follow the pattern of preference for the chairman over the other S.A.C. Public Works Subcommittee members. An analogous table (Table 10.15) is presented for the S.P.W.C.R.H.F.C. Subcommittee. In Table 10.15, we note that 13 of the 20 cases are consistent with the appeals court notion. The difference between this table and the previous one lies in the fact that a majority of the seven deviant cases are incompatible with the

TABLE 10.16

Senate Additions to House Recommendations for States Represented by the R.M.M. Versus Other Members, Excluding the Chairmen, on the S.A.C. Public Works and the S.P.W.C.R.H.F.C. Subcommittees

	R.M.M. gets larger Senate addition than others	R.M.M. gets smaller Senate addition than others
S.A.C. Public Works Subcommittee	6	14
S.P.W.C.R.H.F.C. Subcommittee	6	14

TABLE 10.17

Senate Additions and House Cuts for the R.M.M. Versus Other S.A.C. Public Works Subcommittee Members, Excluding the Chairman

	R.M.M. gets larger Senate addition than others	R.M.M. gets smaller Senate addition than others
R.M.M. gets larger House cut than others	3	6
R.M.M. gets smaller House cut than others	3	8

hypothesis that the subcommittee chairman receives better treatment than the other members receive.

The same comparisons can be made between the ranking minority members. We might expect that, as we found with the chairmen, the R.M.M. of the S.A.C. Public Works Subcommittee would receive higher Senate additions than other subcommittee members more frequently than the R.M.M. of the S.P.W.C.R.H.F.C. Subcommittee would. Table 10.16 presents the comparison. This table indicates no difference between the two committees, and suggests, surprisingly, that ranking minority members do not seem to be favored over other subcommittee members. When the ranking minority members of the two subcommittees were compared directly, it was found that in nine of the 20 years the R.M.M. of the S.A.C. Public Works Subcommittee received the larger percentage increase by the Senate. The R.M.M. of the S.P.W.C.R.H.F.C. Subcommittee received the larger Senate increase seven times. In the remaining four years to be accounted for the two ranking minority members received the same treatment.

Table 10.17 presents the cross-tabulation of Senate additions and House cuts for the R.M.M. of the S.A.C. Public Works Subcommittee versus other subcommittee members. While 11 cases out of 20 are

TABLE 10.18
Senate Additions and House Cuts for the R.M.M. Versus Other
S.P.W.C.R.H.F.C. Subcommittee Members, Excluding the Chairman

	R.M.M. gets larger Senate addition than others	R.M.M. gets smaller Senate addition than others
R.M.M. gets larger House cut than others	4	7
R.M.M. gets smaller House cut than others	2	7

consistent with the appeals court hypothesis, only three of nine deviant cases are consistent with the theory that the R.M.M. does better than other subcommittee members. In essence, the party difference (for example, the difference between the chairman and the R.M.M.) is substantial enough to cancel out whatever general seniority effect is at work.

The same table has been constructed for the R.M.M. versus the other members of the S.P.W.C.R.H.F.C. Subcommittee (see Table 10.18). This table demonstrates even less preference for the R.M.M. over other subcommittee members than does the previous table. We may conclude that the R.M.M. of the S.P.W.C.R.H.F.C. Subcommittee does not receive better treatment from the S.A.C. Public Works Subcommittee than other members receive. Whatever effects result from holding the ranking minority membership on the subcommittee, they appear to be of less importance than the effect of being a member of the minority party.

The results of this exposition are fairly unambiguous. The subcommittee chairmen get better treatment from both the H.A.C. and the S.A.C. Public Works Subcommittees than other subcommittee members get, but this is not the case with the ranking minority members. In each comparison, the chairman and the R.M.M. of the S.A.C. Public Works Subcommittee fared better than their counterparts on the S.P.W.C.R.H.F.C. Subcommittee.

For the sake of completeness, we must still examine the actual appeals court decision rules themselves. This analysis proceeds, as did the analysis in the previous section, by estimating the regression equation of Senate additions (in millions of dollars) to House cuts. Table 10.19 presents the regression coefficients, the $\bar{R}^2$s, and the mean House cuts for the chairman, the R.M.M., and the other members of the S.A.C. Public Works Subcommittee. Utilizing the figures in this table, it is possible to compute the expected Senate addition if

TABLE 10.19

*Results of Regression Analysis for the Members of the
S.A.C. Public Works Subcommittee*

Member	a (millions of dollars)	β	$\bar{R}^2$	Mean House cut (millions of dollars)
Chairman	$3.212	.480	.491	$ 1.545
R.M.M.	1.018	.656	.641	3.034
Other members	7.736	.945	.990	18.532

NOTE: a represents the estimated Senate addition if the House has made no cut; β represents the estimated proportion of each dollar of House cuts that the Senate restores.

TABLE 10.20

*Size of House Cuts Necessary to Ensure That the Senate Addition
Remains Below the Original Budget Request: The S.A.C.
Public Works Subcommittee*

Member	Size of cut (millions of dollars)	Number of occurrences
Chairman	$6.70	3
R.M.M.	1.54	5
Other members	8.20	7

the House produces its mean budget cut. For the chairman this Senate addition is $3.961 million, or 256 percent of the average House cut. For the R.M.M. the Senate addition is 197 percent of the House cut; 157 percent is the figure for the other subcommittee members. If the Senate is following its estimated appeals court rule, the states of the chairman and the R.M.M. will end up getting an amount below the original budget request if the House cut is large enough. Table 10.20 indicates both the size of the House cut large enough to keep a state below its budget estimates and the number of times the House has made such cuts. These data indicate that if the Senate follows its normal way of considering these budget requests, the budget for the state of the chairman ends up below the initial request only three times out of 20. From this analysis we can conclude that on the S.A.C. Public Works Subcommittee the appeals court rule for the chairman is better than that for the R.M.M. and the other subcommittee members, given House behavior on the budget requests.

The regression results for the S.P.W.C.R.H.F.C. are shown in Table 10.21. Just as was true for the S.A.C. Public Works Subcommittee, on the average the Senate adds more than the House cuts

TABLE 10.21

Results of Regression Analysis for the Members of the
S.P.W.C.R.H.F.C. Subcommittee

Member	a (millions of dollars)	β	$\bar{R}^2$	Mean House cut (millions of dollars)
Chairman	$1.040	.649	.749	$20.841
R.M.M.	.810	.454	.795	22.485
Other members	6.860	.543	.719	28.722

NOTE: a represents the estimated Senate addition if the House has made no cut; β represents the estimated proportion of each dollar of House cuts that the Senate restores.

TABLE 10.22

Size of House Cuts Necessary to Ensure That the Senate Addition
Remains Below the Original Budget Request:
The S.P.W.C.R.H.F.C. Subcommittee

Member	Size of cut (millions of dollars)	Number of occurrences
Chairman	$ 1.61	7
R.M.M.	1.77	5
Other members	12.55	6

for all subcommittee members. On the other hand, when a table is computed showing the size of the House cut necessary to keep the Senate addition below the initial budget request, no clear ordering among the chairman, R.M.M., and other subcommittee members is found. Table 10.22 indicates that under the estimated appeals court rule the Senate figure for the state of the chairman is expected to remain below the budget request more frequently than is the case with the states represented by the R.M.M. or by the other subcommittee members. This apparent anomaly can be accounted for by examining deviations from the estimated appeals court rule. Of the seven predicted cases in which the Senate addition for the chairman's state was expected to be below the initial budget request, it was actually below the request on only two. There is only one other observed deviation for members of the S.P.W.C.R.H.F.C. Subcommittee. Apparently, the estimated appeals court rule is not a good approximation of Senate behavior for the state of the S.P.W.C.R.H.F.C. Subcommittee chairman, although it works well for all the other states examined.

The conclusions to be drawn from this analysis are the following:

first, the chairman of each subcommittee does better in both types of benefits than either the R.M.M. or the other subcommittee members do; second, the chairman and the R.M.M. of the S.A.C. Public Works Subcommittee do better in both types of benefits than their counterparts on the S.P.W.C.R.H.F.C. Subcommittee; third, the ranking minority members of both subcommittees get somewhat better treatment from the H.A.C. Public Works Subcommittee than other members get, but they do no better in the Senate.

Conclusions

In some ways the analysis of the Senate has yielded more intuitive results than was the case with the House. All of the hypothesized relations were in the expected directions. For example, it was found that senators gained something from subcommittee membership, and they gained more from membership on the S.A.C. Public Works Subcommittee than they gained from S.P.W.C.R.H.F.C. Subcommittee membership. Democrats were shown to benefit more than Republicans and chairmen more than other subcommittee members. The only finding that was even a little outside this pattern was the realization that ranking minority members did no better than other subcommittee members. This can be accounted for by the hypothesis that party effects are more significant than the seniority effect.

There were major differences between the analyses of the House and of the Senate. When House new starts were examined, institutional variables (committee membership, party, seniority) explained very large portions of the variance. In the Senate, however, only a small part of the explanation for the distribution of Senate new starts would appear to originate in the institutional variables. Rather, it was found that the institutional variables in the Senate were most helpful in explaining the Senate's treatment of the House budget recommendations themselves, largely within the framework of the Senate as an appeals court. In retrospect, it is possible to argue that the House acts as an appeals court for Budget Bureau cuts in agency recommendations; however, since data on that subject were not available for this study, such a possibility must remain unexplored.

When the results of Part Two are considered, we should not be surprised that much Senate behavior is "explained" by the temporal position of the Senate in the appropriations process. The House, as it turns out, may be viewed as an initiator of public works policy in some ways independent of the Budget Bureau (but in conjunction with the Corps of Engineers). The Senate's appropriations behavior, on the other hand, is so heavily characterized by its appeals court role that the institutional effects are reflected mainly in the kind of appeals court pattern the Senate committees deign to produce. This fact has made the Senate analysis more labored and tortuous than that of the House, where it made sense to conceive of new starts as primarily a function of institutional variables.

Conclusion: Comments on a Theory of Congressional Behavior on Divisible Policies

The empirical propositions that have emerged from this study would seem to require some sort of coherent explanation. They would also seem to have consequences for many theories, both descriptive and normative, of congressional policy-making. Therefore, this conclusion will informally attempt to provide some theoretical foundations for the results that have been adduced and to assess the consequences these results may have for other theories.

The findings of this study fall principally into two categories. The first category encompasses those findings that establish the favored treatment by Congress of the program and budget of the Corps of Engineers. This special relationship was examined mainly in the budgetary arena, where advantage could be taken of Fenno's work for comparative purposes. Additional evidence was presented to indicate that the Corps received other sorts of advantages from the Congress in the agency's continuing struggles with the President, other agencies, and the Budget Bureau. Strong congressional support has enabled the Corps of Engineers to employ a very low discount rate compared to that used by other agencies (the Bureau of Reclamation and the Defense Department agencies other than the Corps have always had to employ much higher discount rates). This congressional support has also allowed the Corps to retain its own criteria for evaluating transportation projects in the Transportation Act of 1966, to employ liberal benefit criteria in project evaluation, and to routinely circumvent the Budget Bureau in its presentations to the appropriations committees.

The second category of findings indicates that the distribution of the Corps of Engineers' projects is related to the distribution of influence over the Corps of Engineers within the Congress. Among the propositions in this category that were supported by the data were the following: (1) members of the public works committees of both chambers get more new projects than nonmembers do; (2) members of the public works subcommittees of the appropriations committees get more new projects than nonmembers do; (3) appropriations subcommittee members receive better treatment than authorization committee members (by several different measures) in both chambers; (4) the committee leaders of the public works committees (subcommittee and full committee chairmen and ranking minority members) receive more favorable treatment for their state's budget requests than nonleaders on the committees do in both chambers and for both the authorization and the appropriations committees; (5) within the appropriations subcommittees of both chambers the budgets of states represented by Democrats fared better than those of states represented by Republicans.

It was suggested in Chapter 9 that these propositions have not always been true for members of the H.A.C. Public Works Subcommittee. It was demonstrated that, prior to 1955, H.A.C. Public Works Subcommittee members' states received fewer new starts and had smaller budgets than nonmembers' states did. The hypothesis put forward in that chapter was that as long as the members of the H.A.C. Public Works Subcommittee represented states with little interest in water projects, the Corps of Engineers' budget requests could be expected to receive deep cuts. This pattern of severe cutting was in fact observed during the period when the H.A.C. Public Works Subcommittee had few members with interests in projects. In the period after 1955, when the subcommittee was made up of congressmen with major constituency interests in water resources development, the Corps of Engineers received greatly increased committee support and no longer had its budget requests deeply cut.

It is noteworthy that even before 1955, when the Civil Functions Subcommittee (predecessor of the Public Works Subcommittee) had very limited constituency interests in the Corps' program, the chairman and the R.M.M. of the subcommittee generally did much better than the other subcommittee members. They had relatively large Corps budgets in their states, and these budgets were not cut deeply. Thus we might conclude that the preeminent position of committee leaders in getting favorable treatment for their constituencies is largely independent of the existence of a subgovernment. In other words, even while the Civil Functions Subcommittee conceived its role as one of vigorously reducing the "pork barrel" expenditures of the Corps of Engineers and of opposing the general expansion of the Corps' mission and budget, the subcommittee leaders were busily getting disproportionate shares of pork barrel expenditures for their own states. Consequently, it seems that the theory that accounts for why leaders of the H.A.C. Public Works Subcommittee receive more benefits than nonleaders must apply equally to situations where the subcommittee supports the Corps (especially against the Budget Bureau) and to situations where it opposes the Corps.

Two basic questions remain to be answered. First, what is it about Congress (or any voting body) that leads to pork barrel expenditures?* Second, what is it in Congress that leads to the particular kinds of distributions of expenditures observed in this study? These are largely separate questions, and each of them has been dealt with elsewhere by scholars. The first has been analyzed by economists and by game theorists who have investigated the properties of "voting games" or voting institutions. The second has received far less treatment, but some fruitful lines of inquiry have been put forth by political scientists and economists.

Political Bases for the Pork Barrel

Let us consider a simple legislature consisting of N representatives from geographical districts governed by simple majority rule. The legislature is considering the question of internal improvements. For simplicity, let us assume that each district would like to receive a given amount of funds to be spent on "improvements" within the district (roads, harbors, dams, and so on). Each district's proposal may be thought of as a separate bill, and all the districts will be taxed to pay for the improvements. This situation is similar to ones analyzed by Buchanan and Tullock, Barry, and others.[1] It has much the same structure as an N person majority rule game analyzed by Raoul Bott[2] and others, except that direct side payments are not permitted.

Evidently, if a bill calling for improvements in a single district is put up, it will not pass since all the districts must pay and only one will benefit. Consequently, only an omnibus bill proposing expenditures in at least a majority of the districts has a chance of passage. Some additional assumptions are needed in order to carry out the analysis. Let us say that the benefit accruing to the individual district

---

* The definition of pork barrel expenditures used here is simply expenditures that are not justifiable on strict economic grounds: those with total costs greater than total benefits.

if a project is built will be \$60, and that the total cost to the society of making improvements in one district will be \$100 (so that none of the projects is economically beneficial). Now suppose that the legislature contains 100 members and that by law each district bears an identical share of the costs of financing an internal improvement (\$1 each in this case). If 51 legislators then formed a coalition to enact an omnibus bill containing projects for their districts alone, the total tax their districts would have to pay would be \$51, but the benefits for each of the participating districts would be \$60. The coalition would in such a case be beneficial to its members. Can one then say that such a coalition would form and that society would expend \$5,100 on pork barrel projects?

It is on this point that there is disagreement. Buchanan and Tullock argue that such a coalition would form and build the projects. Then, at the next opportunity, another (partly overlapping) winning coalition would form and decide to build more of the uneconomical projects (along with some newly eligible uneconomical projects), so that eventually many uneconomical projects would be built. Barry argues, however, that if an initial majority coalition formed, one of two things would happen. Either it would stick together and agree within itself that none of its members would defect to another coalition, or, failing that, it would break apart with the result that another coalition would form and repeal the first appropriation and substitute another. In Barry's model, then, either only one coalition gets its projects built or an endless cycle of bills is passed by one coalition and repealed by the next so that nothing ever gets built.

The root difference between these two scenarios is institutional. In Buchanan and Tullock's model, once the majority passes an appropriations bill the money is spent, the projects are built, and new projects subsequently become eligible for funding. The facts that the money is spent before the majority coalition breaks up and that new projects become eligible are necessary to produce the Buchanan and Tullock result. The importance of the first of these two features is that it prevents Barry's endless cycle. The second feature permits the minority to induce former members of the majority to form a new coalition to build new projects.* If the second feature does not hold

---

* Barry, *Political Argument*, p. 250. It is well to point out that Buchanan and Tullock do not need to explicitly introduce the device that new projects become eligible. This is so since the "projects" in their example are not fixed-cost but variable-cost expenditures. Consequently, more money can always be spent in a given district, and it is presumably possible to convince members of a winning coalition to defect to another coalition in order to obtain even more expendi-

but the first does, the initial majority will form to build its projects and no other majority will form. Consequently, the total pork barrel expenditure will be $5,100.

Which of these institutional structures—Buchanan and Tullock's, or Barry's—most nearly characterizes Congress? There are rules in both the House and the Senate that arbitrarily end consideration of a bill. In addition, once a bill is signed into law it is not reconsidered (though there have been cases where a subsequent law has essentially repealed an earlier one). Most districts would also seem to have a substantial list of projects requiring funding. On this elementary basis we might conjecture that the Buchanan-Tullock institutions seem to be plausible.*

On the other hand, observation of which congressional districts benefit most from the Corps of Engineers' budget would seem to indicate that essentially the same coalition forms each year (or at least many members are always in the winning coalition). This would seem to give some support to Barry's conjecture that the coalition will "agree" to stick together. Casual observation does not seem to indicate that one model is preferable to the other.

One difficulty with this reasoning is that it is based on the assumption that the legislature makes its decisions by simple majority rule. Evidently, if a two-thirds rule is instituted with all other features remaining the same, the initial two-thirds coalition that formed would find that each member district would pay a tax of $67 and receive only $60 in benefits. Consequently, no projects would be built. This is only a small improvement, however, since nothing will stop the legislature from building projects with benefits of $70 and costs of $100.

Decision-making in Congress departs from simple majority rule in two principal ways: first, Congress is bicameral; second, the committee system is operative. These two features of the congressional decision-making structure serve to lodge a veto power over particular pieces of legislation in the hands of certain congressional participants. Dahl and Lindblom argue that "many strategically placed leaders who represent minorities are in a position to insist on their demands through bargaining."[3] Which congressional participants

---

tures. This device leads to complications, however, which the authors fail to analyze. For that reason the model presented here is even simpler by virtue of the assumption that all projects have fixed costs.

* Buchanan and Tullock argue elsewhere in their book that requirements for extraordinary majorities (more than 51 members in this case) provide a protection against gross inefficiency in public spending.

hold vetoes over the passage of the Corps of Engineers' appropriations? If we can answer this question, then theoretically at least we can make a list of essential members of any winning coalition.

Dahl and Lindblom describe the piecing together of appropriations for the Corps of Engineers as a form of logrolling: "Logrolling is a means of getting the acquiescence of every leader who has enough control to block or weaken your policy proposal, by trading your consent to the proposal of another leader for his consent to your proposal."[4]

Strictly speaking, in either chamber a unified majority can have its own way; in one sense, therefore, there are no absolute vetoes within Congress. In practice, however, each chamber refers legislation to committees and considers only (with very rare exceptions) legislation that is reported out of the relevant committee. In addition, the chairmen of committees exercise largely unchallenged authority to call committee meetings, schedule hearings, set up agendas, draft proposals for committee consideration, staff subcommittees, and so on. It is no great violation of the facts, therefore, to argue that the committee chairman holds a "relative" veto over legislation in his bailiwick. The term "relative" is employed because if a majority of a committee is united behind a proposal, it can force committee consideration of it. By the same token, if a majority of the House or the Senate favors a bill, it can be called out of committee through various extraordinary procedures.

The extreme rarity with which these events occur makes it possible to list the congressional actors holding relative vetoes over the appropriations bill for the Corps of Engineers. They include (1) the chairmen of the public works subcommittees of the appropriations committees; (2) the chairmen of the appropriations committees; (3) majorities of the public works subcommittees of both appropriations committees; (4) majorities of the appropriations committees of both chambers; (5) all senators; (6) majorities of both chambers; (7) the House Rules Committee when the H.A.C. requires a special rule waiving points of order; and (8) the conferees from the House and the Senate.

Several features of this list deserve notice. First, the leaderships of both bodies have been omitted since appropriations bills are privileged items that need not appear on legislative calendars in order to receive floor consideration. Second, members of the authorization committees have not been listed. They would only be considered as having a veto if the object of analysis were the individual project rather than the whole appropriations bill. After all, we know that no project can be constructed without legislative authorization. However, for the present purposes only items already authorized are considered to be eligible for appropriations, and so no discretion is lodged with the authorization committee.* Third, all senators are said to have vetoes in the sense that any one of them might choose to filibuster a bill if he felt strongly enough about it.

Not all the possible vetoes are of equal strength, credibility, or likelihood. For example, one of the public works subcommittees would never "veto" an appropriations bill; if the subcommittee did not like it, it would change it. The full committee would not veto the bill either, partly for the same reason (it can change the bill) and partly because of the expectation of reciprocity among subcommittees. If a majority on the floor does not approve of the committee proposal, it can amend the bill to conform to majority sentiment. Evidently, then, many of the bodies that could veto a bill if they so desired find it more advantageous merely to amend it. For all veto-holding bodies with the ability to amend a bill a veto is extremely unlikely. Does this mean that these groups would not be contained in the minimal coalition? One would think not. After all, these groups merely change the bill to conform more closely to their own desires, after which they presumably become supporters of the bill.

Though all senators are listed as holding a relative veto in the form of the threat of a filibuster, this threat is not a particularly credible one. Since nearly every state receives Corps appropriations, mounting a filibuster would seem to be extremely costly to a senator since he would face widespread support for the bill and resentment at the filibuster. Only when a senator stood to gain a lot from a successful filibuster would such a veto be credible, since the costs seem relatively fixed and the probability of success low. Nevertheless, we might hypothesize a situation in which a filibuster would be a credible enough threat to place a constraint on the amount of inequality between states exhibited in the Senate budget recommendations. (No such inequality-reducing mechanism is at work in the House, though.) This conjecture is consistent with the data presented in Chapter 10, where we found that the distribution of benefits in the Senate was relatively equal.

* In the case when certain items in the appropriations bill have not yet been authorized, then the bill requires a rule waiving points of order from the House Rules Committee in order to go to the House floor. The Public Works Committee could in this eventuality fail to authorize these items and force the Appropriations Committee to go to the Rules Committee for the special rule.

The prevalence of relative vetoes over legislation means that the rule by which decisions are made in Congress is not a simple majority rule. To be sure, a particular majority of both chambers—one containing all congressional actors holding relative vetoes—could pass any particular piece of legislation it desired without trouble. The distribution of relative vetoes constitutes a restriction on which majorities may form; in particular, those majorities that command majorities of the members of the relevant committees, virtual unanimity in the Senate,* and so on are able to work their will with minimal costs. In other words, not all majorities incur the same costs in gaining passage of legislation desired by their members. A majority coalition that does not include a majority of the members of the House Committee on Appropriations may have to resort to extraordinary and costly methods to bring a bill to the House floor. In addition, once the bill passes the House and the Senate the House conferees must be persuaded to produce a conference bill acceptable to the majority.† Unless the majority stands to gain a great deal by passage of the bill, these costs will effectively restrict the set of coalitions that might form to those containing the most holders of relative vetoes.

This simple model of the congressional decision structure amends the simple majority model by restricting the set of "formable winning coalitions." It is not clear whether the introduction of relative vetoes throughout a bicameral legislature with a committee system will act to increase overall spending levels or not. Once again, there are several divergent views on this question. Barry's position is that the dispersion of relative vetoes (not his term) moves the system closer to a unanimity requirement. He observes, "The nearer a system comes to requiring unanimity for decisions, the more prevalent we may expect to find the 'pork barrel' phenomenon."[5] Buchanan and Tullock, and subsequently J. Roland Pennock,[6] using the logic described earlier in this section argue that as a system comes closer to a unanimity requirement there are reduced incentives to undertake inefficient (pork barrel) projects. The Buchanan-Tullock argument has already been given. Barry's argument will be given now.

---

* The requirement of virtual unanimity in the Senate means simply that no senator will feel sufficiently aggrieved by the appropriations bill to resort to the extreme of a filibuster.

† In the case of appropriations for public works, the actual divisions of benefits are spelled out in the reports accompanying the bill. Consequently, the conferees must be persuaded to produce an acceptable conference report as well as an acceptable bill.

Barry claims that a system requiring unanimity will contain more incentives for a pork barrel than a system with less than a unanimity requirement. His argument proceeds as follows. Since all participants must agree before a given expenditure can be made, each participant has an incentive to misrepresent his true desires and to claim that he would not vote to build X (something presumably of interest to the whole society) unless Y (an inefficient project of interest only to his own constituency) would be built as well. Each legislator can therefore threaten to withhold his vote on X unless his district receives a special project (which is inefficient); then depending on just how big an improvement for society X is, and on how inefficient the special projects are, either X and all of the inefficient projects will be built, or no projects at all will be built. To make the needed empirical linkage, Barry asserts that "the United States comes nearer to a 'unanimity system' than any other western democracy."[7] The outcome in Barry's model is inconclusive: either too many or too few projects will be built.

Buchanan and Tullock have no effective reply to this argument. A unanimity-requiring system vests "monopoly power" in everyone's hands, with the result that threats and strategic behavior are beneficial to the participants. The preferences of the actors (or constituents) will not be revealed by rational legislators; therefore, efficient expenditure levels cannot generally be determined. Other theorists (principally Wicksell,[8] who seems to have been among the first to discover this difficulty with a unanimous voting system) have proposed a slight retreat from an absolute unanimity requirement that might remove the incentive for threats from a voting system. It is unfortunate for this point of view that, while it may have some truth if the proposed system only requires that any nine-tenths of the legislature agree for a proposal to pass, the particular departure from unanimity observed in the United States Congress is that certain actors (for example, committee chairmen of the relevant committees) are in each formable minimal winning coalition.* Thus, employing the earlier terminology, each actor with a relative veto still has some monopoly power over the passage of the appropriations bill (the amount depending on the credibility of his threat to block the legislation and force costly countermeasures). Therefore, threats are rational for these particular actors, and they can insist on bribes before acceding

---

* "Minimal winning" coalitions can be interpreted as winning coalitions with the smallest possible number of members.

to generally desired legislation. By this argument, inefficient projects will be built and there will be a pork barrel.

Yet another theory leading to pork barrel incentives has been proposed by William Niskanen.[9] His analysis rests on some sociological assumptions about what coalitions will form. On each issue the legislature is divided into three equal-sized groups—those with high demand for the public service, those with medium demand, and those with low demand. When discussing water projects, the high-demand group would include those congressmen whose districts contain many rivers, harbors, and other waterways and who desire improvements to be made on them. The low- and medium-demand groups can be defined as well. The major assumptions Niskanen makes are the following: first, those congressmen in the high-demand group will dominate the committee that writes the legislation; second, those congressmen in the medium- and low-demand groups will not find it worth their effort to form a coalition to substantially change the committee's proposed bill on the floor. According to Niskanen's model, each district pays a share of the costs of the program through taxes; however, the high-demand group of districts benefits most from the program, the medium-demand group receives the next largest benefits, and the low-demand group receives the least. Each group also prefers a different level of expenditures on the program—the high-demand group prefers the highest expenditures, the low-demand group prefers the lowest.

The legislators, being economic actors, determine their preferred expenditure levels by choosing that level which equates marginal benefits to marginal costs for their own districts. The high-demand group, by the first assumption, controls the committee (presumably the Appropriations Committee's Public Works Subcommittee in this case), and so it chooses the proposed agency budget according to the following rule. If its preferred budget level (the one for which marginal costs and benefits are equal) leaves the members of the medium-demand group with positive net benefits, then the committee bill will reflect this figure. By the second assumption, this bill will successfully pass the chamber unchanged, since the members of the medium-demand group will not find it worthwhile to devote their resources to amending or defeating the bill.* On the other hand, if the pre-

---

* Those in the medium- and low-demand groups in public works would probably be in the high-demand group in urban housing, agriculture, defense, or some other legislative area. Thus a reciprocity argument would help to explain why oppositional floor coalitions are seldom mobilized.

ferred budget of the high-demand group should leave the medium-demand group with negative net benefits, then the latter group, along with the low-demand group, would oppose the bill on the floor. In this case, the high-demand group will initially propose the largest possible budget subject to the constraint that the members of the medium-demand group receive positive net benefits. This bill would then, under the model assumptions, successfully pass the floor.

In Niskanen's model it is not clear whether inefficient projects are built or not. There is no mechanism in the model to ensure that such projects will not receive funding if they are located in the districts of members of the high-demand group. A simple numerical example will show that Niskanen's model produces a pork barrel phenomenon.

Once again there are 100 legislators. Thirty-three are in the high-demand group, whose districts each contain projects costing $100 to build and yielding $80 in benefits to their constituents. Each of the 33 members of the medium-demand group has a project in his district costing $60 to build and producing $53 in benefits. The 34 members of the low-demand group have no projects in their districts. Since the high-demand group dominates the committee, the bill contains projects for all the districts in both the high- and the medium-demand groups. The total tax bill is $5,280; retaining the assumption that each district has the same tax bill, this comes to $52.80 per district. Net benefits are $27.20 for those in the high-demand group, $.20 for those in the medium-demand group, and −$52.80 for those in the low-demand group. All of the projects are inefficient by assumption (the costs exceed the benefits), but all would be built under Niskanen's model. Therefore, the model can produce pork barrel behavior.

The models put forth above suggest several independent bases for pork barrel behavior (for example, the building of inefficient projects) that are inherent in various structural features of the Congress:* first, the instability of winning coalitions (Buchanan and Tullock); second, the prevalence of monopoly power over legislation attributable to relative vetoes (Barry); and third, the domination of legislative committees and appropriations subcommittees by representatives of those districts with the most to gain from the program (Niskanen).

---

* It is worth noting parenthetically that the economic basis of the pork barrel in each of these theories rests on the divergence of private and total costs and on the concentration of benefits. The individual congressional district bears only a small fraction of the total costs of a project built in the district but receives nearly all of the benefits.

Each of the aforementioned theories isolates a different feature of the structure of Congress and demonstrates that that feature can produce the pork barrel phenomenon. It is of course possible for all these theories, or for any combination of them, to be correct. Unfortunately, the first two theories rely on features that are temporally invariant in the Congress. The first is a characteristic of a voting decision rule for making decisions. The second rests on a distribution of influence that has not changed substantially for many years. On the other hand, the data presented in this study can be brought to bear on the Niskanen theory, since it rests on the assumption that high-demand groups dominate the committee, which has not always been the case.

Prior to 1955, as we have pointed out repeatedly, the H.A.C. Public Works Subcommittee (then the Civil Functions Subcommittee) was effectively dominated by members of what Niskanen would call the low-demand group. In this case Niskanen's logic would be turned around. The smallest possible budget that still would leave the medium-demand group better off than it would be without the bill would be proposed. In the numerical example given earlier, only the projects in the districts of the members of the medium-demand group would be built. The net benefits would be $-\$19.50$ for members of the high- and low-demand groups and \$32.50 for members of the medium-demand group. There would still be a pork barrel, but it would be a smaller pork barrel. In 1955 the recruitment criteria for the H.A.C. Public Works Subcommittee changed, and since then the subcommittee has been dominated by members of the high-demand group. If Niskanen's theory is correct, after 1955 we should find a marked jump in appropriations, fewer floor amendments calling for additional projects, and greater expenditures in the districts of H.A.C. Public Works Subcommittee members. Each of these predictions was fulfilled, as is documented in Chapter 5 and Chapter 9. These observations thus provide some empirical support for Niskanen's theory.

The Distribution of Expenditures to Districts

In the previous section we attempted to locate incentives in the structure of Congress (the voting rules on the floor and in committees) that lead toward the building of inefficient public projects (which we called pork barrel expenditure). The same structural features may be shown to have distributive implications as well. In other words, the decision-making structure in Congress may determine not only *that* inefficient projects will be built but also *which* inefficient projects will be built. The same theories dealt with earlier will be examined in this section in an attempt to determine, in a set of simple theoretical models, some of the distributive biases inherent in the structure of the Congress.

Are there particular distributions of benefits implied by the practice of simple majority rule? Game theorists have examined the elementary game in which a group of individuals must divide a fixed amount (of money) among themselves by majority rule.[10] Without going into technicalities, one solution to the game consists of allocations of the following sort: each of the members of a minimal winning coalition obtains an equal share of the money and everyone else receives nothing.* The theory that predicts that this "solution" will occur naturally does not predict which minimal winning coalition will prevail—and there are large numbers of such coalitions. In this majority rule game, the actual division of benefits among legislators is unpredictable since each legislator is in the same number of minimal winning coalitions. We might conclude from this discussion that the fact that floor decisions in Congress are made by a majority is of little help in predicting which coalition will form and, therefore, which districts will receive projects.

Consideration of a slightly different majority rule model may modify this conclusion. Let each district represented in a 100-member legislature contain precisely one project eligible for funding, and let us order the districts by the total costs of the projects. That is, district one will have the least costly project, district two the next least costly project, and so on. The lowest-cost winning coalition (L.C.W.C.) is the winning coalition whose total project cost is less than the total project cost for any other winning coalition. In this model the L.C.W.C. is simply a coalition of districts one to 51. Finally, the benefits from a project are assumed to go entirely to the district in which that project is located, though the costs are spread equally among all the districts.

To enable us to make a simple analysis, some restriction consistent with actual congressional behavior will be put on the range of choice

---

* This is the "symmetric solution" to a zero sum game that is strategically equivalent to the constant sum game in the text analyzed by Bott. The term "solution" is used in the game-theory sense as a set of proposals (allocations to the players) satisfying two properties: first, for any proposal (allocation) not in the solution there is a proposal in the solution that is preferred to it by a majority; second, no proposal in the solution is preferred by a majority to any other proposal in the solution. It can be shown that the set of symmetric proposals (the ones in which a minimal winning coalition divides up the money equally among its members) is a "solution" in the above sense.

a coalition may exercise. In particular, if a certain winning coalition forms, it will choose to build projects in each of its members' districts. It will not execute a full search over all the possible states of affairs that it could conceivably institute on its own and then choose the optimal policy from that set. This restriction constitutes an assumption of limited search capacity. The importance of this assumption is discussed in a footnote following the analysis of the model.

Two definitions will prove useful for our analysis of this model. First, a winning coalition is called *locally stable* if no one-member changes in its composition are possible to increase the net benefits to all members of the resulting coalition over their net benefits prior to the one-member change. Second, a winning coalition is called *globally stable* if there does not exist another winning coalition such that all members in both coalitions would be better off in the second coalition than in the first. From these definitions it is evident that if a coalition is globally stable it is locally stable. The meanings of these two properties should be apparent. If a coalition is locally stable, then no "small" change in it will benefit its members. If a coalition is globally stable, then no other coalition can form that will be capable of taking members away from the initial coalition. If we can show that only one coalition possesses both of these properties, then this coalition will form according to the assumptions of the model. Thus in this model the exact distribution of projects will be predicted under simple majority rule.

The following two propositions are easily proved: first, a lowest-cost winning coalition is locally stable;* second, a lowest-cost winning coalition is globally stable.† If the L.C.W.C. is unique, then the sec-

---

* Proof: L (the L.C.W.C.) is minimal so that we need only consider replacing one member of the coalition, j, with a nonmember, k. The benefits for all other coalition members are the same (B_i, $i \in L - [j]$), but the costs are

$$\frac{1}{N} \sum_{i \in L-[j]} c_i + \frac{(c_k - c_j)}{N} ;$$

the last term is nonnegative by assumption. Thus no replacement will take place. Q.E.D.

† Proof: Assume that the proposition is false. Then there exists a winning coalition N such that each individual i in both coalitions is strictly better off in N than he is in L. We can write

$$\left(B_i - \frac{1}{N} \sum_{i \in N} c_i \right) > \left(B_i - \frac{1}{N} \sum_{i \in L} c_i \right) \text{ for } i \in N \cap L \neq \phi ,$$

or $\frac{1}{N} \sum_{i \in N} c_i < \frac{1}{N} \sum_{i \in L} c_i \sum_{i \in N} c_i < \sum_{i \in L} c_i .$

But this contradicts the assumption that L is the lowest-cost winning coalition. Q.E.D.

ond proposition implies that it is the only winning coalition that possesses global stability. This model therefore contains the strong implication that if any projects at all are built by the legislature, only the smallest ones will be built.

The assumptions of this simple model seem to approximate some important features of congressional decision-making on the Corps of Engineers' projects. First, more than a bare majority of congressional districts (218) and states receive benefits from projects in a given year. This may be the result of the "sequential majorities" requirement discussed in the previous section; in any event, the consequences of the majority rule model would still hold—the smallest projects would still be constructed. The requirement of one project per district is too restrictive, but it can be relaxed in various ways such that essentially the same result obtains. There is some interview evidence for this hypothesis. Murphy quotes a staff member of the H.A.C. Public Works Subcommittee: "The small flood control projects are top priority."[11] Several other quoted remarks in the works of Murphy, Fenno, and Horn suggest that small projects have less stringent criteria to meet than large ones do for inclusion in the budget. We may tentatively conclude that majority rule alone (with its consequent necessity of building a majority when putting a bill together) produces a small-projects bias. Of course, much empirical work will need to be done in order to fully evaluate this hypothesis (see Appendix C).

The two other models set forth, Barry's and Niskanen's, can be discussed together without doing much violence to either. The essential component in Barry's system is the distribution of (relative) veto power among various participants in congressional decision-making. Niskanen's model rests on the central role of the committee in formulating legislative proposals and on the hypothesis that nonmembers of the committee do not find it advantageous to try to effect large changes in committee bills on the floor. Each of the two models has explicitly distributive implications.

The distribution of benefits predicted by Barry's theory can be seen in the following quotation:

Suppose that a bill will, if passed, benefit the bulk of each congressman's constituents; why should not a congressman who is (by himself or with a group of others) able to hold up the bill by his strategic position along the legislative pipeline threaten to do just that unless he gets another base in his constituency? On this theory the most "pork" will go to the constituents of those congressmen who are in the best position to hold the Administration and the rest of Congress to ransom by threatening to block legislation and appropriations of national importance.[12]

One of the particular implications of this argument is that members of the H.A.C. Public Works Subcommittee should obtain more benefits than nonmembers from Corps projects. If we introduce a modification of Barry's theory that states that members of Congress should benefit from Corps expenditures *in proportion to* their ability to exact "ransom" from the whole Congress, more implications follow, among which are the following: first, the chairman of the S.A.C. Public Works Subcommittee should obtain more benefits than both other members of Congress and other subcommittee members; second, the majority party on the subcommittee should benefit more than minority party subcommittee members and other members of Congress; third, the H.A.C. Public Works Subcommittee members should receive more Corps projects than other H.A.C. members.

A similar set of implications follows for the Senate. In addition, the ranking minority member of the H.A.C. Public Works Subcommittee may receive more benefits in relation to the extent that his concurrence in the subcommittee bill substantially aids its passage without amendment in the full committee and on the floor.

Each of these propositions generated by Barry's theory has received some confirmation in Chapters 9 and 10. It was remarked in those chapters that the differences were generally smaller and more marked by random variation in the Senate than in the House. Barry's theory would account for this result as well, since individual senators possess a weak relative veto over the appropriations bill. Many other predictions also follow from this theory. For example, the chairman of some entirely separate committee (say Veterans Affairs) may threaten to hold up a piece of legislation important to many congressmen if he does not receive certain Corps projects in his district. According to this line of reasoning then, members of Congress in a position to exercise a relative veto over any legislation important to many (or most) congressmen would be expected to receive a disproportionate share of projects. This hypothesis can be examined by observing whether states represented by committee chairmen receive more projects than other states do (after controlling for membership on water-resource-related committees). In Chapter 9 this analysis was done and a slightly negative relationship was obtained. It can be tentatively concluded from that analysis that the possession of a relative veto over unrelated legislation is of little assistance in obtaining Corps projects.

Niskanen's theory focuses explicitly on the committee (in this case the H.A.C. Public Works Subcommittee). He argues that since members from districts with "high demand" for water-resource projects dominate the committee, an agency budget that is "too large" will be proposed by the committee. Although he does not explicitly treat the case of divisible expenditures, it is a small step to the proposition that the committee will propose a disproportionate number of projects in its own members' districts (both because they come from high-demand districts and because they are the ones who actually write the bill).

Niskanen's theory can be extended in the following way. Members of high-demand (for water-resource projects) districts will tend to dominate both the H.A.C. Public Works Subcommittee and the H.P.W.C. When the H.A.C. Public Works Subcommittee puts the Corps of Engineers' appropriations recommendations together it recommends "too large" a budget (in the sense of the previous section) and puts projects disproportionately in the high-demand districts. Thus members of both the H.A.C. Public Works Subcommittee and the H.P.W.C. benefit overly from the proposed appropriations bill. The Niskanen theory can thus explain the phenomenon whereby H.P.W.C. members receive favorable treatment at the hands of the H.A.C. Public Works Subcommittee. According to this line of thought, the H.P.W.C. members do better than other congressmen not because of explicit cooperation between the committees but because of the abundance of eligible projects in the districts of H.P.W.C. members.

In Barry's theory, the fact that H.P.W.C. members receive a greater share of House new starts than nonmembers do must be accounted for by the ability of the H.P.W.C. to exact "ransom" from the H.A.C. Public Works Subcommittee. In particular, since each project must be authorized by the H.P.W.C., if the H.A.C. Public Works Subcommittee were not to give favorable treatment to the members of the H.P.W.C., a reciprocal threat to withhold desired project authorizations could be enforced by the H.P.W.C. Barry's theory would account for such a phenomenon by pointing to the threat structure available to the two committees as a result of sharing authority over the same agency. Niskanen's explanation lies primarily in the area of recruitment to the committees. Can the two theories be examined side by side, so to speak, with an eye toward accepting one and rejecting the other?

To the extent that the category of states with "high demand" for water-resource projects is a stable one, it is possible to examine the hypothesis that the sole reason that H.P.W.C. members obtain more House new starts than other members do is because they come from states with "high demand." This question was addressed in Chapter 8, and we found that current H.P.W.C. membership had a sizable effect on the number of House new starts allotted (the surrogate variable for favorable treatment by the H.A.C. Public Works Subcommittee) independent of the measures of "demand" by state. We can conclude from this analysis that the "extended-Niskanen" view rests on a weak empirical foundation. The evidence seems to argue for the existence of a significant independent effect of negotiation (whether implicit or explicit).

Therefore, the principal reason that the H.A.C. Public Works Subcommittee accords preferential treatment to H.P.W.C. members is that the H.P.W.C. controls project authorizations, which are important to H.A.C. Public Works Subcommittee members since they come from high-demand districts and states that need authorizations for new projects. A further empirical result along this line is the finding that prior to 1955—when the H.A.C. Public Works Subcommittee was composed of members from states without major interests in water projects—the subcommittee did not treat the H.P.W.C. members' states better than it treated other states. These remarks all tend to lend credence to Barry's view (which is consistent with the arguments of Dahl and Lindblom) that the current possession of a relative veto over related legislation explains why H.P.W.C. members receive favored treatment from the H.A.C. Public Works Subcommittee.

Can a unified theory of the distribution of expenditures be constructed from the partial models of Barry and Niskanen, and from the theories of majority rule and logrolling? It would seem so. The outlines of such a theory can be briefly stated here. To a great extent the models of Niskanen and Barry overlap, though Barry's model seems capable of producing nearly the full range of empirical outcomes observed in this study, while Niskanen's model does not. Each of the two models produces one notable failure: The extension of Niskanen's theory (which seems faithful to his analysis) predicts that the favored treatment of H.P.W.C. members should be accounted for by the fact that they come from states which "need" a lot of projects. This is not empirically true. Barry's theory implies that anyone holding a strong veto over any "important" legislation should be able to extract a disproportionate number of new starts for his district or state. This relationship was not found when states represented by House committee chairmen were examined.

It seems that to remedy the defect in Barry's theory we need to introduce an assumption that makes it more like Niskanen's. The reverse appears to be true as well. The difficulty in Niskanen's theory can be alleviated by introducing an entire new set of relationships among committees, which would in the end make his model look more like Barry's. On the other hand, if congressmen are assumed to join the committees in which they have the most interest (as they are in the Niskanen model), the failure of committee chairmen to obtain new starts may simply be the result of a relative absence of projects eligible for funding in their states or districts. If there were a significant number of projects in their states, then their state delegation would most likely have another member on either the H.P.W.C. or the H.A.C. Public Works Subcommittee. To the extent that this were true, there would not be an observed relationship between a state's having a committee chairman and obtaining new starts. Thus, putting the two theories together seems to solve the problems of each.

The majority rule theories contribute one basic proposition that neither of the other theories appears to be capable of producing—that is, that there will be a preference on the part of the H.A.C. Public Works and the S.A.C. Public Works subcommittees for choosing small projects. Though there seems to be some interview data consistent with this hypothesis, statistical analysis still must be carried out. In any event, the simple majority rule theory can be combined with the theory of Barry and Niskanen, though the appropriate relative weighting of these theories will need to be determined by further analysis.*

The analysis carried out here has introduced a relatively simple theory capable of explaining the empirical findings presented in this study. If this theory constitutes a more or less accurate description of the way the institutional structure of Congress determines the policies produced by Congress, then it also forms the basis for a critical analysis of congressional decision-making. The primary result produced here from a normative viewpoint is that there are several mechanisms operative in Congress that guarantee that inefficient projects

---

* The models of majority decision-making presented here do not constitute even a partial survey of results in this field. Some interesting results have been obtained by investigators who have examined a legislature as a simple exchange economy for votes. The most thorough published analysis to date is Wilson's "An Axiomatic Model of Logrolling." Wilson succeeds in setting up a model which produces a market for votes on legislation (and incidently a price system). His model has some distributive implications as well, the most notable of which is that projects with high benefit-cost ratios are more likely to pass (to the degree that his model correctly represents congressional decision-making, the pork barrel tendency is inhibited). Wilson's analysis is too technical to describe here, but if his analysis were applied to the three-person model in Appendix C, none of the projects would pass the legislature (note that none of them has a benefit-cost ratio greater than one).

will be built. The institutional forces that produce this tendency toward what ought to be considered "poor policy" do not rest too heavily on the much-maligned seniority system, on the power of committee chairmen, or on the overrepresentation of the South in positions of power. Rather, the principal institutional features leading to overspending in public works are those that constitute the very basis of representative government as it exists in the United States: geographic representation, majority rule, and the committee system.

The theoretical arguments presented here would seem to apply with equal force to the making of any divisible policy. Other investigators have reported empirical results in the areas of defense and urban-renewal expenditures similar in many respects to those produced here.[13] In each of these policy areas, the same theory would seem capable of explaining the principal findings. It seems, then, that what we have uncovered here is a set of biases operative in congressional policy-making in the divisible policy area. It is possible to argue that much of the policy made in Congress either is purely divisible (in such areas as public works, military construction, urban housing policy, and Interior Department policy) or has major divisible components (defense expenditures, agriculture, veterans affairs, and so on). As a result, the findings reported here have serious and far-reaching implications for a critical analysis of congressional decision-making.

Appendixes

Structure of the Appropriations Process

Chapters 4–7 constituted a sketch of the aggregate behavior of the major budgetary actors from 1948 to 1969. Later chapters looked beneath the gross yearly movements in budgets, numbers of new starts, and floor amendments to behavior on a project-by-project basis. Only glimmerings of that perspective were visible in the early chapters. The movements of the aggregates are in a sense epiphenomenal, in that they are the sums of the small decisions on hundreds of projects. These movements are indicative—sometimes surprisingly so—of the structure of operating rules of the budgetary bodies. This appendix presents a summary of the structure of these rules. This effort will allow inferences to be drawn regarding the principal points of leverage or decision-making in the appropriations process for the Corps of Engineers.

The simple models of the budgetary process found in the works of Fenno and Wildavsky indicate the following sequence. The House Appropriations Committee considers the difference between last year's budget and this year's budget request. The House then cuts in proportion to the size of the increment. The base—last year's budget—is accepted as it stands, and only the increment over it is critically examined. The equation representing this model follows:

(1) H.A.C. cut in budget $= 44.51 + .315$ change in budget
$\qquad\qquad\qquad\qquad\quad (2.81) \qquad (2.14)$ request over
$\qquad\qquad\qquad\qquad\qquad\qquad\qquad\qquad\qquad$ last year

$$\bar{R}^2 = .143$$

The House floor's (H.F.) reaction to the H.A.C. recommendation is not estimated, but is written as

(1') $\text{H.F.} = \text{H.A.C.} + K_1 + \epsilon_1$

where K is a constant and ϵ is a disturbance. The Senate subcommittee's response is estimated using the simple "appeals court" model. The Senate's change in the house recommendation depends simply on how much the House cut the budget by. The equation is

(2) Senate change over $=$ 55.71 $+$ .442 House change
     House figure   (9.88)   (7.00) from budget
                                                     figure

$$\bar{R}^2 = .700$$

The relationship of the Senate floor (S.F.) and the committee is written

(2′) S.F. = S.A.C. $+ K_2 + \epsilon_2$

Finally, the conference committee's decision model was estimated. The postulated model was that the conference committee chose some mixture of the Senate and House figures. The equation is written

(3) Conference figure $=$ .43 Senate floor $+$ .57 House
                              (11.54) figure   (14.44) floor
                                                              figure

$$\bar{R}^2 = .999$$

This system of equations allows for an estimate of how much a small change in behavior by one of the acting bodies would affect the final budget figure. There are five interdependent points of decision in the process prior to the conference committee: the Budget Bureau, the two appropriations committees, and the floors of the two chambers. Each of these bodies, with the exception of the Budget Bureau, has its behavior at least partially induced by prior decisions. To the degree that the behavior of a decision-making unit is "determined" by earlier decisions, there is less discretion for change unrelated to prior decisions. The change in the conference outcome resulting from a one-dollar change by each of the five bodies is written as follows:

Budget Bureau	$.54
H.A.C.	.81
H.F.	.81
S.A.C.	.43
S.F.	.43

These figures indicate that a one-dollar change in the Corps' budget made by the House Appropriations Committee will have a larger effect on the final conference committee outcome than a one-dollar change made by any of the other decision-making bodies. These figures might be considered *marginal* influences. The trouble is that these numbers contain no information to show the degree of ease of adding a dollar on the House floor relative to the degree of ease of adding a dollar in the House committee. Observably, the budget seldom changes much on the floor although it frequently undergoes sizable change in committee.

We want to determine how much independent influence each decision unit can bring to bear on the Corps' budget—independent, that is, of the structure of relationship between itself and the other bodies. The numbers that will be used are estimates of the standard deviation of what will be considered the independent influence variable: the error terms in the equations. These terms, for example, are the part of the decisions made by the House floor that cannot be explained by the actions of the House Appropriations Committee. Using these standard deviations, the 95 percent confidence intervals can be obtained. These numbers indicate the range of discretion within which 95 percent of the discretionary decisions of the body under consideration fall (assuming statistical normality). Using these confidence intervals and the marginal influence coefficients, 95 percent influence coefficients are obtained, which indicate in millions of dollars the 95 percent discretionary effects of each of the bodies. That is, 95 percent of the actual decisions will have discretionary effects within these bounds (this computation requires the discretionary behavior of each body to be independent of the others; below, this assumption will be slightly relaxed):

	Millions	
Budget Bureau	$102.0	($59.5)
H.A.C.	106.0	
H.F.	19.8	
S.A.C.	23.6	
S.F.	2.0	

The column figures indicate the 95 percent range of influence exercised at each stage of the process. There are two figures for the budget: in the first, the entire change in the budget is caused by discretionary factors; the second represents the situation if the change over last year depends only on employment and inflation in the construction industry as well as on how well the budget did last time in Congress. This model gives much less discretionary range to the budget; the House Appropriations Committee appears relatively even more dominant in the process.

This way of conceptualizing influence produces at least two propositions, one of which accords with previous literature and one of which does not. The first is that the House Appropriations Committee dominates the budgetary process to a significant extent. The second is that the House committee is more influential in conference than the Senate committee. The second result is generally in accord with the analysis contained in Chapter 7, and is in conflict with both Fenno's and Vogler's findings, which claim to exhibit Senate dominance in conference.

The regression analysis reported here has a possible source of weakness. Fenno's work on "economy moods" and "spending moods" that act on the whole Congress suggests that there might be some variable (i.e. mood) that acts to lower the Senate and House figures together in some years and to raise them in others. If this is true, the model that was employed would overestimate House committee influence, since the observed drop in the House recommendation would be a causal factor in explaining Senate behavior.

Another model was postulated that contained a "proxy" variable for mood. This proxy was a linear function of unemployment in the economy and inflation in the construction industry. The theory was that when unemployment was low and inflation high, the conditions were set for a cutting mood. The new model is written

(4) House cut in   = 213.1   +   .43   change in bud-   +   mood
     the budget   (2.96)   (2.88)   get request from
                                              last year

$$\bar{R}^2 \;=\; .283$$

(5) Senate change = 55.52   + .332   change in President's
                       (1.69)   (2.81)   budget

                   + .293   mood + .514   separable House
                      (2.11)   (6.64)   influence other
                                                 than mood

$$\bar{R}^2 \;=\; .703$$

Equation (3), the conference equation, remained the same. The new estimates of influence can be summarized as follows:

	Marginal	95 percent influences, millions
Budget Bureau	.553	$104.0 ($62.4)
H.A.C.	.780	94.0
H.F.	.780	19.2
S.A.C.	.430	23.6
S.F.	.430	2.0

Again, there are two figures in the 95 percent influence estimate for the Budget Bureau. The second represents the estimate when the components of budget increase due to change in conditions in the construction industry and to the previous year's congressional treatment of the budget are separated out. These new estimates indicate

that House Appropriations Committee influence was only very slightly overestimated.

The aggregate model produced here corresponds roughly to the
impressions given in Chapters 4–7 and constitutes an adequate summary of the appropriations process for public works. Chapters 8–10
disaggregated these data to some extent in an attempt to achieve a
better picture of the many small mechanisms that operate to produce
this one aggregate mechanism.

Distribution of Institutional Authority

In order to measure or assess the impact of the distribution of institutional authority in Congress on the public works budget, we must construct a plausible model to show how much in public works funds or in new starts each state would have received were these institutional factors not present. There appear to be two general ways of doing this. First, we can utilize the Army Corps of Engineers' calculations of benefits to construct a hypothetical "optimal" distribution of expenditures. Then any deviation from this package would be considered to result from political factors. Second, we can utilize other information to construct a surrogate variable for the "need" of a state in the area.

The second alternative was the one chosen for this study, for two major reasons. To begin with, the calculations of benefits and costs favor certain types of projects systematically. For example, navigation projects and recreation projects will generally have benefit-cost ratios that are too high. Second, there would appear to be a significant amount of political influence exercised in the actual calculation of these ratios, and the biases introduced here are unknown. It is of some interest to note that when the 1969 House new starts from the 1968 Rivers and Harbors and Flood Control Bill were examined, the correlation between benefit-cost ratio and project choice was found to be under .20. When the equation was controlled for navigation projects versus others, the relation fell to zero. It appeared that whether a project was a navigation project or not determined (weakly) whether it was chosen and how high a benefit-cost ratio it had. The magnitude of these relations, and interviews with various participants, sufficed to eliminate from consideration any model based on a naïve acceptance of the benefit-cost ratio.

These difficulties forced the choice of another tack altogether.

There seems to be an infinite number of ways to measure a state's "need" for water projects—nearly all of them bad for one reason or another. One way might be to utilize estimates of flood damage by state and to treat this variable as a measure of need for flood-control expenditure. One difficulty with this measure is that it is fairly unstable from year to year, so that averages would have to be used, preferably over long periods of time. The idea behind this is that flood-control needs are in reality fairly constant over time for each state. Washington, Oregon, Louisiana, and Kentucky "needed" large federal expenditures for these purposes both in 1945 and in 1965, despite the fact that a lot of money had been spent between those years. In addition, this measure would have to be supplemented by others for water supply, power benefits, navigation benefits, and so on. The task of estimating potential benefits for all of these areas is so formidable as to be virtually impossible.

A final approach was settled upon—an approach that appears to have the virtue of simplicity. The price paid in using this approach is that several simplifying assumptions must be added. The major assumption employed was that the "need" of a state for water resource investment was relatively constant over time. This variable could change, to be sure, but not in relation to the same variable in other states. The model in this chapter is written

(1) $\quad NS_{rt} = aP_{rt} + bN_{rt} + \epsilon_{rt}$,

where $\quad NS_{rt} =$ the number of new starts in the rth state for year t;

$\quad P_{rt} \quad =$ political variables (committee membership, seniority, class, etc.) for state r, year t;

$\quad N_{rt} \quad = N_r$, need variable for the rth state; and

$\quad \epsilon_{rt} \quad =$ random error.

An additional assumption is now introduced that simplifies the exposition but does not significantly restrict the analysis. Each project has a construction schedule N period long, and the total federal expenditures for the project are allocated over time according to the proportions

$$(\lambda_1, \lambda_2, \ldots, \lambda_N) \quad \text{where } \lambda_i \geqq 0 \text{ and } \textstyle\sum \lambda_i = 1$$

That is, if C is the total federal cost of a project, then $\lambda_1 C$ is spent the first year, $\lambda_2 C$ is spent the second year, etc. The current *budgeted* construction (Budcon) for the rth state can now be written

(2) $\quad \text{Budcon}_{rt} = \sum_{i=1}^{N} \lambda_i \, (NS_{rt-i} \, C_{rt-1})$,

where Budcon$_{rt}$ = the construction budget in dollars for state
r, year t;

C_{rt} = average cost of a new start in state r, year t.

Using equation (1) the following relation is obtained:

(3)   Budcon$_{rt}$ = $\sum \lambda_i [aP_{rt-i} + bN_r] C_{rt-i} + \sum \lambda_i \in_{rt} C_{rt-i}$

  = $a\sum \lambda_i P_{rt-i} C_{rt-i} + bN_r \sum \lambda_i C_{rt-i} + \sum \lambda_i \in_{rt-i} C_{rt-i}$.

If the average federal cost of new starts is constant over time and
states, equation (3) can be further reduced to

  Budcon$_{rt}$ = $aC\sum \lambda_i P_{rt-i} + bCN_r + C\sum \lambda_i \in_{rt-i}$,

  where C = C_{rt} for all r and t .

If equation (1) is the true model (i.e. if lagged values of the political variables have no direct effect on new starts), and if the errors of
equation (1) are uncorrelated over time, Budcon$_{rt}$ can be used as a
proxy variable for N_r , the need for water projects in the rth state.
There is some considerable measurement error in this variable that
will produce some bias in the estimates.* In general, this bias will
produce *smaller* coefficients and smaller correlations than would be
obtained under the true model of equation (1).

If past political variables do have an independent effect, then there
will be a further source of bias in the estimates. This situation will
lead to the attributing of effects to need that should properly be
attributed to past political variables. This sort of bias is "conservative" in the sense that it works against accepting the hypotheses presented here. There are various methods that could be used to estimate the magnitude of this bias under different models of the phenomena, but such attempts would take this study too far into a
technical realm.

* See Malinvaud, *Statistical Methods of Econometrics*, pp. 326ff.

The Majority Rule Model:
Nonstable Outcomes

It is important to realize that the majority rule model does not necessarily produce stable outcomes if the restriction on coalitional rationality is dropped—that is, if each coalition chooses its most preferred state of the world out of all conceivable states. A simple three-person example will demonstrate this. Each of the districts in a three-man legislature has an eligible project. District one has a project costing $10 and yielding $10 in benefits. District two's project costs $18 and produces $12 in benefits. District three's project costs $30 and its benefits are valued at $20. Assuming taxes are shared evenly, the table below lists the net benefits to each district under the eight possible states of the world. The numbers in parentheses are the legislators' ranking of outcomes.

By the definition given in the Conclusion, the coalition of legislators representing districts one and two is the lowest-cost winning coalition, and it will choose to build a project in each district. However, note that if a coalition of districts two and three should form and build only the project in the second district, both districts would be better off than under the original proposal. Continuing, a coalition of one and three could propose to build only the project in the first district, which results in a better outcome for both coalition members. But then a coalition of two and three could propose no projects at all and improve their situation. In that case, however, a coalition of one and two could form and build projects in both districts—and the situation is where it began. This cycling phenomenon is eliminated by the limitation placed on coalitional rationality. It is worth noticing that the cycle obtained in this situation includes the L.C.W.C. as defined in the Conclusion as well as alternatives that are even less expensive than that (since they each involve not building projects in members' districts).

Projects built	District one net benefit rank		District two net benefit rank		District three net benefit rank	
0	0	(3)	0	(3)	0	(5)
1	20/3	(1)	−10/3	(4)	−10/3	(6)
2	−6	(5)	6	(1)	−6	(7)
3	−10	(7)	−10	(7)	10	(1)
1,2	2/3	(2)	8/3	(2)	−28/3	(8)
1,3	−10/3	(4)	−40/3	(8)	20/3	(2)
2,3	−16	(8)	−4	(5)	4	(3)
1,2,3	−28/3	(6)	−22/3	(6)	2/3	(4)

The analysis can be extended to the case where there are no restrictions on the coalitions' choice. In particular, a theorem by Joseph Kadane in his article "On Division of the Question" can be used to establish that either the allocation corresponding to no projects being built is globally stable or, if it is not, there is a cycle and it is in the cycle. Further, if when the L.C.W.C. forms

$$B_i - \frac{1}{N} \sum_{i \epsilon L} > 0 \text{ for all } i \text{ in } L ,$$

then L is in any cycle since building all the projects in L dominates building no projects, and since by Kadane's theorem there is a sequence of allocations each of which dominates the previous one beginning with L and ending with no projects being built.

Reference Matter

Notes

Introduction

Epigraph: Richard Fenno, "The Internal Distribution of Influence: The House," in David Truman, ed., *The Congress and America's Future*, p. 52.

1. The most famous example was Clare Hoffman (Republican–Michigan), who was chairman of the Government Operations Committee in the 83d Congress. He is reputed to have run the committee "... with an iron hand, primarily through the use of *ad hoc* subcommittees appointed by Hoffman with little consultation. The members revolted and voted to give virtual autonomy to five subcommittees, which would have broad powers to hire staffs and conduct investigations." See Jewell and Patterson, *The Legislative Process in the United States*, pp. 227–28.

2. Clarence Cannon (Democrat–Missouri), former chairman of the House Appropriations Committee, was not able to dictate who went on his committee or, perhaps more importantly, who did not get to go on. See Fenno, *The Power of the Purse*.

3. Lasswell, p. 13.

4. Interviews were conducted with a former director of the Bureau of the Budget, a former political appointee in the Budget Bureau who also had been a deputy director for several years, and four high-ranking officials in the Office of Management and Budget who were in the natural resources section. Sixteen House members were interviewed, of whom six were high-ranking members of the House Public Works Committee, four were members of the House Appropriations Committee's Subcommittee on Public Works, one was a high-ranking member of the Interior Committee, and one was close to the leadership. Three staff aides to House members were interviewed, as were three committee staff members. On the Senate side interviews were conducted with three staff members of the Senate Public Works Committee and with a staff member of the Senate Appropriations Committee's Public Works Subcommittee. In addition, two senators and six staff members were interviewed. Nine employees of the Corps of Engineers, two leaders of environmental groups, two lobbyists, several economists at work in water-resources economics, and a newspaper reporter who works in the

environmental area for a major newspaper were interviewed as well. The interviews lasted from 25 minutes in one session to five or six hours over several sessions. No set schedule of questions was put to respondents during the interviews since the author wanted to take advantage of their unique perspectives on water-resources legislation.

Chapter 1

Epigraph: Arthur Maass, *Muddy Waters*, p. 37.

1. U.S. Congress, Senate. *Policies, Standards, and Procedures in Formulation, Evaluation, and Review of Plans for Use and Development of Water and Related Land Resources,* prepared under the direction of the President's Water Resources Council. Sen. Doc. 97, 87th Cong., 2d sess., 1962.

2. Maass, *Muddy Waters*, p. 40.

3. *Ibid.*, p. 127. If a project receives a negative report, it must receive a committee resolution for restudy from either the House or the Senate Public Works Committee. A project is eligible for a restudy resolution by the House Public Works Committee after at least three years have elapsed since the filing of the negative report. A project can receive a restudy resolution from the Senate Public Works Committee, though, after only one year has elapsed.

4. U.S. Congress, House, House Committee on Public Works. *The Omnibus Rivers and Harbors and Flood Control Bill of 1968, Hearings.* 90th Cong., 2d sess., 1968, p. 529.

5. U.S. Congress. *Congressional Record.* CVIII, 87th Cong., 2d sess., 1962, p. 22,168.

Chapter 2

1. Marglin, *Public Investment Criteria*, p. 20.

2. Fox and Herfindahl, p. 202.

3. Baumol, "On the Social Rate of Discount"; Tullock, "The Social Rate of Discount and the Optimal Rate of Investment"; Hirshleifer, "Investment Decision Under Uncertainty: Choice-Theoretic Approaches."

4. See Marglin, "The Social Rate of Discount and the Optimal Rate of Investment."

5. Baumol, p. 789.

6. Marglin, "The Social Rate of Discount," p. 95.

7. Maass, "Benefit-Cost Analysis: Its Relevance to Public Investment Decisions," pp. 216–17.

8. Marglin, "The Social Rate of Discount," p. 99.

9. *Ibid.*, p. 111.

10. Baumol, p. 798.

11. Marglin, "The Social Rate of Discount," p. 102.

12. See Arrow and Lind, "Uncertainty and the Evaluation of Public Investments."

13. *Ibid.*, p. 375.

14. See Samuelson, "Social Indifference Curves."

15. See Lindblom, *The Intelligence of Democracy.*

16. See Haveman, "Evaluating Public Expenditures Under Conditions of Unemployment."

17. There are several other arguments for this point of view. Some of them are given in Maass, "Benefit-Cost Analysis."

18. This seems to be the position of Weisbrod in "Income Redistribution Effects and Benefit-Cost Analysis."

19. See Haveman, *The Economic Performance of Public Investments.*

Chapter 3

1. See Schumpeter, *Capitalism, Socialism and Democracy,* and Dahl, *A Preface to Democratic Theory.*

2. Dahl and Lindblom, p. 285.

3. Bailey and Samuel, p. 169.

4. Clapp, p. 122.

5. Smith, p. 134.

6. *Ibid.,* pp. 160, 129.

7. *Ibid.,* p. 81.

8. Martin, pp. 57–59.

9. Maass, *Muddy Waters,* p. 51.

10. Bailey and Samuel, p. 170.

11. Wallace, p. 287.

12. *Ibid.,* p. 305.

13. U.S. Congress, Senate, Senate Appropriations Committee. *Public Works Appropriations Bill for Fiscal Year 1967, Hearings,* before the Public Works Subcommittee. 89th Cong., 2d sess., 1966, pp. 2307–8.

14. Michael, p. 3.

15. *Ibid.*

16. See Downs, *An Economic Theory of Democracy.*

17. See Schlesinger, *Ambition and Politics.*

18. For important recent work and short bibliographies see Clausen, "Home State Influence on Congressional Behavior," and Matthews and Stimson, "Decision-Making by U.S. Representatives: A Preliminary Model."

19. Donald Matthews and James Stimson have generously allowed the author to quote freely from their 1969 and 1970 interviews with a selected list of 108 congressmen.

20. This quotation and those in the next three paragraphs are all from Deckard, "State Party Delegations" (dissertation), chap. 4.

21. Miller, pp. 16–17.

22. Deckard, chap. 4.

23. *Ibid.*

24. See Bullock, "The Influence of State Party Delegations on House Committee Assignments.

Chapter 4

1. Schultze, p. 168.

2. Galloway, p. 106.

3. Davis, Dempster, and Wildavsky, pp. 285–87.

4. Lewis, p. 19.

Chapter 5

1. Fenno, p. 102. (All citations for Fenno throughout the remaining chapters refer to his book *The Power of the Purse* unless otherwise noted.)

2. *Ibid.,* p. 106.

3. *Ibid.,* Table 8.1.

4. *Ibid.,* p. 109.

5. *Ibid.,* p. 16.

6. *Ibid.,* pp. 86–88.

7. *Ibid.,* p. 420.

8. Miller, p. 17.

9. Fenno, p. 88.

10. U.S. Congress, House, House Appropriations Committee. *Public Works Appropriations Bill for Fiscal Year 1968, Hearings,* before the Public Works Subcommittee, 90th Cong., 1st sess., 1967.

11. Fenno, p. 120.   12. *Ibid.,* pp. 85–86.
13. Schultze, p. 166.   14. *Ibid.,* p. 167.
15. Wildavsky, p. 88.

16. U.S. Congress, House, House Appropriations Committee. *Public Works Appropriations Bill for Fiscal Year 1967, Hearings,* before the Public Works Subcommittee. 89th Cong., 2d sess., 1966, p. 467.

17. U.S. Congress, House, House Appropriations Committee. *Civil Functions Appropriations Bill for Fiscal Year 1954, Hearings,* before the Public Works Subcommittee on H.R. 2181, 83d Cong., 1st sess., 1953.

18. Fenno, p. 144.
19. *Ibid.,* p. 430.
20. Smith, pp. 191–92.
21. *Congressional Quarterly Almanac,* 1962, p. 181.
22. *Congressional Quarterly Almanac,* 1963, pp. 178–79.
23. Fenno, p. 493.
24. *Ibid.,* pp. 495–96.
25. This quotation is from the author's interview of a source who wished to remain anonymous. Henceforth, all interview material obtained by the author and quoted in this study will not be identified.
26. Smith, p. 193.

Chapter 6

Epigraph: Henry Adams, *The Education of Henry Adams,* p. 261.

1. Fenno, p. 503.
2. *Ibid.,* p. 505.
3. *Ibid.,* p. 515.
4. U.S. Congress, Senate. Senator McKellar speaking for the Appropriations Bill for Army Civil Functions for Fiscal Year 1953. 82d Cong., 2d sess. *Congressional Record.* LXXXXVIII, pp. 7586–87.
5. See Horn, *Unused Power.*
6. Fenno, p. 540.
7. Horn, p. 92.

Chapter 7

1. Fenno, p. 628.
2. See Gilbert Steiner, *The Congressional Conference Committee.*
3. See David Vogler, "Patterns of One-House Dominance in Congressional Conference Committees."

Chapter 8

1. The House Committee on Public Works is a semiexclusive committee. It is not a prestigious committee by the conventional rankings of committees —ranking below Banking and Currency, Education and Labor, and Judiciary, and above Interior, District of Columbia, Post Office and Civil Service, and Government Operations. See Jewell and Patterson, *The Legislative Process in the United States,* p. 206. The average number of years of prior ser-

vice before assignment to the committee was 1.16 for Democrats and 1.62 for Republicans. Thirty-five of the 55 Democrats assigned to the committee from 1947 to 1970 were freshmen. For Republicans, 42 of 58 were freshmen.

There is some indication of state "claims" to committee seats, but there are so many exceptions that it cannot be regarded as a firm rule. It would be very difficult for a nonprestigious committee to perpetuate a norm such as this since there is not a long list of representatives waiting to get on the committee each year. Even so, some states appear always to have a certain number of congressmen on the committee. California generally has two or three members, as does New York. Pennsylvania and Ohio very often have two members, and Texas generally has one or two. Oklahoma usually has a member, as do Louisiana, Washington, New Jersey, and Tennessee.

There does appear to be an attempt to keep regional representation on the committee in rough accord with regional representation in the House. For comparative purposes, the representativeness score (the sum of the absolute values of the differences between the House percent and the committee percent) is 11. This compares with scores of five for Appropriations, 12 for Ways and Means, 23 for Post Office and Civil Service, and 77 for Interior.

The figures reported here mask significant secular changes. The relative strength of the South among committee Democrats has generally been declining while it has been rising among committee Republicans. The West has become stronger over time in the Democratic contingent and weaker among Republicans.

The leadership does not intervene frequently in recruitment to the committee. However, there have been some significant exceptions in the past. Frank Smith claims that he was asked for his views on issues before the committee—specifically on the St. Lawrence Seaway. This is not surprising since the H.P.W.C. is a highly partisan committee. Smith gives an example of intervention by the leadership in recounting how in 1952 Truman got four members who were opposed to the Seaway to transfer off the committee. See Smith, *Congressman from Mississippi.*

2. Murphy, "Partisanship and the House Public Works Committee," p. 12.

3. Fenno has found that the members of the Post Office and Civil Service Committee and of the Interior Committee tend to have as their principal goal helping their constituents in order to ensure reelection. This contrasts both with the goals of members of the prestigious Ways and Means and Appropriations committees, who are apparently most interested in maximizing their influence in the House, and with the goals of members of the Education and Labor and Foreign Affairs committees, who appear to want to help make "good" public policy. Evidently the goals of members of the Public Works Committee are most similar to those of members of the Interior and the Post Office and Civil Service committees. See Fenno, "Congressional Committees: A Comparative View."

4. Smith, p. 186.

5. *Ibid.*

6. One possible objection to this measure is that if a very large project is started the state's budget will remain high for several years even though not many smaller projects are available to be initiated in the state. In practice this objection is not too serious because there are two kinds of projects

that can achieve a massive scale: navigation projects and multiple-purpose (flood-control, hydroelectric, recreational) projects. If a navigation project is constructed, many smaller projects will follow principally for the dredging, widening, and clearing that must be done at frequent intervals during the project's life. Thus the construction of a navigation project has the effect of making many other projects eligible for construction.

A similar reasoning extends to large multiple-purpose projects, especially hydroelectric projects. Typically these projects will actually consist of several separable projects (see Wallace on the Roanoke River Basin project). For example, if a hydroelectric project is built, only part of its generated power is considered to be "primary" power while the rest is secondary or "dump" power. This is because if only one dam exists, power generation must bear some relation to natural stream flow; since power cannot be stored efficiently, "prime" power is the maximum amount that can be generated during the period of least natural stream flow. "Dump" power can be sold only at very low rates or not at all. The building of upstream dams allows the storage of water that can be released over the year to the hydroelectric dam, thus converting "dump" to "prime" power salable at market rates. Thus the building of a hydroelectric facility frequently makes smaller upstream flood-control, recreation, water supply, or power dams more economically beneficial than they might have been otherwise. Once again, the building of a large project tends to make several smaller projects eligible for construction. Examples of this phenomenon can be found in Krutilla and Eckstein, *Multiple Purpose River Development.*

7. See Murphy, "Partisanship and the House Public Works Committee."

8. See Murphy, "The House Public Works Committee: Determinants and Consequences of Committee Behavior."

9. See Smith, *Congressman from Mississippi*, and Murphy, "The House Public Works Committee."

10. Smith, p. 182.

11. See Fenno, *The Power of the Purse.*

12. Arthur Maass develops this concept at some length in his book *Muddy Waters.*

13. As one Budget Bureau official said, "There is a public works club in the Congress. The guys in the club do well no matter what." The question of whether there is a "club" or not has been confronted in other areas by students of Congress. If a necessary condition for the existence of such a club is continuous and conscious collusion in policy-making and lack of internal disagreement over a broad range of policy questions, then it would be difficult to prove that one operates in the public works issue area. For our present purposes a much weaker set of conditions is imposed in order to speak of the existence of a club (or as it is known in the larger context of national politics, a subgovernment). The conditions are (1) that the proposed club must dominate the centers of effective decision-making (in this case the committees and subcommittees); (2) that its members must be shown to benefit from the arrangement; and (3) that there must not be evidence of internal dissatisfaction (for example, there should be few floor amendments by club members, and club members should not oppose recommendations of other members).

If these conditions are taken to constitute the definition of a club, it seems reasonable to expect that a rivers and harbors club has existed since 1955. In this study conditions (1) and (2) are being demonstrated. If, as seems likely, (3) can be shown to be true after 1955 (though probably not before), then it might seem useful to identify a set of congressmen as members of a rivers and harbors club.

An additional difficulty remains, however. Is it sensible to speak of a rivers and harbors club made up principally of members of the House and Senate Public Works committees along with the Public Works subcommittees of the Appropriations committees, or should the idea of a "public works" club be considered also to include the members of the Interior committees? The Budget Bureau officials who were interviewed tended to refer to the latter group interchangeably with the former. This may be partly a consequence of the internal organization of the Budget Bureau, for the same staff considers both Interior and Corps of Engineers' projects. This question of boundaries was not investigated here, and so the idea of a public works club or a rivers and harbors club must remain a useful shorthand concept, but one lacking precision.

14. See Halperin, "Why Bureaucrats Play Games."

15. There are, of course, many places where the personalities of the actors may have a very significant effect on the distribution of public works projects. One example that comes to mind is the fact that the chairman of the House Appropriations Committee, Clarence Cannon, decided along with John Taber to keep congressmen with strong constituency interests off the Public Works Subcommittee of the H.A.C. for a period of years prior to 1955. This decision had a pronounced effect on how many and which projects were built. The argument put forward here is that the nature of constituency benefits from public works projects makes even the resolution of the very strong-willed Cannon an unstable one in the long run. After several years, the House expressed its dissatisfaction with the Cannon-Taber norm with the result that it was dropped (the next chapter documents this allegation in detail). The nature of the policy would therefore seem to determine in part the distribution of benefits from it. A strong-willed committee chairman may temporarily impose his own standards and force a deviation from what may be considered as the natural or normal distribution of benefits, but this attempt must eventually fail, for it undermines the incentive structure of the House.

This situation contrasts with one where the policy being formed does not distribute significant constituency benefits. Cannon's appointment of Otto Passman (Democrat–Louisiana) to the chairmanship of the Foreign Operations Subcommittee of the H.A.C. over Vaughn Gary (Democrat–Virginia) undoubtedly had severe and long lasting effects on the appropriations for foreign aid. In the foreign-aid policy arena there is no strong force (such as constituency influence) that helps shape the program externally irrespective of the will of the chairman.

Chapter 9

1. Fenno, chap. 8.

2. *Ibid.*, p. 458.

3. *Ibid.*, p. 368.

4. See Cater, *Power in Washington.*

5. Fenno, p. 85.
6. *Ibid.*, p. 71.
7. *Ibid.*, pp. 85–86.
8. *Ibid.*, p. 175.
9. *Ibid.*, pp. 86–87.
10. *Ibid.*, pp. 145–46.
11. See Barry S. Rundquist, "Congressional Influence on the Distribution of Prime Military Contracts."
12. See Carol Goss, "Congress and Defense Policy: Strategies and Patterns of Committee Influence."
13. See Cater, *Power in Washington.*
14. See Berkman and Viscusi, *Damming the West.*
15. See Price, "The Congressional Career—Then and Now."
16. See Polsby, "The Institutionalization of the U.S. House of Representatives."

Chapter 10

Epigraph: Ralph Huitt, "The Internal Distribution of Influence: The Senate," p. 181.
1. *Ibid.*, p. 180.
2. Jewell and Patterson, p. 206.
3. Polsby, *Congress and the Presidency*, p. 40.
4. See Horn, *Unused Power.*
5. Fenno, p. 556.
6. Horn, p. 52n.
7. *Ibid.*, p. 137.
8. *Ibid.*, p. 101.
9. *Ibid.*, p. 129.
10. Bolling, p. 92.
11. See Polsby, Gallaher, and Rundquist, "The Growth of the Seniority System in the U.S. House of Representatives."
12. See Hinckley, *The Seniority System in Congress.*
13. See Horn, *Unused Power.*
14. *Ibid.*
15. See Fenno, *The Power of the Purse.*
16. See Polsby, Gallaher, and Rundquist, "The Growth of the Seniority System in the U.S. House of Representatives."
17. See Murphy, "The House Public Works Committee: Determinants and Consequences of Committee Behavior."
18. See Wolanon, "Subcommittee Chairmen and Seniority: 1917–1967."
19. Horn, p. 135.
20. *Ibid.*, pp. 139–40.

Conclusion

1. See Buchanan and Tullock, *Calculus of Consent*; Tullock, "A Simple Algebraic Model of Logrolling"; Barry, *Political Argument.*
2. Bott, "Symmetric Solutions to Majority Rule Games," pp. 319–23.
3. Dahl and Lindblom, *Politics, Economics, and Welfare*, p. 337.
4. *Ibid.*, p. 339.
5. Barry, p. 317.
6. See Pennock, "The 'Pork Barrel' and Majority Rule."
7. Barry, p. 317.
8. See Wicksell, "A New Principle of Just Taxation."
9. See Niskanen, *Bureaucracy and Representative Government.*

10. See Bott, "Symmetric Solutions to Majority Rule Games"; Luce and Raiffa, *Games and Decisions*; and Riker, *A Theory of Political Coalitions.*

11. Murphy, "The House Public Works Committee: Determinants and Consequences of Committee Behavior," p. 378.

12. Barry, p. 318.

13. Particularly important is the work of Rundquist, "Congressional Influence on the Distribution of Prime Military Contracts." Also see Goss, "Congress and Defense Policy: Strategies and Patterns of Committee Influence," and Plott, "Some Organizational Influences on Urban Renewal Decisions."

Bibliography

Adams, Henry. The Education of Henry Adams. Boston, 1918.

Arrow, Kenneth, and Robert Lind. "Uncertainty and the Evaluation of Public Investments," *American Economic Review*, 60 (June 1970), 364–78.

Bailey, Stephen K., and Howard D. Samuel. Congress at Work. New York, 1962.

Barry, Brian. Political Argument. New York, 1965.

Baumol, William. "On the Social Rate of Discount," *American Economic Review*, 58 (September 1968), 788–802.

Berkman, Rick, and Kip Viscusi. Damming the West. Washington, D.C., 1970.

Bolling, Richard. House Out of Order. New York, 1955.

Bott, Raoul. "Symmetric Solutions to Majority Rule Games," in H. Kuhn and A. Tucker, eds., Contributions to the Theory of Games, vol. 2. Princeton, N.J., 1953.

Buchanan, J., and Gordon Tullock. Calculus of Consent. Ann Arbor, Mich., 1962.

Bullock, Charles. "The Influence of State Party Delegations on House Committee Assignments," *Midwest Journal of Political Science*, 15 (August 1971), 525–46.

Cater, D. Power in Washington. New York, 1964.

Clapp, Charles. The Congressman: His Work as He Sees It. New York, 1964.

Clausen, Aage. "Home State Influence on Congressional Behavior." Paper presented at the American Political Science Association Meeting, September 1970.

Dahl, Robert A. A Preface to Democratic Theory. Chicago, 1956.

Dahl, Robert A., and Charles Lindblom. Politics, Economics, and Welfare. New York, 1953.

Davis, Otto, M. A. H. Dempster, and Aaron Wildavsky. "On the Process of Budgeting: An Empirical Study of Congressional Appropriations," reprinted in The Planning-Programming Budgeting System: Progress and Potentials. Hearings Before the Subcommittee on Economy in Government of the Joint Economic Committee, 90th Cong., 1st sess., 1967.

Deckard, Barbara. "State Party Delegations in the House of Representatives." Unpublished Ph.D. dissertation, University of Rochester, 1969.

———— "State Party Delegations in the U.S. House of Representatives—A Comparative Study of Group Cohesion," *Journal of Politics*, 34 (1972), 199–222.

Downs, Anthony. An Economic Theory of Democracy. New York, 1957.

Elazar, Daniel J. American Federalism: A View from the States. New York, 1966.

Fenno, Richard. "Congressional Committees: A Comparative View." Paper presented at the American Political Science Association Meeting, September 1970.

———— "The Internal Distribution of Influence: The House," in David Truman, ed., The Congress and America's Future. Englewood Cliffs, N.J., 1955.

———— The Power of the Purse. Boston, 1966.

Fox, Irving, and Orris Herfindahl. "Attainment of Efficiency in Satisfying Demands for Water Resources," *American Economic Review: Papers and Proceedings of the Annual Meeting of the American Economic Association*, 54 (May 1964), 198–206.

Galloway, George B. The Legislative Process in Congress. New York, 1955.

Goss, Carol. "Congress and Defense Policy: Strategies and Patterns of Committee Influence." Unpublished Ph.D. dissertation, University of Arizona, 1971.

Halperin, Morton. "Why Bureaucrats Play Games," *Foreign Policy*, 2 (Spring 1971), 70–90.

Haveman, Robert. The Economic Performance of Public Investments. Baltimore, 1972.

———— "Evaluating Public Expenditures Under Conditions of Unemployment," in Robert Haveman and Julius Margolis, eds., Public Expenditures and Policy Analysis. Chicago, 1970.

Heins, A. J. "A Reconsideration of the Economic Aspects of the Oakley Reservoir Project," in John Marlin, ed., A Battle for the Sangamon. Champaign, Ill., 1971.

Hinckley, Barbara. The Seniority System in Congress. Bloomington, Ind., 1971.

Hirshleifer, Jack. "Investment Decision Under Uncertainty: Choice-Theoretic Approaches," *Quarterly Journal of Economics*, 79 (November 1965), 509–36.

Horn, Stephen. Unused Power. Washington, D.C., 1970.

Huitt, Ralph. "The Internal Distribution of Influence: The Senate," in Ralph Huitt and Robert Peabody, eds., Congress: Two Decades of Analysis. New York, 1969.

Jewell, Malcolm, and Samuel Patterson. The Legislative Process in the United States. New York, 1966.

Kadane, Joseph. "On Division of the Question," *Public Choice*, 13 (Fall 1972), 47–54.

Krutilla, John V., and Otto Eckstein. Multiple Purpose River Development. Baltimore, 1958.

Lasswell, Harold. Politics: Who Gets What, When, How. New York, 1958.

Lewis, Wilfred, Jr. Federal Fiscal Policy in the Postwar Recessions. Washington, D.C., 1962.

Lindblom, Charles. The Intelligence of Democracy. New York, 1965.

Lowi, Theodore. "American Business and Public Policy, Case Studies and Political Theory," *World Politics*, 16 (July 1964), 677–715.

Luce, R., and H. Raiffa. Games and Decisions. New York, 1957.

Maass, Arthur. "Benefit-Cost Analysis: Its Relevance to Public Investment Decisions," *Quarterly Journal of Economics*, 80 (May 1966), 208–26.

——— Muddy Waters. Cambridge, Mass., 1951.

Malinvaud, E. Statistical Methods of Econometrics. Chicago, 1966.

Manley, John. The Politics of Finance. Boston, 1970.

Marglin, Stephen. Public Investment Criteria: Benefit-Cost Analysis for Planned Economic Growth. Cambridge, Mass., 1967.

——— "The Social Rate of Discount and the Optimal Rate of Investment," *Quarterly Journal of Economics*, 77 (February 1963), 95–111.

Martin, Joe. My First Fifty Years in Politics. New York, 1960.

Matthews, Donald, and James Stimson. "Decision-Making by U.S. Representatives: A Preliminary Model," in Sidney Ulmer, ed., Political Decision Making. New York, 1970.

Michael, Terry. "Both Candidates Support Oakley Project: Almost Identical Positions De-emphasizes Potentially Explosive Issues," *Champaign-Urbana News Gazette*, May 7, 1972.

Miller, Clem. Member of the House: Letters of a Congressman (John Baker, ed.). New York, 1962.

Murphy, James T. "The House Public Works Committee: Determinants and Consequences of Committee Behavior." Unpublished Ph.D. dissertation, University of Rochester, 1969.

——— "Partisanship and the House Public Works Committee." Paper presented at the American Political Science Association Meeting, September 1968. Revised July 1969.

Niskanen, William, Jr. Bureaucracy and Representative Government. Chicago, 1971.

Pennock, J. Roland. "The 'Pork Barrel' and Majority Rule," *Journal of Politics*, 32 (1970), 709–16.

Plott, Charles. "Some Organizational Influences on Urban Renewal Decisions," *American Economic Review*, 58 (May 1967), 306–21.

Polsby, Nelson. Congress and the Presidency. Englewood Cliffs, N.J., 1964.

——— "The Institutionalization of the U.S. House of Representatives," *American Political Science Review*, 62 (March 1968), 144–68.

Polsby, Nelson W., Miriam Gallaher, and Barry S. Rundquist. "The Growth of the Seniority System in the U.S. House of Representatives," *American Political Science Review*, 63 (September 1969), 787–807.

Price, H. Douglas. "The Congressional Career—Then and Now," in Nelson W. Polsby, ed., Congressional Behavior. New York, 1971.

Riker, William. A Theory of Political Coalitions. New Haven, 1962.

Rundquist, Barry S. "Congressional Influences on the Distribution of Prime Military Contracts." Unpublished Ph.D. dissertation, Stanford University, 1973.

Samuelson, Paul. "Social Indifference Curves," *Quarterly Journal of Economics*, 70 (February 1956), 1–22.

Schlesinger, Joseph. Ambition and Politics. New York, 1966.

Schultze, Charles. Setting National Priorities. Washington, D.C., 1970.

Schumpeter, Joseph A. Capitalism, Socialism and Democracy. 3d ed. New York, 1962.

Smith, Frank E. Congressman from Mississippi. New York, 1964.

Steiner, Gilbert. The Congressional Conference Committee. Urbana, Ill., 1951.

Tullock, Gordon. "A Simple Algebraic Model of Logrolling," *American Economic Review*, 60 (June 1970), 419–26.

——— "The Social Rate of Discount and the Optimal Rate of Investment," *Quarterly Journal of Economics*, 8 (May 1967), 331–36.

Vogler, David. "Patterns of One-House Dominance in Congressional Conference Committees," *Midwest Journal of Political Science*, 14 (1970), 303–20.

Wallace, Earle. "The Politics of River Basin Appropriations." Unpublished Ph.D. dissertation, University of North Carolina, 1959.

Weisbrod, Burton. "Income Redistribution Effects and Benefit-Cost Analysis," in Samuel Chase, ed., Problems in Public Expenditure Analysis. Washington, D.C., 1968.

Wicksell, Knute. "A New Principle of Just Taxation," in R. A. Musgrave and A. T. Peacock, eds., Classics in the Theory of Public Finance. London, 1958.

Wildavsky, Aaron. The Politics of the Budgetary Process. Boston, 1964.

Wilson, Robert. "An Axiomatic Model of Logrolling," *American Economic Review*, 59 (June 1969), 331–41.

Wolanon, Thomas. "Subcommittee Chairmen and Seniority: 1947–1967." Paper presented at the Midwest Political Science Association Meeting, Ann Arbor, Mich., April 1969.

Index

Adams, Henry, 106
A.D.E., 162–65
Aerospace Committee, Senate, 199
agencies, 36, 87f, 92–94, 157–59, 172.
  See also Army Corps of Engineers;
  Fenno, Richard
Agency for International Development,
  158
Agriculture, Department of, 99, 103–4,
  142
Agriculture Subcommittee (of H.A.C.),
  172–73
Alabama, 146
Allerton Park, Illinois, 59
Allott, Gordon, 147, 150
Alum Creek Reservoir, Ohio, 90
"appeals court" role: of House, 76, 83,
  87, 100, 115, 188, 231; of Senate,
  106–7, 111–15 *passim*, 119, 126, 209–
  17, 226–32, 256
appropriations, 9–11, 18–24, 75, 76n,
  92–93, 199
Appropriations Committee, House, 1,
  3–4, 87–115 *passim*, 157–94, 196, 234,
  248; and 1955 floor revolt, 7, 97,
  101–3; goals of, 87, 97, 159–60, 271;
  conference committee and, 116–17;
  chairman of, 116, 159, 162–65, 168,
  169n, 238; subcommittee system in,
  140, 159, 162, 168, 169n, 172; seniority
  in, 151, 219–22; relative veto of, 238–
  40; decision model, 255–58; mentioned, 66, 131, 155, 177, 233, 239n.
  See also Public Works Subcommittee
  (of H.A.C.) *and individual subcommittees by name*

Appropriations Committee, Senate, 1,
  23n, 106–16 *passim*, 125–26, 158, 202;
  state delegations and, 66; procedure
  in, 73–74, 77, 129, 131–32, 196; Budget
  Bureau and, 177, 233; status of, 198–
  99; seniority in, 219ff; relative veto
  of, 238–39; decision model, 256–58.
  See also Public Works Subcommittee
  (of S.A.C.) *and individual subcommittees by name*
Arkansas, 146, 174
Armed Services Committee, House,
  73, 191, 196
Armed Services Committee, Senate,
  73, 196, 198
Armed Services Subcommittee (of
  S.A.C.), 196
Army Civil Functions Appropriations
  Bill for 1953, 109–10; hearings, 110–11
Army Civil Functions Subcommittee (of
  H.A.C.), 168, 180
Army Corps of Engineers, 1, 5–10, 15n,
  18–24 *passim*, 56, 256–57; chief of,
  10, 19, 73–74; benefit evaluation in,
  19ff, 25, 28, 44, 46, 52, 54ff, 66; district engineer of, 19, 66, 173n; division engineer of, 19, 173n; budget
  for, 69–86; House and, 87–105, 232–
  39, 247–49; Senate and, 106–15, 233–
  39, 247–49; and conference committee, 116–26; H.P.W.C. and, 127–56;
  H.A.C. and, 157–94; Senate committees and, 195–232
Arrow, Kenneth, 38–39
Atomic Energy Commission, 1, 96
authorization, 3, 9–11, 19–21, 30, 73,

199; time, 130, 134; active, 178n. *See also* Public Works Committee, House; Public Works Committee, Senate
average per district expenditure (A.D.E.), 162–65

Bailey, Stephen K., 49, 54
Barry, Brian, 235–37, 240–41, 243, 247–51
Baumol, William, 31f, 35, 37f
benefit-cost analysis, 9, 19–21, 25–46, 55, 58, 79–80, 130, 260; by Budget Bureau, 23, 79–81, 145
benefit estimates: economic, 46, 52, 80, 233; political, 47–68
Boggs, Caleb, 21
Boland, Edward, 167–68, 178
Bolling, Richard, 207
Bonneville Power Administration, 161
Bott, Raoul, 235, 245n
Brooks, Overton, 165n
Buchanan, J., 235–37, 240f, 243
Buckley, Charles, 65, 140
Budget, Bureau of the, 6, 9, 19–24 *passim*, 66, 71–87 *passim*, 191f, 231–32; H.P.W.C. and, 131ff, 143–54; H.A.C. and, 170–71, 173, 177–78, 180–81, 185, 188, 190; Senate committees and, 206f, 215, 223; decision model, 256ff; mentioned, 17, 92, 233, 235
Budget and Accounting Act, 94
budget estimates, reduction of, *see* economy norm
Bureau of Reclamation, 1, 8f, 96, 158, 161, 164, 200, 233
Burke, Edmund, 33

California, 38, 61, 64, 66, 134, 146, 210, 271
Cannon, Clarence, 88–89, 96, 99, 103, 168n, 169n, 184f, 190, 222; -Taber norm, 161–65, 172, 273
career advancement, congressional, 47–49, 62, 193f, 198; reelection, 48–51, 194, 271
Carolina Power and Light Company, 55
Casey, Robert, 168
Cassidy, Gen., 75n–76n
Cater, Douglas, 165, 192
certainty equivalent, 36–37
Champaign-Urbana News Gazette, 60
Champaign County, Illinois, 60
Chicago, Illinois, 63
Civil Functions and Military Construc-

tion Subcommittee (of H.A.C.), 163. *See also* Public Works Committee (of H.A.C.)
Civil Functions Appropriations Bill for 1954, 94
Civil Functions Subcommittee (of H.A.C.), 96, 164, 169n, 234–35, 244. *See also* Public Works Subcommittee (of H.A.C.)
Civil Functions Subcommittee (of S.A.C.), 234–35
Clapp, Charles, 50
Clausen, Aage, 63
coalition, 55, 236–43, 245–47; conservative, 197n, 207; model, 263–64
Columbia River states, 146
Commerce, Department of, 99, 103–4
committee chairman: influence of, 3–4, 140, 190–92, 196, 238, 252, 273; benefits to, 7, 234; choice of, 140, 218–19; and subcommittee power, 162–65, 168, 172, 181, 199, 219, 221–22; influence on other committees, 192, 248
committee system: and decision-making, 3–4, 48, 68, 237, 240, 242, 247, 251–52; member cooperation in, 61, 90, 101, 112–13; state delegation and, 63, 67; in House, 89, 101, 107, 133–38, 155–56, 168–71, 190, 193, 231; in Senate, 107, 196, 208, 219; effect of membership, 133–38, 168–71, 190, 193, 208, 231. *See also* committees by name
concurrent resolutions, 74–75, 81
Conference Committee, 23, 116–26, 158–63, 174, 217–18, 240, 256–58; Appropriations Bill, 1, 10
Congress, U.S., 1–6, 8–9, 15, 18f, 24, 76–87 *passim*, 173, 233–48 *passim*, 251–52; 74th, 18; 80th–83d, 161–63, 184, 212, 218; 84th–88th, 18, 63, 134, 137, 164, 184; 89th–91st, 137, 184; 92d, 15n, 59; 93d, 59; benefit-cost analysis and, 45; and president, 92, 153, 162–65, 233; new starts in, 132, 143–44, 147–48, 151; committee membership in, 136, 139–40; other agencies' budgets and, 159f; mentioned, 48, 106, 116, 192–94. *See also* House of Representatives, U.S.; Senate, U.S.
Congress at Work, 49
"Congressional Committees: A Comparative View," 160
Congressional Record, 11, 109
conservative coalition, 197n, 207

constituency interests, 129–30, 147, 172, 241, 273; in H.A.C., 87–97 *passim*, 103, 105, 159–67 *passim*, 168n, 175, 183, 234; in Senate committees, 106, 126, 208
construction industry, 50, 54, 58, 82, 257f
construction program, 5, 7–10, 22–24, 72–75, 81, 77, 92, 132, 178n; speed of, 5, 8, 24, 74, 90, 94, 132, 133n, 214; executive determination of, 71–86; in budget model, 261–62. *See also* public works budget
Cooley, Harold, 56
Coolidge, Calvin, 51
Cooper, John Sherman, 1, 148, 199, 208
Corps of Engineers, *see* Army Corps of Engineers
cost estimates: political, 47–68. *See also* benefit-cost analysis
Cramer, W., 141

Dahl, Robert A., 35, 47, 62, 237–38, 250
dams, 38, 41, 52–53, 55, 65, 152, 272
Davis, Glenn, 164, 168, 180, 184–85
Davis, Otto, 79
Davis-Bacon Act, 45
Decatur, Illinois, 59–60
decision rule, 121, 213–14, 217, 228, 244
Deckard, Barbara, 62n, 64–66, 180
Defense, Department of, 73, 233
Defense, Secretary of, 73
defense spending, 5, 67, 192
Defense Subcommittee (of H.A.C.), 172–73
Defense Subcommittee (of S.A.C.), 199
Deficiencies and Army Civil Functions Subcommittee (of H.A.C.), 162–64. *See also* Public Works Subcommittee (of H.A.C.)
Deficiencies Subcommittee (of H.A.C.), 161
Delaware, 42
Delta region, Mississippi, 50f, 61, 166
democracy, theory of, 47–48
Democratic Study Group, the, 197
Democrats, 50, 64, 66, 96, 114–15, 163f, 231, 234; on conference committee, 117; on H.P.W.C., 131, 138–42, 144–45, 150–52, 154, 198, 212; "external support" and, 163; on H.A.C., 167–70, 179–81, 188, 191, 212, 215; on S.P.W.C., 198, 215–18, 227–28; on S.A.C., 199, 212–15, 227–28

Dempster, M. A. H., 79
Devine, Samuel, 90
Dirksen, Everett, 114
discount rate, 29–46 *passim*, 79–80, 233
distributive policies, 7, 190–94, 214, 244–52, 273
District of Columbia, 42
divisibility, 6, 19, 65, 181, 190–92, 252; defined, 4–5
Douglas, Paul, 56–58, 114
Downs, Anthony, 62

economy norm, 87, 91, 94, 97, 103, 126, 159–65 *passim*, 172
Education and Labor Committee, House, 220f, 271
efficiency, project, 26–28, 30, 32, 38, 42, 44–45
Eisenhower, Dwight D., 81, 84, 92, 163f, 180
Elazar, Daniel, 63n
electric power production, *see* power benefits
Ellender, Allen, 1, 57–58, 148, 201–2
"eminent domain," 53
employment, 32, 40–41, 43, 45, 81–82; in decision model, 257f
environmental impact statement, 15n
environmentalists, 53, 59f, 193
Environmental Protection Agency, 9
Evins, Joe, 1, 166–68, 178
executive role, 9, 20, 71–86, 146–47, 150f, 170, 195. *See also* Army Corps of Engineers; Budget, Bureau of the; president
"external support," 160, 163–64, 182

F.A.B., *see* fixed-agency-budget system
"fair-share" budget model, 76–79
Fallon, George, 140
Fall River, Massachusetts, 51
feasibility study, 18
Federal Bureau of Investigation (F.B.I.), 9, 158
Fenno, Richard, 1, 3–4, 7, 87–108 *passim*, 113–22 *passim*, 158–61, 233, 247; on subcommittee power, 169–72, 181ff, 200f; budget model, 255, 258
filibuster, 239, 240n
Finance Committee, Senate, 196, 198f
fixed-agency-budget system, 39–40, 43
Flood Control Act: (1936), 25; (1944), 55; (1962), 21

Flood Control Committee, House, 55
flood-control projects, 2, 8, 81; 144–46; irrigation, 8, 38, 52, 193; dams, 38, 41, 52–53, 55, 65, 152, 272; benefits of, 38–39, 41, 46, 52–55, 59, 261, 272
Flood Control Subcommittee (of H.P.W.C.), 19, 142–44, 153–54, 157–58
floods, 10, 87, 135n
Florida, 64, 146
Fogarty, John, 96, 167
Foreign Affairs Committee, House, 220, 271
Foreign Operations Subcommittee (of H.A.C.), 169n, 172, 273
Foreign Relations Committee, Senate, 198
Fox, Irving, 30, 40
Friends of the Earth, 53
funding: year-by-year, 24n, 73–75; "full," 72–73, 90, 92; breakdown of, 132

Galloway, George B., 75
Gary, Vaughn, 169n, 273
geographic representation, 4, 56, 190, 192, 252
Georgia, 56
"grandfather clause," 46
gross national product, 28, 37

H.A.C., *see* Appropriations Committee, House
Halperin, Morton, 152
Hand, T. Millett, 166
Harlow, Bryce, 146
Hartke, Rupert Vance, 57
Haveman, Robert, 41, 46
Hayden, Carl, 158–59, 201–2
Health, Education, and Welfare, Department of, 99, 103–4
Herfindahl, Orris, 30, 40
Highway Trust Fund, 193
Hill, Lister, 201–2
Hinckley, Barbara, 219
Hirshleifer, Jack, 31, 37f
Hobbes, Thomas, 33
House floor revolt of 1955: constituency service after, 7, 164–67, 273; Public Works Subcommittee (of H.A.C.) after, 94–97, 188, 234, 244, 250; House floor and H.A.C. relations after, 101–5, 125, 165; Senate response after, 109–11, 113, 205–6
House of Representatives, U.S., 1–4, 8, 20, 48–49, 75, 87–106, 111, 116, 157–63 *passim*, 237–38, 240, 248; institutions of, 4, 61–62, 64, 68, 194, 206–7, 231–32; as appeals court, 76, 83, 87, 100, 115, 188, 231; floor, 97, 99–105, 113–15, 155–65 *passim*, 239, 244, 247, 255–58; budget cuts in, 106f, 109–13, 115, 208–17, 223–30, 255–58; committee system of, 106–8, 193–97, 219–23, 231; log-rolling in, 112–13, 122f, 125, 138; in conference committee, 116–26; new starts in, 132–45, 148–54, 167–75 *passim*, 179, 190, 231, 249–50; Senate response to, 203–6, 209–11, 213–17, 225–32. *See also* Appropriations Committee, House; Public Works Committee, House; *and by committee*
Horn, Stephen, 111, 114, 199ff, 219, 222–23, 247
H.P.W.C., *see* Public Works Committee, House
Huitt, Ralph, 195, 197, 206
hydroelectric power, 46, 55, 135, 272

Illinois, 56, 59–61, 63, 93–94
Illinois Waterway, 46
Independent Offices Subcommittee (of H.A.C.), 96, 164
Indiana, 56
inflation, 76, 79, 82–84, 257f
institutional hypothesis, 7, 194, 206–7, 231–32, 236–37; variables of, 3–4, 252
interest groups, 63, 71, 76, 80, 173
interest rate, market, 29–32, 35, 37–39
Interior, Department of the, 99, 103–4, 150n, 158–60, 200f
Interior Appropriations Subcommittee (of S.A.C.), 114–15
Interior Committee, House, 103, 164, 271
Interior Department Appropriations Bill, 161
Interior Subcommittee (of H.A.C.), 89, 96, 164, 165n
Iowa, 91, 190
irrigation, 8, 38, 52, 193
Itschner, Gen., 73–74

Jensen, Ben F., 89, 166, 185, 188, 190
Johnson, Lawrence, 59–60
Johnson, Lyndon B., 72, 147, 150
Joint Economic Committee, 79
Judiciary Committee, House, 196
Justice, Department of, 99, 103–4, 170

Kadane, Joseph, 264
Kaldor-Hicks efficiency criterion, 27–28, 38, 43
Kennedy, John F., 18, 114
Kentucky, 2, 41f, 146, 261
Kerner, Gov. Otto, 93
Kerr, John, 162, 184
Kerr Reservoir, the John H., 46
Kerr, Robert S., 21, 199, 200–201
Kirwan, Michael, 1, 75n–76n, 96, 99, 114–15, 148, 166f, 178, 184f
Knowles, Montana, 21

Labor, Department of, 99, 103–4
Labor and Health, Education, and Welfare Subcommittee (of H.A.C.), 172–73
Lasswell, Harold, 5
Lausche, Frank J., 114–15
Legislative Reorganization Act (1947), 157, 161
Lewis, Wilfred, 82
Lincoln Reservoir, Illinois, 56–57
Lind, Robert, 38–39
Lindblom, Charles, 35, 39–40, 47, 237–38, 250
lobbying, 146; public interest, 193
local opposition and support, 19, 22, 55–56, 58, 60–61; interest groups, 63, 71, 76, 80, 173
logrolling, 2, 66, 112–13, 122–25, 138, 238, 250
Los Angeles, California, 61
Louisiana, 2, 57, 148, 261, 271
Lowi, Theodore, 193n

Maass, Arthur, 8, 15, 18f, 33, 54
Macon County, Illinois, 59–60
Madigan, Edward, 59–60
Magnuson, Warren, 1
Mahon, George, 140
Maine, 210
majority rule, 235, 237, 240, 245ff, 250ff, 263–64
Manatos, Mike, 147, 150
Manley, John, 182n
marginal utility, 34, 36
Marglin, Stephen, 27–28, 31, 32–33, 35–36, 38
market rate of interest, 29–32, 35, 37–39
Marshall, Fred, 96
Martin, Joe, 51
Maryland, 42
Massachusetts, 51, 65

Matthews, Donald, 11, 63f, 66
McClellan, John, 174
McCormick, Sam, 65
McKellar, Kenneth, 109–10
McNamara, Pat, 208
Mellon, Andrew, 51
Members of Congress for Peace Through Law, 197
Michael, Terry, 60
Military Construction Subcommittee (of H.A.C.), 172–73
Miller, Clem, 66
Mills, Wilbur, 182n
minority member, ranking, 7, 231, 234–35; in House, 117, 138, 153, 162, 172, 182–85, 188–90, 195f, 201, 248; in Senate, 207n, 221–31
Mississippi, 2, 8, 50, 57
Mississippi Delta region, 50f, 61, 166
Mississippi River, 76n
Mississippi Valley Association, 93–94, 146
Missouri, 146, 163, 185, 190
Montana, 21
Mount Carmel, Illinois, 56
Muddy Waters, 8
multi-purpose projects, 41, 271–72
Mundt, Karl, 49–50
Murphy, James T., 129, 138–39, 220, 247
Murray, James, 166
Muskie, Edmund, 199

Nader, Ralph, 193
National Environmental Policy Act (1969), 15n
navigation projects, 2, 8, 39, 45n, 46, 52, 54, 143, 260; Budget Bureau evaluation of, 79ff, 143, 146, 152, 154f, 178; Congress-initiated, 143–45, 271–72
"need," 135–36, 153, 250, 260–62
New Jersey, 271
new starts: planning 22, 76n, 77; in House, 23, 92–94, 111–12, 116, 132–45, 151f, 170, 175, 179–84, 191, 231–32, 249–50; Congress-initiated, 23f, 83–86, 92–94, 111–12, 116, 119, 125, 132–45, 151, 170, 175, 179–84, 191, 202–12 *passim*, 231–32, 249–50; state delegation and, 68; executive review of, 71–72; construction, 76n, 92, 100, 132, 170; under Eisenhower, 81, 84, 92, 164; Budget Bureau and, 81, 143–53, 171, 177–78, 180–81, 185, 188; in Senate, 92, 202–12 *passim*, 231–32;

in conference committee, 122–23;
floor revolt effect on, 125; H.A.C.
membership and, 132–33, 170f, 175,
177–81, 191; H.P.W.C. membership
and, 133–38, 148–50, 154–55, 191,
249–50; costs of, 135f, 149f; political
party and, 138–39, 150–52, 191, 212,
231; seniority and, 139–42, 151–53,
231; and subcommittee membership,
142–45, 153–56, 182–85, 188
New York, 19–20, 65, 66–67, 162n, 163,
180, 271
Niskanen, William, 242–43, 244, 247–51
Nixon, Richard M., 146
North Carolina, 56, 162n, 185

Oahe Dam, South Dakota, 50
Oakley Dam, Illinois, 59–60
Office of Management and Budget, 9,
20–21, 24, 153, 206. *See also* Budget,
Bureau of the
Ohio, 2, 90, 146, 148, 185, 271
Oklahoma, 146, 210, 271
O.M.B., *see* Office of Management and
Budget
Omnibus Rivers and Harbors and Flood
Control Bill, 19, 20–21, 129, 142, 153,
207; (1968), 19, 68, 143–44; (1970), 20,
153; *also called* Omnibus Rivers and
Harbors Bill, 16, 18; Rivers and Har-
bors Bill, 155 (1956), 180; Rivers and
Harbors and Flood Control Bill
(1968), 10, 18, 260
ongoing projects: executive review of,
71–72; funding for, 72–75, 92, 119
opportunity cost, 32, 40–42, 46
Oregon, 135–36, 261

Passman, Otto, 101, 169n, 172, 273
Patman, Wright, 195
Pennock, J. Roland, 240
Pennsylvania, 64, 66, 271
permeability, 113–15, 118
Phillips, John, 166
Pick, Lewis, 131
Pike, Otis, 19–20
Pillion, John, 180
planning, 10, 21–23, 55f, 71–86, 100,
109–10, 132, 178n. *See also* authorization; new starts
political considerations, 6, 47–68, 146–47
political party: in state delegation, 63ff;
effect in House, 133, 138–39, 144–45,
150–52, 154, 231, 234; effect in Senate,

211–18, 225, 228, 231, 234. *See also*
Democrats; Republicans
Polsby, Nelson, 218–19, 220
"pork barrel legislation": public works
as, 1–2, 4, 167–68, 180, 234–35, 247;
question of, 25, 43–46, 235n; reelection and, 50–52; political bases for,
218, 235–44
Port Jefferson Harbor, New York, 19–20
Post Office and Civil Service Committee, House, 271
Powell, Adam Clayton, 195
power benefits, 52, 54–56, 81, 146, 272;
hydroelectric, 46, 55, 135, 272
Power of the Purse, The, 87, 159f, 182
power of the purse, 87, 97, 159
President, the, 2, 9, 71f, 77, 86, 171, 197n,
233; budget of, 1, 22, 92ff, 109, 258;
review by, 20–21, 71–72, 147, 171;
Congress and, 92, 109, 153, 162–65,
233
Price, H. Douglas, 194
Price, Melvin, 93
proportional growth model, *see* "fair-
share" budget model
Proxmire, William, 114–15
public good, 6, 25, 35, 44–45
Public Works Appropriations Bill, 1–2,
8, 10, 23, 74, 99, 103, 178; hearings
on, 1, 10, 66, 90, 201; state delegation and, 66; and House floor revolt,
97, 101–3, 110, 125–26; Senate response to, 110–11; conference committee and, 119; (1959), 86, 180;
(1969), 68
public works budget, 1–11; decision-
making for, 13–24, 233–52; benefit-
cost analysis for, 25–46; political evaluation of, 47–61; state delegation and,
61–68. *See also* Army Corps of Engineers
"public works club," 148–49, 150n, 151–
52, 155, 165n, 272–73. *See also* "subgovernment"
Public Works Committee, House, 129–
58; membership in, 4, 7, 50f, 61, 68,
171, 191–92, 234, 271; subcommittees,
19, 142–44, 153–55, 157–58, 196; procedure in, 19–20, 75, 77, 89–91, 93;
1955 change in, 97, 103, 164–67;
H.A.C. and, 107, 164–67, 171, 207,
249–51; political party in, 133, 138–
39, 144–45, 150–52, 212, 218; seniority
in, 151, 220f; prestige of, 198, 270;

relative veto of, 239n. *See also* Omnibus Rivers and Harbors and Flood Control Bill

Public Works Committee, Senate, 7, 196–200, 207–11, 234; procedure in, 19, 75, 77, 107; conference committee and, 116f; Rivers and Harbors and Flood Control Subcommittee, 208–11, 215–18, 223–31; seniority in, 221

Public Works Subcommittee (of H.A.C.), 7, 83–105 *passim*, 172–81, 190–91, 234–35, 247–51; procedure in, 22ff, 77, 132, 159, 242, 273; state delegation and, 65, 68; Senate committees and, 111–12, 206–8, 210–11, 228, 231; and conference committee, 117; H.P.W.C. and, 130–32, 133n, 134, 138, 144, 164–68, 234, 249–51; 1955 change in, 164–68, 169n, 234–35, 244; power of, 169n, 205; political party in, 179–81, 191; seniority in, 181–88; relative veto of, 238–39

Public Works Subcommittee (of S.A.C.), 7, 56, 197–207, 242, 248, 251; and budget from Corps, 22ff, 83, 92–93, 106–15; and House budget, 23, 108, 111–13, 158, 174, 230–31, 256; conference committee and, 116, 125–26; chairman of, 116, 158, 231, 238; S.P.W.C. and, 208–11, 231, 234; political party in, 212–16; seniority in, 222–29; relative veto of, 238–39

railroads, 45n, 52, 54, 80, 143n
Randolph, Jennings, 1, 148, 199, 208
recession, 79, 81, 83
reciprocity norm, 3, 66, 119, 239, 242; in Senate, 108, 114, 212, 222; in House, 130, 169–70, 182f, 197, 249
"reclama," 23, 112
recreation facilities, 8, 38–39, 52ff, 58f, 145n, 146, 260, 272
redistribution of wealth, 44–45, 80, 194
Red River, Louisiana, 2
reelection, 48–51, 194, 271. *See also* career advancement, congressional
regression equation terms, 108
Republicans, 110, 163, 219, 231, 234; on H.P.W.C., 131, 138–41, 144–45, 150–52, 154, 212; on H.A.C., 168–70, 179–81, 188, 191, 212, 215; on S.P.W.C., 198, 215–18, 227–28; on S.A.C., 199, 212–15, 227–28

Resources for the Future, 30
restudy resolution, 17, 138, 268
R.H.F.C. Subcommittee, *see* Rivers and Harbors and Flood Control Subcommittee (of S.P.W.C.)
Rhodes, John, 147f, 150, 167f, 178, 180, 185
risk, investment, 36–39
Rivers and Harbors, Board of Engineers for, 19
Rivers and Harbors and Flood Control Subcommittee (of S.P.W.C.), 208–11, 215–18, 223–31
"rivers and harbors club," 139, 141n, 179, 192, 273. *See also* "subgovernment"
Rivers and Harbors Committee, House, 157
Rivers and Harbors Subcommittee (of H.P.W.C.), 19, 142–44, 153–55, 157–58
R.M.M., *see* minority member, ranking
Roanoke River project, 55–56, 272
Robison, Howard, 168, 180
"rolling" of H.A.C., 155
Rousseauian theory, 33, 47n
Rules Committee, House, 131, 238, 238n
Russian River, California, 38

S.A.C., *see* Appropriations Committee, Senate
Samuel, Howard D., 49, 54
Sangamon River, Illinois, 59–60
Savannah River, 56
Schlesinger, Joseph, 62
Schultze, Charles, 92
Schumpeter, Joseph A., 47, 62
Senate, U.S., 1–4, 8, 20, 48, 106–16, 157–63 *passim*, 193–232 *passim*, 237–40, 248; as appeals court, 23n, 106–7, 111–15 *passim*, 119, 126, 209–17, 226–32, 256; committee system in, 106–7, 196–97, 219–22, 231f; logrolling in, 112, 122f, 125; floor, 113–16, 162f, 239, 244, 247, 256–58; in conference committee, 116–23, 126; new starts in, 132–33, 143, 203–16 *passim*, 231; response to House, 174, 203–17 *passim*, 225–30, 256, 258. *See also* Appropriations Committee, Senate; Public Works Committee, Senate; *and by committee*
Senate Document 97, 18
seniority: system, 3–4, 219, 221, 252; in House, 131, 133, 139–42, 151–53,

169n, 179–90, 193f, 231; in subcommittee, 181–90, 193, 219, 221–22; in Senate, 107n, 196, 199, 203, 211, 218–31
shipping, bulk, 45n, 52, 54, 80, 143n
Sierra Club, 53
small-projects bias, 247, 251
Smith, Frank, 50f, 103, 131, 139f, 165n
South (U.S.), overrepresentation of, 4, 252, 271
South Carolina, 56
South Dakota, 50
Southeast region, 41f
Speaker of the House, 116
Springer, William, 59–60
S.P.W.C., *see* Public Works Committee, Senate
State, Department of, 99, 103–4
state delegation, 146, 197, 251, 271; cooperation of, 61–68, 90–91, 112, 180n; chairman of, 63, 173–75
Steiner, Gilbert, 117–18
Stennis, John, 1
Stimson, James, 11, 63f, 66
subcommittees: committee chairman influence in, 3, 157–58, 162–65, 168, 172, 190–91, 238; chairman of, 3–4, 138, 140, 158, 181–88, 190, 212, 219–31, 234–35; cooperation between, 91; membership in, 133, 142–45, 153–56, 209–11, 222, 231, 248; seniority and, 140, 219–22; and committee goals, 172; power within, 193, 196, 248; assignment to, 199, 211–12, 219ff. *See also by name*
"subgovernment," 165, 192f, 205–7, 216, 218, 234, 272; "rivers and harbors club," 139, 141n, 179, 192, 273; "public works club," 148–49, 150n, 151–52, 155, 165n, 272–73; "water resources club," 166

Taber, John, 89, 96, 117, 161–65, 172, 180, 273
Taunton River, Massachusetts, 51
taxation, 31, 34, 37, 242
Tennessee, 2, 41f, 64, 146, 271
Tennessee Valley Authority, 200f

Texas, 64, 134, 146, 271
time preference, 29, 37f
Tombigbee River states, 146
Transportation Act (1966), Department of, 80, 233
Treasury, Department of the, 99, 103–4
treasury, federal, 23, 87, 97, 132, 150–60
Truman, Harry S., 271; administration, 163
Tullock, Gordon, 31, 35, 235–37, 240f, 243

unanimity requirement, 240–41
Unused Power, 200

veto power, 86, 237–41, 243, 247f, 250
Vietnam War, 84
Virginia, 42, 56, 66
Virginia Electric Power Company, 55
Vogler, David, 117ff, 121f, 258

Wabash River, 56
Wallace, Earle, 55
Washington, 2, 64, 261, 271
water-quality control, 52ff
water resources development, 1–2, 8, 15, 49–50, 144, 146, 152. *See also* Army Corps of Engineers *and by type*
Watershed Development Subcommittee (of H.P.W.C.), 142
water supply, 52ff, 58f, 272
Ways and Means Committee, House, 50, 131, 182n–183n, 271
Wednesday Club, the, 197
West (U.S.), 41, 271
West Virginia, 2, 42, 210
Whitten, Jamie, 51, 166f, 178
Whittington, Will, 140
Wicksell, Knute, 241
Wigglesworth, Richard, 185
Wildavsky, Aaron, 76–77, 79, 93, 255
Wilson, Henry Hall, 147, 150
Wilson, Robert, 251n
Wisconsin, 114–15, 180, 185
Wolanon, Thomas, 220
Wright, James, 148